The Life and Teams of
Johnny F. Bassett

The Life and Teams of Johnny F. Bassett

Maverick Entrepreneur of North American Sports

DENIS M. CRAWFORD

McFarland & Company, Inc., Publishers
Jefferson, North Carolina

LIBRARY OF CONGRESS CATALOGUING-IN-PUBLICATION DATA

Names: Crawford, Denis M., author.
Title: The life and teams of Johnny F. Bassett : maverick entrepreneur
  of football, hockey and tennis / Denis M. Crawford.
Description: Jefferson, North Carolina : McFarland & Company, Inc.,
  Publishers, 2021 | Revision of author's dissertation. |
  Includes bibliographical references and index.
Identifiers: LCCN 2020057922 | ISBN 9781476684321
  (paperback : acid free paper) ∞
  ISBN 9781476642956 (ebook)
Subjects: LCSH: Bassett, Johnny F., 1939-1986. | Sports team owners—
  Canada—Biography. | Sports team owners—United States—Biography. |
  Sports franchises—Canada—History—20th century. | Sports franchises—
  United States—History—20th century. | Professional sports—United States—
  History—20th century. | Professional sports—Canada—History—20th century.
Classification: LCC GV697.B38 C73 2021 | DDC 338.7/61796092 [B]—dc23
LC record available at https://lccn.loc.gov/2020057922

BRITISH LIBRARY CATALOGUING DATA ARE AVAILABLE

ISBN (print) 978-1-4766-8432-1
ISBN (ebook) 978-1-4766-4295-6

Front cover image: Johnny F. Bassett watching his Bandits
during pre-game warm-ups at Wembley Stadium in 1984
(Courtesy of Jill Massicotte-Barreto).

Printed in the United States of America

*McFarland & Company, Inc., Publishers
  Box 611, Jefferson, North Carolina 28640
  www.mcfarlandpub.com*

To Amy
There is no one I would rather be a grown-up with.

Table of Contents

Acknowledgments

The support and assistance of the Bassett family is the primary reason for the success of this project. Sue Bassett-Klauber answered a multitude of questions about her late husband and provided access to a treasure trove of scrapbooks, correspondence, and artifacts dealing with the career of Johnny F. Bassett. Her imprimatur allowed me to also discuss the life of Mr. Bassett with all his children: John C. Bassett, Victoria Bassett, Carling Bassett-Seguso, and Heidi Bassett-Blair. Every member of the Bassett family was exceedingly generous and patient in their responses to information requests.

John C. Bassett also acted as a liaison for me while reaching out to many of Bassett's peers, friends, partners, and even rivals. Especially generous with time and documentation were Steve Ehrhardt, Larry Csonka, Mike Tollin, Wayne Gretzky, Peter Eby, Steve Spurrier, Paul Warfield, Peter McAskile, Jim McVay, and Pam Yonge.

The esteemed faculty at Penn State Harrisburg, particularly Charles Kupfer, Charity Fox, John Haddad, and David Williamson, who advised me throughout the research of this work when it started as a dissertation, were a great help. It was an honor to work with them and they not only helped to craft this work, they made me a better writer. Heidi Abbey Moyer, humanities librarian at Penn State Harrisburg was instrumental in helping to navigate all the databases available through the university's wonderful library. Special thanks also to Jon Kendle of the Pro Football Hall of Fame for his assistance in viewing documents in the Hall's archives. I am also thankful to the staffs of Youngstown State University's Maag Library, the Toronto Public Library, the State Library of Pennsylvania, the Tampa Public Library, and the Hockey Hall of Fame for their help.

This book is also a family affair. My wife Amy, in addition to putting up with my obsession with all things Bassett, took on the extra jobs of copy editor and sounding board. Amy granted me the precious gift of time, a gift that I will never be able to adequately repay. I also thank my parents James and Louisa Crawford for providing me with a love of books and reading, a passion that has enabled me to undertake a myriad of writing projects. This book is the result of many people working in concert to achieve an audacious goal, just the kind of team Johnny F. Bassett would have liked.

Preface

This book is a critical biography of Johnny F. Bassett, an edited and reconfigured version of my successful dissertation in the American Studies doctoral program at Penn State University. This work is intended as neither a hagiography nor a hit piece. It is also a deconstruction of North American society in the 1970s and 1980s as well as the economic underpinnings of professional sports during that same era. This is to provide context for the specific universe Bassett operated in.

The methodology of research was two-pronged. The first approach was gathering primary source material on Johnny F. Bassett for a detailed biography of his career between 1973 and 1986. The second was to thoroughly analyze cultural and sporting histories of America and Canada during this era to recreate the world Bassett knew. To complete the first approach, online and library newspaper archives of the *Toronto Star, St. Petersburg Times, Lakeland (FL) Ledger, Sports Illustrated,* and other local and regional periodicals were accessed. Articles were analyzed for references to Bassett, with attention focused on personal profiles, coverage of marketing promotions, coverage of team operations, and coverage of Bassett's public battles with rivals. Questions guiding these analyses included: How was Bassett portrayed by the local and national press? With whom did he clash and/or agree? How did the sporting public respond to his operations? Several dozen telephone and personal interviews were conducted between 2009 and 2015 with surviving family, friends, peers, staffers, and rivals. Interview questions were broad and conversations free flowing. The interviews resulted in anecdotes and recollections not covered in press accounts of the times, which affords a more intimate views of Bassett's life details. This resulted in a narrative that offers the reader an intimate view of Bassett's life. These interviews were cross-referenced with press accounts and other interviews to verify information.

The second approach consisted of critical reading of cultural and sports histories of America and Canada. Specific attention was paid to biographies of other sporting entrepreneurs/figures who were peers of Bassett; books on the history of major sports leagues and upstart leagues, with the added mission of finding Bassett anecdotes/quotes; books and articles on Canadian anti–Americanism in the early 1970s; Toronto's transformation in celebrating multiculturalism; Alabama's historic use of Crimson Tide football as an avatar of the Lost Cause; the rise of Redneck Chic as a national pop culture phenomenon in the 1970s/1980s; Florida's tourist economy and culture in the 1980s; and the economic culture shift in America during the 1980s.

If I have succeeded in this account, the reader will view Bassett as I have: a fascinating yet imperfect man whose dedication to professional sports and spectacle was well-intended but existed in a time of less cultural sensitivity. The history of twentieth century American professional sports cannot be written without mentioning Johnny F. Bassett's many contributions. Unfortunately, it has. Sports historians devote little space to the Canadian-born entrepreneur who fielded teams in three short-lived upstart professional sports leagues: WHA (1972–1979), WFL (1974–1975), and USFL (1983–1985). Bassett's won-loss record as a sports owner is underwhelming in comparison to titans such as Eddie DeBartolo, Robert Kraft, George Steinbrenner, and Jerry Buss, whose teams combined for 28 world championships. Bassett's teams combined to win only one playoff series in his twelve-year run. Bassett's profit-loss record is also not comparable to owners in established leagues guaranteed tens of millions of dollars per year in television revenue by their association with the highly successful NFL, Major League Baseball, and National Basketball Association (NBA). Bassett straddled the thin line between insolvency and liquidity, and each of his teams folded within two to seven years. The lack of titles and windfall profits helps to explain Bassett's relative anonymity. There is a bias against failure in sports as there is in larger American society. As Vince Lombardi, the Hall of Fame coach of the dynastic Green Bay Packers football team, once succinctly put it, "Winning is not everything, it is the *only thing!*"[1]

But what qualifies as winning? If it is strict adherence to a binary scoreboard, then sports histories should only be written about the New York Yankees, New England Patriots, and Los Angeles Lakers. If, as I believe, winning is doing more with less, outmaneuvering and outthinking competitors with more resources, surviving for multiple years in a rigged system, and impacting the way the business of sports is conducted then Johnny F. Bassett was overwhelmingly successful when it came to his outsized impact on American professional sports during his relatively short tenure (1973–1986).

Introduction

Johnny F. Bassett has been a part of my life since the Canadian-born entrepreneur announced the formation of the Tampa Bay Bandits of the United States Football League (USFL) in 1982. The Bandits were Bassett's third attempt to build a professional sports franchise and his third association with an upstart sports league. His previous attempts with the Toronto Toros/Birmingham Bulls of the World Hockey Association (WHA) and Toronto Northmen/Memphis Southmen of the World Football League (WFL) were successful failures: Bassett's teams were competitive and popular, proving the major league viability of new markets in Birmingham, Alabama and Memphis, Tennessee. Unfortunately, the leagues he associated with were overwhelmed by the resource advantage held by the entrenched sporting conglomerates they battled against, respectively the National Hockey League (NHL) and National Football League (NFL). The WHA and WFL folded, taking Bassett's teams, and his personal fortune, with them.

Born and raised in Tampa Bay, I was a twelve-year-old fan when the Bandits started play in 1983. My childhood fascination with the team led to a desire to write a definitive history of the Bandits as I had previously done on the Tampa Bay Buccaneers (aka Bucs) of the NFL. Reading through back issues of the *St. Petersburg Times*, *Lakeland Ledger*, and *Tampa Tribune* I was struck by Bassett's braggadocio, savvy, and business sense, traits that had escaped my adolescent self. I realized the story of Johnny F. Bassett needed to be told because the history of sports in the United States and Canada cannot be told without his biography. That is the book in the reader's hands.

The Bandits proved to be Bassett's third successful failure. In 1984 the Bandits became the only team from the newer and smaller USFL to outdraw its established NFL counterpart: 46,158 fans per Bandits game to 45,732 fans per Bucs game. This figure was buoyed by a season ticket base of 27,000, the largest amount of season passes sold in the USFL during its existence.[1]

The Bandits followed that up with a larger margin in 1985: 45,220 per Bandits game to 38,753 per Bucs game. Furthermore, a 1984 sports apparel survey concluded the Bandits' lone horseman logo was the third most popular team symbol in America, behind only "America's Team," the Dallas Cowboys, and the Washington Redskins, a team coming off back-to-back Super Bowl appearances.[2] Despite Tampa Bay's individual success, the USFL folded, as had the WHA and WFL, taking the Bandits and Bassett's money with it. Ironically and tragically, Bassett died with the USFL, succumbing to brain cancer in 1986.

Bassett's success in competing with wealthier and more powerful sports franchises while possessing relatively modest resources led to the overarching question which guided my research of Johnny F. Bassett the individual: "How did Bassett do it?" The answer I found is that Bassett utilized showmanship and cultivated the persona of the maverick, resulting in a sporting figure I refer to as "The Maverick Showman." A showman is one who sells the product of spectacle, a viscerally charged event which excites the senses. Bassett felt there was little to differentiate between one football or hockey game and another, so he added to their aura by overseeing ahead-of-their-time team-building strategies and never-before-seen promotions. The success of both resulted from their appeal to base human urges.

Bassett in the 1983 Tampa Bay Bandits Media Guide. The 44-year old Bassett found his sporting nirvana in Tampa, Florida. The Bandits were marketed as the "anti–Buccaneers" and "anti–No Fun League," featuring Steve Spurrier's high-octane offense, Hollywood celebrities, a popular lone-horseman logo, and imaginative promotions. The Bandits became the most successfully marketed team in the short-lived USFL, becoming the only team to attract more spectators than their NFL rivals (courtesy Steve Ehrhart).

Team-building examples were placing a premium on boundary-pushing violence in hockey and trickery in football. On the promotional front, Bassett played into a national obsession for material wealth by hosting mortgage burnings, diamond giveaways, and an audacious one million-dollar giveaway. Bassett also tapped into the nation's fascination with celebrities and popular culture, inviting a litany of film, television, music, and sports stars to either participate in the team or to have prominent seats of honor at the games.

The term "maverick" connotes idealistic individualism, the solitary figure following a path of life which runs upstream against the conventional wisdom of their peers. In American business the maverick entrepreneur is also a disruptive and necessary figure, challenging the status quo and forcing an entrenched entity to confront its own ossification. The maverick challenges industries engaging in "closed innovation policies," in which a monopolistic corporation does not prioritize innovation or expansion.[3] The introduction of a maverick into the industry forces the entrenched parties to "learn about new business models ... and respond by incorporating these innovations into their own businesses."[4] Bassett adhered to this dictum by marketing himself and his franchises as the champions of the common fan, agitating against the elitist NFL and NHL, and exploiting regional biases, mores, and cultures to stoke an "us" against "them" environment. His resulting success led to professional football and hockey changing the way they marketed their sports. I propose in this book that Bassett is a forgotten exemplar of the Maverick Showman, a practitioner of the promotional arts on par with Bill Veeck and a sports entrepreneur in the class of Lamar Hunt.

Bill Veeck owned the Cleveland Indians, St. Louis Browns, and Chicago White Sox during his storied career in Major League Baseball. Lacking the resources of New York, Veeck employed maverick showmanship to generate ticket revenue from his small market teams. As owner of the Cleveland Indians, he tapped into a sense of resentment the city's largely working-class majority held towards New York's competitive advantage. Veeck reminded citizens of how the Indians were considered "bush-league" by New York, and literally went door-to-door, holding impromptu meetings in taverns, lodges, bus stops, and cab stands to canvass the citizens on what they wanted in a game day experience.[5] Armed with this data, Veeck produced a stream of promotions catering to the lower and middle class: giving away appliances, automobiles, and even livestock to fans holding a lucky seat ticket. When Veeck sold the Indians and purchased the St. Louis Browns, his methodology intensified, and his promotions became the stuff of baseball legend. Veeck sent the 3'7" Eddie Gaedel to bat, complete with toy bat and uniform number ⅛. He hosted

Grandstand Manager Night in which fans voted on strategy with YES/ NO placards. When Veeck took over the Chicago White Sox he designed an exploding scoreboard which presaged today's Jumbotrons. Veeck also introduced the concept of Ladies' Day, offering free or reduced tickets to women to broaden his fan base.[6] Veeck's promotions paid off. His 1948 Cleveland Indians drew 2,620,627 fans, a record that stood for fifteen years and the Browns and White Sox generated enough revenue for him to compete until his retirement in 1981, including one World Series title and two American League pennants.

Lamar Hunt founded the American Football League (AFL) in 1959 when the NFL refused to grant him an expansion team in Dallas. Using the NFLs tone-deafness to expansion against them, Hunt awarded teams to cities the NFL believed too small: Buffalo, Boston, Dallas, Houston, Denver, Oakland, and San Diego. Hunt also used the NFL's antipathy to revenue sharing against it. Hunt's main proposition was that for the AFL to attract fans and media, all teams needed an equal opportunity for on-field success. To that end, he decreed that all revenue would be split equally between franchises regardless of their on-field success or attendance figures.[7] This sharing of revenue led to competitive parity, a primary reason the AFL attracted the revenue necessary to win a war of attrition against the wealthier NFL.[8]

Lamar Hunt grew a sport and led it to an era of progressivism but also made it difficult for another professional sports league to get off the ground. The AFL's success forced the NFL to accept a merger in 1966. Unfortunately, the merger Hunt forced had the ironic effect of making professional sports more of a monopoly than ever before. His innovative approach to television technically circumvented the Sherman Antitrust Act by allowing the AFL to tie up a network. This required a special exemption to the Sherman Act: the 1961 Sports Broadcasting Act (SBA) which allowed the NFL and AFL to tie up networks exclusively.[9] The SBA has subsequently been put into effect by all four major sports leagues to the detriment of competition. In the years since the AFL-NFL merger there have been several attempts to create upstart professional sports leagues which ultimately failed because of the hold the established leagues have on television. This is a situation that Johnny F. Bassett knew all too well and is what led him to employ promotional wizardry and business acumen in a maverick style.

ONE

||||||||||||||||||||||||||||||||||||||

Young Bassett and the
Show Business of Sports

P.T. Barnum allegedly said, "There is no such thing as bad publicity." The authenticity of this quote is as suspect as Barnum's more famous line: "There's a sucker born every minute."[1]

Regardless of the validity, Barnum's purported quote about publicity certainly did not apply to Johnny F. Bassett on December 3, 1975. Bassett's Toronto Toros suffered a one-sided loss to the Edmonton Oilers the night before and the game was sparsely attended. The poor showing led many to believe Bassett was on the brink of folding his hockey team as he had done with his teams in the World Football League and World Team Tennis (WTT).

Windsor Star columnist Jack Dulmage argued that Bassett's setbacks were proof of the entrepreneur's poor judgment and naiveté. "As an entrepreneur of professional sports, Bassett may wait a long time for his ships to dock," Dulmage wrote. "He is afloat in seas of dreamland."[2] Bassett maintained a positive public persona in the face of this ordeal. He continued to make the argument he had started the year before that Toronto could be a booming market for several professional sports. "What do we have?" Bassett asked rhetorically. "Major league hockey and Canadian football. No annual golf tournaments and only a couple of weeks of tennis. I am convinced that this (his investment in sports) is a worthwhile venture that will eventually provide a return."[3]

Bassett's positivity was viewed with ever increasing skepticism by a local press which viewed him as "a millionaire playboy dabbling in sports with other people's money."[4] The truth, however, was that Bassett's personal fortune was at stake because he violated a standard maxim of show business eloquently explained by the fictional producer Max Bialystock in Mel Brooks' film *The Producers:* "Never put your own money in the show!"[5] The folding of his WFL and WTT teams cost

7

Bassett millions and the floundering Toros were continuing to drain his accounts. The reality of Bassett's financial situation did not derail the portrayal of him as an affable but eccentric dilettante who produced little substance. Bassett's lifetime friend and collaborator Peter Eby summarized the overall perception of Bassett in the early-to-mid 1970s. "I do not know of anyone who disliked Johnny," Eby said. "They may have thought he was crazy, but they did not dislike him."[6] The string of failures led to comparisons with a legendary American showman whose reputation for spectacle and humbug went hand in hand. "He was referred to as Canada's Barnum," said Bassett's son, John C. Bassett.[7] This comparison is more apt than Bassett's contemporary Canadian chroniclers may have thought. Bassett and sports promotion derived naturally from "The Greatest Showman."

P.T. Barnum and Show Business

Phineas Taylor Barnum was a trailblazer in American entertainment and is referred to as an entrepreneur who was "happy to explode established rituals ... and challenge notions of social order."[8] Barnum exemplified the calls for probity, work ethic, and constantly striving for self-improvement, which marked the nineteenth century.[9] At the same time, Barnum argued for the importance of entertaining the masses, an industry that came to be known as show business, stating in his autobiography: "Men, women and children, who cannot live on gravity alone, need something to satisfy their gayer, lighter moods and hours."[10] Barnum dedicated his life to satisfying such needs.

Barnum started his mission as a child, making his own molasses candy and selling it to neighborhood children, saving the profits for future use as if he were a character in a Horatio Alger novel.[11] The son of a farmer and part-time tavern keeper, Barnum grew up far from want and as an early adult settled in as a clerk at a family grocery store. Unsatisfied with the routines of urban life, Barnum quit and set out to make his mark in his own way, explaining: "A salary was not sufficient for me. My disposition was of that speculative character which refused to be satisfied unless I was engaged in some business where my profits might be enhanced, or, at least, made to depend upon my energy, perseverance, attention to business, tact, and calculation."[12]

Barnum took advantage of an era in which the nation was growing less rural and more urban. Farm life, and the self-sufficiency that went along with it, was abandoned in favor of a factory job in the city. This migration created a need for consumer goods to provide the necessities of life that were once produced at home. A key discovery of Barnum's was that a need for entertainment was as important a fulfillment as food and lodging and that those who commercialized entertainment could make a fortune.[13] In order to embark on this career, Barnum liquidated his grocery store, borrowed $500 more and purchased the exhibition rights of Ms. Joice Heth, an African American woman who promoters claimed was the 161-year-old former nursemaid of George Washington.[14] Facing $1,000 in debt, Barnum was thrilled and terrified. His early showings of Heth barely broke even, leading him to pawn his watch for train fare. Despite the rough start, Barnum was having the time of his life, claiming in his autobiography: "I had at last found my true vocation."[15] Soon, Barnum parlayed his purchase of the American Museum and his promotion of the opera singer Jenny Lind into a multi-million dollar business.[16] This same life arc was repeated by Bassett and other sports promoters with the establishment of sport as an industry.

Bassett's Barnum-esque Sports Childhood

Johnny F. Bassett was born February 5, 1939, in Toronto to John White Hughes Bassett, Jr., and Moira Eleanor Bassett. He was the couple's first son, a couple which represented the middle generation of a family referred to on more than one occasion as "The Canadian Rockefellers."[17] Bassett's grandfather, John Bassett, Sr., rose from beat reporter to president of the *Montreal Gazette*.[18] John White Hughes Bassett followed in his father's footsteps, starting as a reporter for the *Sherbrooke Daily Record* and eventually becoming owner of one of the largest newspapers in Canada (the *Toronto Telegram*) and Canada's first commercial television station (CFTO of the CTV network).[19] Both newspapermen parlayed their political and business contacts into lucrative financial deals which culminated in a family fortune estimated in the tens of millions.[20] The Bassett family wealth may have inoculated the young Johnny from a life of want, but it did not inhibit a native entrepreneurial spirit which he shared with P.T. Barnum.

An eight-year-old Johnny F. Bassett, sent away to boarding school at Bishop's College, showed his inclination for selling joy at a precocious age also. Bassett invented a baseball game using dice in his dormitory room. The game became quite popular among the boys at Bishop's, and before long they were paying Bassett ten cents apiece for a "franchise."[21] In addition to inventing the game and selling franchises, Bassett also wrote a weekly newspaper chronicling the previous week's slate of games, complete with game capsules and player profiles. The papers sold for a penny apiece and made Bassett a popular child on campus, as well as a profitable mogul.[22] "I was a sports entrepreneur when I was eight years old and I made money!" he crowed in an interview near the end of his life.[23] Bassett's childhood choice of sport as his product made personal and financial sense given both his passion for sports and the growth of sports as an industry in the twentieth century.

Bassett's childhood was consumed with sports. Like any young Canadian male, Bassett gravitated towards hockey and proved to be a stellar goalie. Bassett became the youngest goalie to ever start for the Upper Canada College team.[24] Bassett excelled to such a level that he attracted the notice of the professional ranks. At the age of fifteen, Bassett was approached by representatives of the Toronto Maple Leafs. A fifteen-year-old goalie being approached by the Maple Leafs in 1954 is akin to an American pitcher of the same age and era being approached by the New York Yankees. The Maple Leafs offered Bassett the chance to leave school and join their top junior team, the Toronto Marlies. There is little doubt among Bassett's family that given his druthers, Bassett would have jumped at the opportunity to begin his life in sports right then and there, but his father had other ideas.

Johnny F. Bassett recalled the story in an interview later in his life. Of course, as he told it, his father did not just refuse to let him sign, but made a special trip to the spiritual home of hockey in Canada to deliver a message to a Hall of Fame executive that his son was not to be tempted about leaving school again. "The Leafs wanted to sign me," Bassett said. "When I took the contract home to the old man, he took it down to Conn Smythe's office at Maple Leaf Gardens. He stood in front of Smythe's desk and tore it (the contract) up. He told Smythe to leave me alone."[25]

At roughly the same time his father was ripping up his offer from the Maple Leafs, Johnny F. Bassett teamed up with Peter Barnard to win the Canadian Open junior doubles tennis championship.[26] The following year, now only sixteen years of age, Johnny F. Bassett became noticed for his ability in singles. In July 1955, Bassett showed a flair for drama during the junior singles championship of the Canadian Open. In the quarterfinals, he lost the first set to Joe Anderson before rallying to win the match 6–8, 6–4, 6–4. In the semi-finals, Bassett faced his doubles partner from the previous year, Peter Barnard. Once again, Bassett dropped the first set in a high-scoring, back-and-forth manner. With an ability to cover the entire court from the baseline to the net and back, the speedy Bassett once again rallied against an opponent, besting Barnard 6–8, 6–4, 6–4. The finals almost proved anticlimactic as Bassett overwhelmed Gord Daly 6–1, 6–2. In writing up the contest for the *Toronto Star*, reporter John MacDonald hailed Bassett as "one of the best prospects" in Canadian tennis.[27]

Between ages sixteen and eighteen, Bassett continued to improve and climbed in the Canadian rankings. In 1957, at the age of eighteen, Bassett was ranked as the number one male tennis player in Ontario, and number two in all of Canada.[28] He earned a spot on the Canadian Davis Cup team and received an invitation to the U.S. Open. Unfortunately for Bassett, his love of all sports led to his time as an elite tennis player being short lived. Bassett injured his right knee while playing quarterback for Upper Canada College in 1957.[29] The injury required the first of three surgeries Bassett had on his leg. The quickness his knee injury depleted proved to be the difference between Bassett being the great tennis player he was on his way to becoming and the very good player he would always be. Bassett gave up sports and focused on academics, qualifying for the Gold Medal at the University of Western Ontario. Western Ontario is also where he met the most important person in his life.

Sue Carling first met Johnny F. Bassett when she was fifteen years old. The great-great granddaughter of Thomas Carling, founder of Canada's Carling Brewery, Sue was attending the annual Shakespeare festival and was introduced to Johnny. "We were quite young," Sue Bassett-Klauber recalled. "We met at the Stratford Festival and I was fifteen and he was seventeen."[30] It would be a couple of more years before they interacted regularly

Twenty-one-year-old Johnny F. Bassett and Sue Carling, his fiancée, in February 1960 while students at the University of Western Ontario. Bassett graduated with honors, earning the Gold Medal for academic excellence, the equivalent of valedictorian, while also holding the office of student president and editor of the college newspaper (courtesy the Bassett family).

as co-eds at the University of Western Ontario. An attractive, intelligent, and sought-after woman from an equally impressive family, Sue Carling was not awestruck by Bassett. A big man on campus, Bassett was well-known for his tennis accomplishments and for being the son of John W.H Bassett. When he met Sue again at the University of Western Ontario in London, he quickly went out of his way to try and catch the eye of the cheerleader and model. They dated briefly during the early fall term, but the relationship stalled due in part to his arrogance.

Bassett kept in pursuit of Sue Carling, embarrassed by his early behavior. He let his true feelings for Sue come out and she was receptive to his admission and they began to date again. By the time final examinations began, Johnny F. Bassett and Sue Carling realized they had a connection that they just could not deny and discussed getting married. Given their respective ages at the time, it is obvious that they were each other's first true love. "By summer's end we were just eighteen and twenty years old and planning our wedding for the following June," Sue Bassett-Klauber said.[31]

Compared to the standards of today's society, engagement at such an early age would be unusual and likely a source of family drama. As far as John W.H Bassett was concerned, he could not have been happier. As Johnny Bassett's son, John C. Bassett, recalled, John W.H. Bassett believed Sue Carling would do what he could not: get his son to finally focus on academics. "If you listened to my grandfather it was his idea so his son would study," John C. Bassett, said.[32]

At the age of twenty, Johnny F. Bassett had proven himself an exemplary athlete with the natural ability to compete at the highest levels of hockey and tennis, winning championships and earning top honors. Unfortunately, his balky right knee ended any hopes he had for a professional playing career. Bassett needed another role to stay in sports. He eventually undertook a role that did not exist just forty years earlier and was only now coming into vogue.

Sports Promotion in the Twentieth Century

P.T. Barnum's marketing of show business was replicated by others in an industry once reviled as seedy and debauched: professional sports. Professional sports underwent a transformation after the age of Barnum. The term "sport" began the nineteenth century as a derogatory term for denizens of taverns who gambled unscrupulously on cards and fights, drank beer with abandon and fornicated outside of marriage.[33] By the end of the century, "sportsmen" became synonymous with men of good breeding who whiled away their leisure time golfing, sailing, swimming, and watching local semi-professional baseball teams.[34] While baseball spectating was a permissible method of leisure, paid participation in sports, particularly baseball, football, and boxing, was viewed as a sign of low economic class.[35] In addition to class, the morality of baseball, football, and boxing was questioned. A series of gambling scandals plagued baseball up to and including the Chicago White Sox throwing of the 1919 World Series. Football struggled under the cloud of several player deaths. Rumors and outright proof of fixed fights and pre-determined outcomes were rampant in boxing. Organizational structures implemented throughout sports in 1920, including the naming of Kenesaw Mountain Landis as the first baseball commissioner and the creation of the NFL, allayed most of the moral and ethical concerns about professional sports and spurred a decade known as "The Golden Age." The age was not just golden because of stars like Babe Ruth, Red Grange, and Jack Dempsey, it was also gold for a new type of sportsman: the promoter.

The vanguard of the modern sports promoter was George Lewis "Tex" Rickard, an erstwhile miner who discovered there was more gold to be made in providing entertainment such as boxing to the denizens of the Klondike and Nevada desert than in prospecting. Rickard realized miners had limited capital to spend on entertainment so he set his sights on broadening the appeal of boxing to a higher-class clientele, eventually succeeding and becoming the first man to promote fights which made in excess of one million dollars.[36] This was done by using the innovative approach of bringing the concept of heroes and villains to a new level. Rickard built passionate rivalries on personality differences as minute as whether fighter Gene Tunney was a snob and enemy of the working class because he liked to read too much or that Jack Dempsey was an unpatriotic draft-dodger.[37] Rickard also established the value of celebrity spectators, discerning that having a well-known politician, performer, or socialite in the stands gave his bouts an appeal to non-boxing fans. Rickard's biography abounds with references to "celebrities from various high and low social planes attending in evening clothes, giving the event the touch of class that Rickard had so long hoped would distinguish his big boxing shows."[38]

Sporting spectacles soon became part of the American entertainment landscape. Middle and upper-class businessmen created sporting spectacle. Professional leagues were founded, uniform rules were codified, a sporting press was nurtured, and the action was beamed from coast-to-coast on radio and then television. The number of sporting spectacles grew exponentially. By the 1960s the sporting calendar in

America was packed with a series of seasonal televised spectacle: the World Series, the Super Bowl, the NBA and NHL Finals, NCAA March Madness, the Indianapolis and Daytona 500, the Masters, and a bevy of New Year's Day bowl games. Not until the Covid-19 pandemic of 2020 did this panoply of offerings end its 60-year run.

Into this world came Johnny F. Bassett.

Two

IIIIIIIIIIIIIIIIIIIIIIIIIIIIIIIIIIIIIII

Show Business
Leads to Sports Business

Bassett dutifully followed into the family business upon graduation, taking a position with his father's communication conglomerate. Bassett hit the ground running, enjoying immediate success by innovating the way his father's mass media outlets covered the news and bringing a new audience to the company.

Following a stint as a beat reporter and production assistant, the 27-year-old Bassett was promoted to promotions manager and producer at CFTO, Toronto's first private television station and the flagship of CTV, Canada's early national network. The next year, he was named assistant editor of his father's *Toronto Telegram*, a politically conservative Tory publication notorious for its coverage of national politics. CFTO was operated by Baton Broadcasting, a company founded by his father and the influential Eaton's, a family which oversaw a retail and construction empire. Bassett proved quite adept at both jobs but saw his hiring as an opportunity to update the mediums. He viewed newspapers not as just a repository of a community's comings and goings, but as a civic asset with a mandate to promote a region socially and economically with a dose of activism added for good measure. Loyalty to one's community was a personal characteristic of Bassett's and he felt the *Telegram* could help Toronto become an even better city. An industrial concept Johnny F. Bassett brought to the *Telegram* was service journalism. Coining the phrase "The *Telegram* Cares," the paper unveiled a range of features.[1]

"Action Line" was developed as an ombudsman service for helping readers deal with the frustrating inefficiencies inherent in government agencies. "Today's Child" was a feature which profiled orphaned children, raising awareness of the issue and leading to many adoptions. Johnny F. Bassett also championed placing more letters to the editor at the expense of staff written editorials, reasoning that people would be more willing to read the paper if they were given a chance to express their own viewpoints.[2]

The feature that Bassett became especially identified with was his supplemental insert designed for teenagers. *After Four* was all Johnny F. Bassett. Acting as editor and columnist, Bassett was completely free to run the section as he saw fit. *After Four*, like his other work on the *Telegram*, is the earliest example of Bassett taking a traditional institution and broadening its horizons. The stodgy, politically oriented *Toronto Telegram* which older and conservative readers clung to remained, but Johnny F. Bassett inserted a hip place for teen-agers into its pages as well. Just as he would with professional sports in the 70s and 80s, Johnny F. Bassett expanded the market for a rigid institution by identifying an underserved demographic and crafting a product and corresponding promotional strategy which brought a new and energetic audience into the fold.

After Four had as its motto "Best Serving the Interests of Youth," and included interviews with local musicians, actors and other assorted artists, music reviews, fashion tips, and a classified section which highlighted a marketplace for teenagers. Advertisements for automobiles, tutoring, and political gatherings abounded in the classifieds. The supplement proved so successful that Bassett transitioned it into a weekly television show on CFTO. The television version of *After Four* aired Saturdays at 4:00 p.m.[3] A cross between Dick Clark's *American Bandstand* and a panel show, the television version of *After Four* was Bassett's first foray into electronic media. Entertainment focused, Bassett sent teenage reporters out in the field to interview incoming music acts whose tours brought them to Toronto. Luminaries such as the Dave Clark Five, Gordon Lightfoot, and the Motown greats were guests on *After Four.*[4]

Bassett did not just cover musical performances, he produced them. In 1969 Bassett brought the incendiary Broadway hit *Hair* to the Royal Alex Theatre. Bassett believed the Toronto theater scene had grown stale after catering to too narrow an audience of social conservatives satisfied with the latest bland musicals. He felt there was a vast and underserved audience hungering for mature political theater which featured vulgarity, nudity, drug use, and anti-war sentiments. Despite criticism from conservative corners that the show was too risqué, Bassett was proved right when *Hair* ran for thirteen months and provided him $3.5 million in gross revenue.[5] Bassett parlayed these proceeds into producing two well-received films: *Face Off* (1971), the story of a Toronto Maple Leaf player falling in love with a counter-culture rock star, and

Paperback Hero (1973), which tells the tale of a minor league hockey player escaping the anxiety of his career ending by surrendering to the delusion that he is a gunfighter in the Old West. *Paperback Hero* became well known for the theme song "If You Could Read My Mind" written by Bassett friend Gordon Lightfoot. Thanks to CFTO, the *Telegram*, and his own productions, Johnny F. Bassett was becoming a household name in Toronto in only his late twenties. Despite this, the lure of sports was too great to pass up.

Lakeshore Racing

The *Toronto Telegram* provided Bassett with connections to civic leaders, entrepreneurs, entertainers, and athletes who all opened his mind to a world of possibilities. The more Bassett learned about professional sports the more he wanted to incorporate his own vision into the industry and provide Torontonians with the best sporting entertainment value possible. A passionate sports fan and proud native of Toronto, Bassett was aghast at the paucity of spectator sports in his hometown. Aside from the Toronto Maple Leafs of the NHL and Canadian Football League Toronto Argonauts, there were scant events for sports spectators in the city. The bare sporting calendar was perplexing to many residents of the city known as the New York of the North for its role as the media capital of the nation and its status as the largest city in Canada.[6] Part of the issue was a provincialism unnatural for a city its size which was so ingrained in the citizens' psyche that Toronto was labeled alternately "Toronto the Good" and "Toronto the Dull."[7] Examples of this mindset included the prohibition of tobogganing on Sundays and the routine padlocking of public playgrounds on "the Lord's Day."[8] Even the two sporting institutions of Toronto, the Maple Leafs and Argonauts, could not play games on Sunday until a city ordinance permitting such games was passed in 1960.[9] It would be another twenty-two years before Toronto allowed beer to be sold at sporting events.[10]

Such rules led Major League Baseball to bypass Toronto and choose Montreal for an expansion team in 1969. Players Maury Wills, Bill Stoneman, and fan favorite Rusty Staub, known as "Le Grand Orange" for his build and hair color, helped the Montreal Expos prove America's national pastime could work in Canada. Toronto watched this from a distance, with many cringing at the thought of Quebec, a province fighting for the right to leave Canada, being the first Canadian city to earn the moniker major league. Montreal further surpassed Toronto as the sports capital of Canada when it was named host of the 1976 Summer

Olympics. It was into this sports desert that Bassett attempted to create an oasis.

His first opportunity came in the form of auto racing. In 1967, at the behest of Johnny F. Bassett, the *Toronto Telegram* sponsored a United States Auto Club (USAC) race at Mosport Park, a two-and-a-half-mile long track built outside of Toronto in Bowmanville, Ontario. Bassett had become enamored with auto racing: the speed, the pageantry, the inherent risk and reward. The Indianapolis 500 was the most popular race in the world, attracting hundreds of thousands of people to Indiana, and Bassett wanted this for Toronto. Bassett organized the Telegram Trophy race in his first attempt to give Toronto an annual spectacle. The race featured the same style cars which participated in the annual Indianapolis 500. The popularity of the Indianapolis 500 led many to call the USAC series the Indy Car circuit. With 10 turns, a back straight of almost a mile in length and plenty of room for spectators, Mosport Park was deemed a "first-class track" upon its opening in 1961 and was ideal for Bassett's initial vision.[11]

The first two Telegram Trophy races at Mosport were modestly attended as Indy Car races did not quite win over the hearts and minds of Canadian sports fans in the mid–1960s as quickly as Bassett hoped.[12] Bassett was not dissuaded, though. An event in Quebec caught his eye and led him to formulate an innovative plan that proved to be too advanced and radical for the Toronto of the time.

In 1968 Labatt Breweries sponsored a street race in Trois-Rivieres, a city located at the confluence of the Saint Maurice and Saint Lawrence Rivers halfway between Quebec City and Montreal. Unlike the road course at Mosport, the Trois-Rivieres race was run on city streets in the same manner as many European Formula One races. The mile-and-a-half long course wound through the city and included two long straights and seven sharp turns, five of which were ninety-degree turns and one hairpin (a turn of almost 180°). The race drew over one-hundred thousand fans. Those that could not sit in the stands watched from upper floor windows or on rooftops of the buildings that lined the course. The attraction for these fans was the danger the course provided for the talented drivers. The everyday objects that commuters passed without notice at 40 to 50 miles per hour on their way to work were risks to great bodily harm at 150–180 miles per hour. "It's not a circuit for the weak of heart," wrote a commentator for the *Canadian Motorsport Bulletin*. "A false move and you can end up in the trees, the curbs, buildings or sidewalks. Drivers have to go through the Duplessis Memorial Arch, which sits threateningly at the bottom of a steep hill right on the apex of a sharp right-hand turn."[13]

Johnny F. Bassett imagined such a race in downtown Toronto and excitedly got to work. In September 1968 Bassett announced his plan to move the Telegram Trophy race to the Toronto lakefront at the Canadian National Exhibition (CNE) grounds, site of Canada's annual national fair. Bassett, along with several other businessmen, including John Eaton, formed Lakeshore Racing. Bassett was head of the company and the architect of a compellingly complex raceway. His vision for a one-of-a-kind course required a unique use of Toronto real estate. The race would run on a circuit of about two miles through the CNE grounds including a 1.1 mile stretch of Lakeshore Boulevard. The most unique twist of the course would allow cars to race over the surface of Exhibition Stadium's playing field, home of the Canadian Football League's Toronto Argonauts.[14] Bassett expected crowds in excess of 100,000 for the Indy Car race in June of 1969 and stated that the success could lead to the Canadian Grand Prix being held on the same course in September of 1969. To accomplish this goal Bassett needed local politicians to okay the logistics of closing public roads and further relaxation of rules prohibiting Sunday sports that were recently granted the Leafs and Argonauts. The proposal was met with much excitement from race fans and civic leaders. There was also a very vocal and powerful opposition to the race as well.

Toronto's Board of Control met to discuss Bassett's proposal shortly after the announcement. A key opponent of the proposal was Controller Allan Lamport. Lamport was adamant that because Mosport had been created for the sole purpose of attracting auto races, it was a waste of taxpayer money to create a temporary racing site downtown, particularly one that would require the closing of Lakeshore Boulevard, a major artery on the shore of Lake Ontario. Lamport also argued about the inconvenience taxpayers would encounter by making an entire section of the city, including a popular waterfront park, inaccessible. Finally, Lamport was also worried about hurting Mosport and other independent tracks financially. "I can't possibly see how we can allow these promoters to use facilities which the taxpayer has paid for," Lamport said. "Are we going to establish facilities such as Mosport? What about these other tracks that pay taxes? Should the city of Toronto put them out of business?"[15]

In addition to concerns over finances and inconvenience, many residents in the Parkdale neighborhood near the site raised concerns over safety, noise, and the old standby of contravening the Lord's Day. The racecourse became a divisive issue. When the Board of Control decided to hold a hearing on the course at the end of October, it guaranteed great local political theater for weeks. Hyperbole was in abundance.

One controller against the course went so far as to worry aloud about children somehow climbing the fence, getting on the track, and being run down.[16]

Bassett tried to assuage everyone's concerns by offering a calm point-by-point response to the most common concerns. "We feel there are only three arguments against it (the track)—safety, cost to the taxpayer and the use of parklands," Bassett told the assembled.

> The track will be one of the safest in the world. We are working closely with Henry Banks, director of competition for the U.S. Auto Club, and Jo Bonnier, president of the Grand Prix's Drivers Association. The entire course will be wide enough to give the drivers protection and we will build fences and guardrails to protect the spectators. Most of the crowd will be well back from the course. We won't be using any parklands. Just some streets in the CNE grounds and Lakeshore Road. We've checked with John Murray, deputy police chief of Toronto, and he claims the races will present no traffic problems.[17]

After weeks of grandstanding by both sides, Toronto's Board of Control met on October 30, 1968, and voted 3–2 in favor of Bassett's racecourse. Shortly after the Board of Control's decision, the Toronto City Council voted in favor of amending its Sunday bylaws to allow two races during the year. Everything looked good for Bassett until a Member of Parliament found the chance to cash in on the discontent of some of his constituents.

Many Parkdale residents organized public pickets and other demonstrations in and around the Toronto lakefront. Boycotts of the businesses supporting the racecourse were held, particularly the *Toronto Telegram* and CFTO. The outrageous nature of some comments in the newspaper was exemplified by a resident who skewered Bassett quite nastily in an article in the *Toronto Star*. "Who would have thought anyone could have such a deranged mind as to even suggest setting up a raceway in the centre of a city, depriving people of the use of their roads," the anonymous resident asked. "Only someone with the power of John Bassett."[18]

Liberal MP James Trotter of the Parkdale Riding viewed this unrest from his office and decided to join in the fray, singling out Bassett for scorn. Calling Bassett a "feudal baron," Trotter opposed the raceway, stating the effort to put on a race on public streets was nothing more than a rich boy using Toronto as his own personal playpen. "Indisputably powerful interests have conspired to inflict this outrage on Toronto in order to satisfy their own egos and greed," Trotter said.[19]

Trotter's attack was answered by Toronto Board of Control Chairman William Allen, who had been a vocal proponent of the track and felt Bassett and his partners were acting in the best interests of Toronto.

Allen had been enamored with the plan from the start, stating the race-track would be a key to "making Toronto a sports capital."[20] "I deeply regret that a group of Toronto businessmen with supreme confidence in the future of this metropolis should have been subjected to such abuse," Allen said.[21]

It was quite a situation Bassett was experiencing. He was engaged in a battle over a sports promotion with a member of his own national government and powerful civic groups. Politely, he continued to tout the economic impact the two races would provide to Toronto. Bassett also was indomitable in his view that Toronto was a world class sports town and that his auto race would be the dawning of an athletic era. While his arguments had won local support from the Board of Control, City Council, and multiple civic groups, Bassett's planned racecourse was ultimately undone by a labyrinth of jurisdictional questions. Bassett could not get a firm commitment from any of the governing bodies which would allow him to move forward. After months of fighting, Bassett finally threw in the towel. "Without necessary consent, we simply cannot go forward," a dejected Bassett told reporters. "In the absence of favorable legal opinion, we cannot invite industrial sponsors, concessionaires, international racing authorities, automotive manufacturers and their racing teams to commit themselves."[22]

Bassett's racecourse was simply too far ahead of its time. The Toronto of 1968 was just not ready for such an endeavor. The *Toronto Telegram* withdrew sponsorship of the race and the Mosport Indy Car race went dormant until 1977. Interestingly, the race was revised in 1986 and moved to the Toronto lakefront and run on almost the exact course Bassett had proposed nearly two decades earlier. The name Johnny F. Bassett became ironically synonymous with Toronto racing after his death. In the late 1980s the Molson Indy Festival Foundation awarded the John F. Bassett Award to "recognize a Canadian individual, organization or event that has made a significant contribution to the development and growth of Canadian motor racing."[23] "They named the trophy after him because the race was his idea," said his son, John C. Bassett.[24]

Basset continued to excel at his job with Baton for a few more years after the Lakeshore battle. He was 34 in 1973 and well established as a newspaperman and television producer. He was employed in a powerful position as his father's right-hand man at Baton, a company which was earning millions in profits annually.[25] Baton Broadcasting was as close to a license to print money as one could have in Canada in the early 1970s. The company went public in 1971, with John W.H Bassett ensconced as the manager and Johnny F. as his heir apparent.[26] The public offering allowed Baton to branch out and own a wide variety of assets. Among these properties were the Montreal Forum, home of the revered Montreal Canadiens of the NHL, and the largest television/radio stations in Saskatoon and Ottawa. With holdings of this magnitude, Baton saw revenues in the tens of millions and profits which reached $3.142 million in 1972.[27] These accomplishments would have contented most men his age, but Johnny F. Bassett was restless. His attempt to bring road racing to Toronto had reawakened a passion for sports. Bassett loved sports more than journalism, television, and theater. The ability of sports to unite a disparate group appealed to the idealist in him, but he found the current state of professional sports in Toronto to be elitist and dismissive of fans. An opportunity for Bassett to alter the nature of what a professional sports team could be occurred in 1973. A floundering team in a newly minted but much scorned hockey league went up for sale in 1973 at the same time a new professional football league was looking for an owner to call Toronto home. This confluence of ownership opportunities led Johnny F. Bassett to undertake a financial risk that most could not fathom.

Selling Out for the Toros and Northmen

The World Hockey Association was founded in 1971 as a competitor to the National Hockey League. The World Football League was founded in 1973 with the same desire to compete with the NFL. Both organizations were founded by Gary Davidson, an American lawyer and businessman who also founded the American Basketball Association (ABA) in 1967. The premise behind all the leagues was similar: Grow their respective sports by providing professional players a viable alternative to the major professional ranks in markets deemed not quite major league. In 1971 the NHL had only fourteen teams centered mostly in Canada and the northern United States.[28] Likewise, the NFL had an America-first allotment of teams and Davidson felt franchises should be placed in Toronto, Mexico City, and eventually Europe and Asia.[29] Davidson's hockey league launched first and of the 12 WHA franchises to take the ice in 1972, none may have been more dysfunctional than the Ottawa Nationals.

At first glance the choice of placing a team in hockey-mad Canada's national capital seemed logical. The city had just built the Civic Centre Arena and had at one time been home to a dominant early NHL franchise, the Ottawa Senators. WHA founders hoped that nearly 40 years after the Senators moved to St. Louis, the hockey fans of Canada's capital city would embrace a new professional team. It became apparent that the WHA was not going to get its wish after the first few weeks of the inaugural 1972-1973 season. Ottawans never embraced the Nationals despite a competitive team. Attendance at the 10,500 seat Civic Centre Arena was sparse at best. When the Nationals did begin drawing crowds during a playoff push, team owners Doug Michel and Nick Trbovich began a dispute with their landlords over future use of the arena. Michel and Trbovich saw their team locked out of the arena by their landlords when neither side could reach an agreement. This action resulted in a most unusual circumstance. The Nationals made the playoffs but were forced to play their home playoff games at Maple Leaf Gardens, an arena 200 miles away. These "home games" were far from convenient for the National players, not to mention out of the reach of their few fans. The road weary Nationals mustered slight resistance as they were routed in the playoffs by the New England Whalers, four games to one.

Johnny F. Bassett attended the Nationals' Toronto playoff games and became enamored with the WHA. A self-proclaimed "creative entrepreneur," Bassett was of a like-mind with the new hockey league.[30] In addition to bringing professional hockey to areas long ignored by the NHL, the WHA played a free-wheeling style of hockey that relied more on speed and skill than brute force and fighting. While the WHA's style of hockey may not have appealed to hockey purists, for an idealist like Bassett it was just the type of sport he could get into. Bassett surmised such a sport may have broader appeal than the NHL's and could bring in the casual fan who found the Maple Leafs dull. Bassett also felt the Maple Leafs had grown complacent and indifferent to their fans as a result of possessing a monopoly on Toronto hockey. Believing as always that there was an audience in Toronto for an alternate form of entertainment, Bassett went to work. Bassett learned that Michel and Trbovich were willing to entertain offers to sell the Nationals. That information was all Bassett needed to spring into action. Bassett had found his mission in life. He was going to be the owner of a professional sports team.

Every facet of Johnny F. Bassett's entry into professional team sports seemed to be contrary to conventional wisdom. The team Bassett purchased could not draw in Ottawa, so he elected to move to Toronto. Toronto just happened to be home to an NHL team with a long tradition and a rabid fan base. That same team also held title to the only hockey arena in the city suitable for professional hockey. And if that was not enough, the Toronto Maple Leafs of the NHL was headed by Harold Ballard, a man with a reputation for cutthroat business practices who squashed opponents like bugs. Nothing about this scenario made sense, but Bassett could not wait to get started. He began making phone calls to friends and acquaintances and before long he had an ownership group totaling an unwieldy 22 members.[31]

Bassett's ownership group was named Can-Sports, Inc., and among its 22 members was Bassett's good friend Peter Eby.[32] Eby recalled the days of late spring/early summer 1973 when Bassett introduced his plans for purchasing the Nationals. Bassett had hired a lawyer to draw up papers for prospective investors to document what they intended to invest. The meeting quickly took a positive yet chaotic turn and within minutes Bassett was able to buy a hockey team:

> When he first developed the idea of bringing a second hockey team to Toronto, a lot of people called to say they would like to join him. To see how real the interest was, we called a meeting in downtown Toronto. Johnny went through his thought process and put out the fact he needed over a million dollars to do this. A lawyer had developed a form for people to fill out how much they would be interested in investing. Someone yelled out, "That's bullshit! If you are interested, write out a check right now!" Lo and behold, there is 20–30 people pulling out checkbooks and writing checks! We had more money than we needed! It was amazing. I was in the investment business and I had never seen anything like it.[33]

A reason for the investor's appeal was Bassett's willingness to put up a significant portion of the purchase price. "He paid the same price I did to invest," Eby said. "Today, a guy like him would not put any money up and own 30% of the team. But he did not do that. If something was not a commercial success, he suffered like everyone else did."[34]

There were not as many investors willing to follow Bassett into professional football, however. The WFL required a franchise fee of $600,000 to be paid before a prospective owner was considered, a steep amount for an upstart league. There was also doubt about the wild ideas Davidson had about how the game should be played. The WFL planned a series of game rules which purists decried as gimmicky, although some were eventually adopted by the NFL:

1. The kickoff was moved from the 40-yard line to the 30-yard line to allow for more returns and fewer touchbacks.
2. The goalposts were moved from the goal line to the back of the end zone.
3. Touchdowns were worth 7 points instead of 6.
4. An "action point" could be scored after a touchdown by a successful run or pass to the end zone, eliminating the point-after-touchdown (PAT) kick.
5. A 15-minute overtime period to decide a winner after a regulation tie.
6. Backs were allowed in motion towards the line of scrimmage before the snap.

7. Only one foot required in bounds for a legal reception.
8. The elimination of fair catches on punt returns.
9. Hash marks moved closer to the center of the field, creating wider spaces for offense.[35]

Whatever reservations one had about Davidson's football league, the legacies of his hockey and basketball leagues offer his WFL efforts legitimacy. The WHA ran for almost a decade and eventually led to the cities of Hartford, Edmonton, Quebec City, and Winnipeg merging into the NHL. Likewise, the ABA lasted for almost a decade and eventually catapulted the cities of San Antonio, Denver, and Indianapolis into the NBA. Whether wary of the WFL experiment or tapped out in buying into the Ottawa Nationals, Bassett's friends and acquaintances largely demurred from following him onto the gridiron.

To afford the start-up costs of a Toronto WFL team and the purchase/relocation of a WHA team, Bassett did what many considered unthinkable: he walked away from the family telecommunications empire. Baton Broadcasting provided Johnny F. Bassett a lucrative financial backstop while designing Lakeshore Raceway but doing so also took up a great deal of his time. Now with the chance to bring his own professional hockey and football teams to his beloved hometown of Toronto, Bassett realized he would need to walk away from his father's company to truly acquire the financial resources and time necessary to make his dream a reality. "He resigned and sold his shares to get involved in sports," his son John C. Bassett said. "He was just very passionate about sports."[36]

It was not an easy decision for either Johnny or his family. John W.H. Bassett had long worked under the assumption that his oldest son would succeed him at Baton, but he also knew his Johnny was a free spirit. The first-born son had a history of shocking his father: contradicting the prefects at his boarding school (which brought him a near-school record for demerits and expulsion), engaging in violent disagreements with his father on strategy during doubles tennis matches (after one of which, John W.H. Bassett pulled the car over and forced Johnny to walk home in his tennis whites), and furiously debating the future of the *Toronto Telegram* (the younger Bassett argued for a change to a tabloid format while the father decided to close the paper down for good).[37] This knowledge explains why the father did not stand in the way. Johnny's brother, Douglas, who went on to take the reins of Baton, remembered a spirited but supportive conversation taking place on the day Johnny announced his intentions to leave. "My father asked him if he was certain he wanted to do it," Douglas Bassett recalled. "Johnny said, 'Yes.' We wished him well. So, he sold his shares to the existing shareholders, the four Eaton brothers and the two Bassett brothers."[38] John W.H. Bassett named his son Douglas the new second-in-command and allowed his oldest to go on his own, a decision that Johnny F. Bassett always appreciated. "My father always told me what I should do in terms of the decisions I should make," Bassett recalled in an interview. "But he's never forced me to make them and invariably, the decisions I made were the ones he did not want. He has probably been more right than wrong. He wanted to do the best by me."[39]

While Douglas did not wish to divulge the exact dollar amount of the transaction for personal reasons, he did confirm that his older brother cleared millions of dollars in the sale.[40] It says something about Johnny F. Bassett's commitment to being a provider of sporting spectacle for Toronto that he was earmarking a majority of this money for the benefit of hockey and football. While he no doubt expected contributions from partners, in true Johnny F. Bassett fashion he put up the lion's share of the cash to increase Toronto's sporting profile. In the past he had had the steady income promised by his role at Baton, but now that was gone, stopped by his resignation. Any money Bassett was going to make would be based on the energy, perseverance, attention to business detail, tact, and calculation he brought to sports and which Barnum had once brought to show business.

Several pundits foresaw a life of suffering for Bassett as he signed the dotted line transferring ownership of the Ottawa Nationals from Michel and Trbovich to Can-Sports in May 1973 and the official start of his WFL football team. *Toronto Star* writer Jim Kernaghan conservatively estimated the hockey team would lose $500,000 under the most ideal circumstances.[41] As for football, even the successful American Football League had teams losing in excess of that amount in its first several seasons, including the near bankruptcy of the New York team.[42] Bassett was named principal shareholder and became the public face of both clubs. Upon receipt of the hockey club Bassett quickly announced a change of venue and name. The Ottawa Nationals were out. The Toronto Toros were in. As for his football team, Bassett chose the moniker Toronto Northmen.

Over the next several years Bassett shook up professional hockey and football. He also shook up his accountants and financial advisors. The $500,000 in losses predicted by the press paled in comparison to what Bassett lost in Toronto. Bassett managed to infuriate, alienate, and energize his competitors along the way. Bassett further shook up Toronto and Canadian politicians with his sporting quest, making the contretemps over Lakeshore Racing seem tame. For better and for worse, Bassett unleashed the Maverick. Toronto and professional sports would never be the same again.

THREE
|||||||||||||||||||||||||||||||||||||||||

Battle for the Hockey
Heart and Soul of Toronto

Johnny F. Bassett's establishment of the Toronto Toros was audacious. The Toros were challenging one of the flagship franchises of the
national sport in the league's own hometown. The Toronto Maple Leafs
of the 1970s very nearly *were* hockey in English–speaking Canada.
Toronto, the Maple Leafs, and the stately Maple Leaf Gardens enjoyed a
status as "the spiritual center of hockey" in addition to being home to the
immensely popular television program *Hockey Night in Canada*.[1] While
the Montreal Canadiens were just as famous and recently more successful, the Leafs were every bit as much of a national phenomenon, with
fans from coast-to-coast and a twelve-month lock on Ontario's attention. The Maple Leafs are one of the six original NHL franchises and
winners of thirteen Stanley Cup championships. A Toronto institution
a half-century in the making, the Leafs always sold out the 16,000 seat
Gardens and were a fixture on national television featuring star players like Frank Mahovlich and Tim Horton. Heading the Leafs was Harold Ballard, a cutthroat businessman with so many political connections
that he received a promotion to team president *after being convicted of
embezzling tens of thousands of dollars from Maple Leaf Gardens*.[2] Ballard was frequently referred to as irascible, which was a polite way of
stating that few in hockey considered him friendly or easy to do business with.

The Leafs' stately arena and television presence gave them a large
advantage over Bassett's team. The Toros played their first season at
the University of Toronto's Varsity Arena, a small 4,700-seat rink on
the northside of the city. A favorable television contract could offset
the limited revenue generated in a small arena. A design quirk of Varsity Arena prevented such a contract from being offered, however. "We
could not televise games at Varsity Arena because the lighting was not

sufficient," Peter Eby said.[3] This meant the Toros were exclusively dependent on ticket revenues and needed to create a buzz to attract some of the hockey crowd away from Maple Leaf Gardens. Bassett created a promotional campaign in which the Toros became the anti–Leafs.

The Anti-Leafs

The Leafs might have been hockey in Canada, but they struggled on the ice and in the daily press in the years preceding the Toros arrival. Several seasons of failing to make the playoffs or suffering early playoff exits soured the fans who were charged the highest prices in the NHL for tickets, a trend that continues into the twenty-first century.[4] The tight-fisted Ballard exacerbated the bad feelings by engaging in public feuds with his star players over contracts and with the local press over their coverage of the team's struggles. Studying this from his office near Varsity Arena, Bassett's promotional method became clear. Everything about the Toros should be marketed as new, fresh, and affordable. Everything about the Leafs should be portrayed as old, dated, and expensive.

Bassett began his quixotic campaign against the Leafs by signing as many local players as he could, specifically targeting members of the immensely popular Toronto Marlboros of the Ontario Hockey Association, a Canadian junior team. The Marlboros, also known as the "Marlies," fielded a team of players between the ages of 16 and 21 deemed promising professional prospects. They were closely followed by many fans, who appreciated their cheaper ticket prices as well as their on-ice success. Leaf fans enjoyed watching the next generation of stars on their way up the hockey ladder. Toronto fans were enamored with two up and coming Marlies, Wayne Dillon and Pat Hickey, thinking the two young players could one day return the Leafs to glory. Bassett interfered with those plans by signing the two to WHA contracts and then took a subtle jab at the Leafs in the press. "The best rookie in Toronto is Wayne Dillon," Bassett said. "And if you want the two best rookies, they are Wayne Dillon and Pat Hickey. I would not trade them for any two Leaf rookies."[5]

The second phase of Bassett's plan was to make attending a Toros game at Varsity Arena the most unique hockey experience in Ontario. On October 7, 1973, the Toros opened the season at Varsity Arena against the Chicago Crusaders. The teams skated to a 4–4 tie before 4,753 curious onlookers. Two nights later, the Toros skated to another draw, 3–3 against the New York Blades. Another near-capacity crowd attended. The quality of the play was better than most expected and the atmosphere at both games was unlike any professional hockey game the city had seen. The unique atmosphere was Bassett's view of what professional sports could be come to fruition. Bassett wanted the game to be a joyous evening out, with the flavor of watching the Toros at a local bar, not the "night at the opera" feeling one got at Maple Leaf Gardens. "You had to go to Maple Leaf Gardens in a jacket and a tie," recalled John C. Bassett, who was a pre-teen in 1973. "The Toros were cheaper than the Leafs and a lot more family fun. In fact, their motto was 'Good Hockey, Good Fun.'"[6] In this case, Bassett took aim at the old stereotype of "Toronto the Good," that is of the city being stolid, conservative, and generally not much fun. He clearly saw a future in which Toronto would be vibrant and dynamic, and wanted the Toros to help usher in that era. The patrons at the game came in casual attire: jeans, sneakers, and windbreakers. Not content to provide the fans a mere hockey game, Bassett also provided cheerleaders: The Toro-ettes along with Miss Toronto Toro, 18-year-old Ann Marie Sten. Bassett also invited everyone at the game to attend the team's morning skate, offering free tickets to the second game of the season to the first 100 fans to make the 9:30 a.m. practice.[7] This was done to encourage parents to bring their children to visit Toro players up close.

Bassett took advantage of a local reporter's quest for "man on the street" reactions to the team's debut by passing himself off as an anonymous fan out for the evening. "This is so much more exciting (than the Leafs)," the clandestine owner told Elaine Kenney of the *Toronto Star* in a creative bit of guerrilla marketing. "The people are part of the show. It's like comparing a coffee house to the Royal York Hotel."[8] Bassett finally confessed to his subterfuge, but his point was well made and repeated often by the other fans Ms. Kenney interviewed. The fans were actively engaged and right on top of the action. The fans were so close that one reporter noted, "The fans were as close to the game as a bettor at a cockfight."[9] For Bassett only one thing could have made opening weekend more of a success: his team could really have used a better rink. The lack of decent ice haunted the Toros all year and forced Bassett to constantly negotiate with rinks in the greater Toronto area for ice time.

The quality of play during opening weekend far exceeded the quality of ice at Varsity Arena. A recently installed ice-making machine sputtered and strained to provide the playing surface. The uneven surface led to "sluggish passes, unbelievable bounces and bizarre rebounds."[10] The arena was also more squared than oval which led to clearing passes that caromed unexpectedly into unintended directions. This should have been a home ice advantage for the Toros. Unfortunately, the Toros could not practice regularly at the facility. The Toros were joint tenants with the University of Toronto. The college team held priority status for the university-owned ice. This meant that the Toros always scrambled to find an available ice rink for practice. The team regularly secured ice time at George Bell Arena, a community center in Toronto's Runnymede Park. Even home games were not guaranteed, which made the team nervous. The Toros had set up a home schedule of 25 Sunday night games and 14 Thursday night games. Due to the University's needs, Varsity Arena was not available for multiple Thursday night dates. This forced the Toros to play "home" games in a most ironic venue. The Toros played nine games at Ottawa's Civic Centre, the very facility they had vacated the year before. It was an awkward arrangement that pleased no one.

The reason for the Toros' plight was that Toronto was not quite ready for the second iconoclastic Johnny F. Bassett enterprise. Just as Bassett's quest for a downtown Toronto auto race was about twenty years too early, his belief that Toronto could support two professional hockey teams also outpaced the city's logistics and political will. The arena and stadium building craze occurring in the United States in the 1970s had not crossed the Northern border, leading Bassett and the Toros to spend the season as a wandering band of hockey gypsies.

Vagabond Hockey

There was little doubt that Toronto could support two hockey teams based on population and demographics. Bassett had statistical proof to back him up. Bassett contracted a study by the market research firm Martin Goldfarb to determine how much of an impact his marketing of the Toros was having on Torontonian sports fans. The results were very heartening for Bassett. Two hundred hockey fans under the age of 35 from various economic brackets in both the city and suburbs were surveyed. Of the 200, 171 said they were aware of the Toros. Eighty-six of the respondents said they had a favorite WHA club and of those, 74 said that club was the Toros. This was equivalent to the 163 who said they had a favorite NHL club and of those, 136 said the club was the Maple Leafs. One hundred seventy two respondents said the Toros had a bright future, 114 said they were worth the price of admission and 93 felt they were being underappreciated by the press.[11] Bassett gleefully shared other categories and their impact with the media. "The way I analyze those figures, they tell me we're about halfway to where the Leafs are in popularity after only 4½ months and to me, that's not too damned bad at all. It proves we're on the right track," Bassett said. "22 of the respondents said they had seen a game in person and 111 said they had seen a game on television, which I consider excellent market penetration. 130 had read about the Toros. Moreover, 109 were able to name a few of our players. The work was done six weeks ago when we were in fourth place. Now we're scrambling for first, so we could be even better off."[12]

The survey only strengthened Bassett's belief that Toronto could be a two-team town. As precedent he pointed to New York which had two franchises in each major sport as well as Chicago and Los Angeles, which were also home to multiple teams in the same sport. Bassett viewed Toronto as the New York, Chicago, or Los Angeles of Canadian sports. He had to be proud that his upstarts were carving out a reputation for themselves in a large and sophisticated hockey market. Ballard and the NHL had hoped that Toronto fans would scoff at a so-called inferior brand, but Bassett saw signs that his Toros were making real headway. It is worth noting that, in the early twenty-first century, efforts continue to place a second NHL team in Markham, near Toronto. Also, the Marlies have morphed into a member of the highest-level minor leagues, playing in the American Hockey League (AHL) and drawing enthusiastic crowds, proving Bassett's prediction that Toronto could support two teams correct.

No matter how much hockey passion the population of Toronto possessed there was one simple, incontrovertible fact that countered the emotion. Toronto only had one viable arena suitable for major league hockey and it was in use by the Maple Leafs. Rumors began to circulate that the Toros were approaching the Leafs about leasing Maple Leaf Gardens for possible home playoff games. The operators of the Gardens had been willing to rent the facility to the Ottawa Nationals for their playoff games, so it was conceivable they would be open to renting it to the Toros. One thing these rumors did not factor in was the fact the Toros were marketing themselves as the anti–Leafs. How would it look if the Toros took residence in a facility named after the very team they were lambasting? Bassett dismissed the rumors, stating that his priority was working with Toronto to build a permanent home for the Toros. "We've had five different bona fide developers come to us about a permanent facility all in different parts of the city," Bassett said. "I think the Gardens is for the Maple Leafs. It's an institution. I'd rather play somewhere else with fewer seats where we could establish ourselves."[13] Developers may have approached Bassett, but no one with the means to transform an architectural drawing into a concrete and steel reality.

Property cost was generally the overriding factor in the Toros' inability to build a new venue. Sites in downtown Toronto were expensive and Bassett did not find a lot of civic authorities too keen on contributing to the construction fund. Bassett was too early for public financing of an arena in Toronto. Civic financing of sporting venues began in Toronto just a year after Bassett's struggles to build a home for the Toros led him to relocate. Toronto contributed half of the ren-ovation costs of Exhibition Stadium to bring it up to standards for the Toronto Blue Jays' first season as a member of Major League Baseball.[14] The full-scale arena craze hit Toronto a decade later. Governmental entities ranging from Parliament to the City of Toronto spent more than 500 million Canadian dollars to build SkyDome (now Rogers Centre) for the benefit of baseball's Toronto Blue Jays.

The struggle for ice may have been frustrating for Bassett but it had no effect on the Toros' performance. After a slow start, the team came together in the second half of the season, displaying a knack for timely shooting and defense. The Toros scored 304 goals on the season, fourth in the league and goalie Gilles Gratton, nicknamed "Gratoony the Loony," stopped enough pucks to make leads stand up. The Toros won their final six games, including a clinching 3–2 victory over the Edmon-ton Oilers in their final home game. Their 41–33–4 record was good for second place in the Eastern Division.

The Toros were not alone in the playoffs. The cross-town Maple Leafs had secured the fourth spot in the NHL East Division and were preparing for an opening round battle with the Boston Bruins. The Leafs had missed the playoffs the year before and had been mired in mediocrity during the first half of the 1970s. From an outsider's point of view, it seemed there was more reason to be excited about the prospects of the Toros with one large caveat. Although the Toros were growing into a competitive team, the Leafs at least knew where they were going to play and practice.

The success of the Toros making the playoffs and extending their season also meant a lengthening of their vagabond existence. Var-sity Arena was no longer available because exams at the University of Toronto took precedence.[15] The Toros no longer even had George Bell Arena as a practice site. In April, the city of Toronto took up the ice surface to prepare for the public center's use as a spring/summer rec-reational facility.[16] The Toros bounced around Ontario for practices. They scrimmaged in Sudbury, more than 300 kilometers from Toronto. They even travelled to upstate New York to practice at Seneca Arena. Fortunately for the Toros, their head coach was not a believer in going full-scale in practice or else they would have been exhausted. Coach Bill Harris had a motto: "Don't Leave Your Game on the Practice Rink," and according to the coach it worked out well for the well-travelled team. "There is a philosophy that teams will play as hard as they train. I don't agree with that," Harris said. "In our case, with a difficult schedule, it's almost impossible to work in any hard practices."[17]

Bassett reached a breaking point while looking for temporary quarters after Varsity Arena became unavailable. The small city of Oshawa, a lakefront town 60 kilometers from Toronto, turned the Toros down because the WHA playoff schedule conflicted with the junior hockey playoffs.[18] Quickly running out of options as the post-season approached, the normally positive Bassett was exploring options that ranged from major metro areas to suburban enclaves. "I have no answer as to where we'll play at the moment," Bassett told the *Toronto Star.* "Buffalo. Kitchener. Markham."[19] Just when all hope seemed lost Bassett found a landlord willing to give him and his roving band of hockey players some semblance of home during the post-season. The landlord was an unlikely ally for the Toros: Harold Ballard.

Strange Bedfellows

The President of the Maple Leafs invited the Toros to host their 1974 playoff games at the Gardens. Additionally, the Gardens and Bassett reached an agreement to lease the arena for all Toro home games in the 1974–1975 regular season. Bassett stated the situation plainly and glumly at a press conference in which a smug Harold Ballard sat nearby: "It was verbally agreed to in a telephone conversation I had with Harold Ballard that the Toros would be playing next season at the Gardens."[20]

Ballard's move was far from magnanimous. The infamous businessman may have been annoyed by Bassett, but there was little doubt as to the reason he was willing to turn over the legendary arena to an upstart rival: profit. "The building has got to be made to pay," Ballard told an interviewer when explaining his view on letting a rival play in his building. "I don't care whether you come in here with a flea circus. I would be glad to have the Toros here for a fee."[21]

It was interesting that Ballard used the flea circus analogy. Ballard long maintained the view that the impact of the Toros on his Leafs was about the same as the impact of a flea on an elephant. "They are not a threat," Ballard said, citing that no matter what Bassett did, the Toros were denizens of an inferior league. "They could draw 10,000–12,000 people. They could have a hell of a team and draw a lot of people, but you have to have somebody to play against. Their opponents have to fill their rinks, too. You can't go to Chicago, where they get 3,000 to 4,000 people and balance this against your own success."[22] The pain of the press conference was abated for Bassett somewhat by the results of the NHL and WHA playoffs. The Leafs were swept in the first round of the playoffs by the Boston Bruins. The early elimination meant hockey-starved Toron-tonians flocked to see the Toros, which won its first round series with the Cleveland Crusaders before falling in a thrilling seven-game series against the Chicago Cougars. The Toros averaged well over 8,000 fans at the Gardens during their post-season run. For better or for worse, the Toronto Toros had permanent home ice. Any excitement Bassett had over the arrangement was quickly torpedoed when he experienced Bal-lard's notorious business practices. "Harold may have screwed over my dad on rent," John C. Bassett recalled.[23]

The Toros agreed to pay a five-figure sum to Ballard for every game played at Maple Leaf Gardens. One would expect that in exchange for such an exorbitant rental amount, the Toros would have access to all the facilities of Maple Leaf Gardens. That would be logical for most ten-ants, but not for those who had Harold Ballard as a landlord. Ballard read the agreement as meaning the Toros got access to the ice and little else. The Toros were given the same locker room that the visiting oppo-nents of the junior league Toronto Marlies used to dress. Ballard even had the cushions of the players' bench removed after Leaf games, leav-ing the Toros to sit on a hard surface.[24] The real squeeze came when Bal-lard determined that if the Toros wanted amenities, such as lights, they needed to pay extra. This detail only came out minutes before the Toros' season opener, a nationally televised game against the New England Whalers.

"We had a contract to play at Maple Leaf Gardens and we paid $15,000 to $25,000 a game to rent the arena," said Peter Eby, one of Bas-sett's partners in the Toros. "So, we go to opening night and it is dark in the arena. The game is going to be televised and Harold won't turn on the lights. So, a group of us and our legal counsel go up to talk to Har-old and his legal counsel. Harold says he won't turn on the lights unless we give him $15,000 more in cash. This is an hour before game time!"[25] Johnny F. Bassett was just 60 minutes away from the grand debut of his team as a co-tenant of arguably the most famous venue in hockey and he was being extorted by Harold Ballard.

As a rival entrepreneur, Bassett appreciated the position of strength Ballard held in their rivalry. Given the battles he was waging with Bal-lard and his own competition for Toronto's hockey dollar, this episode may have been unwanted, but it could not have been totally unexpected. "My Dad always respected Harold," John C. Bassett said. "After all, why would Harold have wanted another hockey team in Toronto?"[26]

The demand for cash placed Bassett in a tough spot, but not so tough that he could not overcome it. "To get $15,000 cash even in today's age would be difficult," Peter Eby said. "It was not an easy trick, but Bassett pulled it off with the help of the Eatons (partners with the elder Bassett in Baton Broadcasting)."[27] Ballard accepted the excess cash and turned on the lights. None of the 9,261 in attendance knew about the shenanigans that had taken place. Instead the fans enjoyed Toronto's 6–2 victory over New England to open the season. In addition to celebrating the Toros' victory, Bassett also received a reluctant refund from Ballard. "We got the money back because Harold Ballard's lawyer said it just wasn't right," Peter Eby said.[28] The lighting fiasco only lasted for one game, but another Ballard trick plagued the Toros daily. The crusty arena owner regularly under-staffed the ticket office on the nights of Toro games, forcing Toro employees to walk the streets surrounding the arena with spools of tickets in their hand to sell on a cash basis.[29]

Any concern that Bassett was Harold Ballard's rube was dispelled in the season-opening victory. The most valuable player of the Toros' game was Frank Mahovlich, a former star for the Toronto Maple Leafs. If Ballard stayed in the arena after his extortion attempt, he witnessed Mahovlich have a spectacular game. The Mahovlich signing was just one of many coups by Bassett designed to magnify the difference between the Toros and Leafs, a magnification assisted by Bassett's Barumuesque carnival barking. In addition to bringing back a Leafs' legend, Bassett also signed Paul Henderson, a national hero who scored the game winning goal in the 1972 Summit Series, an eight-game exhibition between the Canadian and Soviet national teams. Bassett also reached behind the Iron Curtain. He assisted Czech Olympians Vaclav Nedomansky and Richard Farda in defecting and then signed the star players to the Toros. Bassett explained his rationale for signing the biggest available names in hockey. "We've got nearly 17,000 seats to fill at Maple Leaf Gardens compared to less than 5,000 at Varsity Arena," Bassett told reporters before the season opener. "We know we've got a hell of an exciting team, so we think we'll need every one of those seats."[30]

Bassett put together a highly entertaining team but was about to learn a classic lesson from sports: offense may sell tickets, but defense wins championships ... and most other games as well.

Four

No Defense, No Discipline, No More Toronto

Bassett committed to hundreds of thousands of dollars in payroll which caught the eye of the fans and press. Bassett also improved the Toros operation in less opulent ways. In 1973-1974, the Toros held their home games primarily on Friday and Sunday evenings. This often conflicted with Maple Leaf games, Toronto Marlboro junior hockey action, and even local college hockey. Bassett rearranged his home game dates for the 1974-1975 season, choosing Tuesday and Friday to avoid conflicts. This gave Bassett a weeknight that would not always have a Leafs game to compete with and the opening night of the weekend generally not taken up with junior and amateur games. "We've established Tuesdays and Fridays as our regular nights for home games," Bassett explained. "We think that will be a successful pattern, especially Friday, which is an open night for just about everybody."[1] Bassett also lined up a better television contract for his team. In 1974-1975 more Toros games were shown on the Global Television Network. Bassett also obtained O'Keefe Ale as a major sponsor of the broadcasts.

The Defense Rests

The Toros were exciting but trouble was on the horizon. A weakness in Bassett's star strategy to sign locally known players to a team geared toward offense was its impact on the defensive end. The Toros were incapable of playing any defense. Bassett's focus had been on creating a high-scoring, free-wheeling team which would make for exciting nights and counter the mundane Leafs. With little regard to defense, however, the Toros became one dimensional and goalie Gilles Gratton paid the price. Over the course of the season the Toros scored 349 goals, second most in the WHA, but they gave up a whopping 304 goals against with Gratton being the victim most of the time.[2]

The team drew between 7,000 and 8,000 fans for their home dates in October and November. This was better than the year before at Varsity Arena, but still less than half capacity of the cavernous Gardens. Things got marginally better in December as two dates against former playoff opponent Cleveland drew 8,019 and 10,317, respectively. Two days after Christmas, the Toros set a new home attendance record as 12,366 attended a game against the Chicago Cougars. The attendance was spurred by a Bassett marketing stroke. The Toros admitted any child to the arena for only $1.00 as a Christmas present to the youth of Toronto. While the gesture was generous, the severely discounted ducats could not paper over the fact that Bassett and his partners were not getting the revenue needed to go head-to-head with a Leafs team which continued to sell-out despite a lackluster squad.

Unfortunately for the Toros, the defense continued to rest. The nadir of the Toros' defensive deficiencies occurred in a pre-game marketing promotion during the 1974-1975 season. American daredevil Evel Knievel was invited by Bassett to take part in a goal-scoring contest before a Toros game at Maple Leaf Gardens against reserve goalie Les Binkley. Knievel, who had become internationally famous for his motorcycle jump over the fountains of Caesars Palace in Las Vegas and his failed attempt to jump the Snake River Canyon in an experimental rocket, was a big get for Bassett, but the promotion did not go according to plan. "Knievel was to take six shots on goal," explained Peter McAskile, the Toros' publicity director.

> We would give $5,000 to Evel for every goal he scored and $1,000 for every save we made. This is right after his fall in Snake River Canyon and ABC was trying to revive his career. *Wide World of Sports* came to town with Frank Gifford and billed this thing. We budgeted for him scoring two goals, worst case scenario. Well, his first shot missed but his second one went in and I looked at Johnny, and even though we budgeted, he's looking uncomfortable. The third shot was stopped, but the fourth shot goes in. The puck went right between the goalies' legs. I look at Johnny and he has his head in his hands, he's spending $5,000 he did not budget for.[3]

An April 4 meeting with the Winnipeg Jets set a franchise attendance record as 16,316 came to see the great Bobby Hull skate in Maple Leaf Gardens. The Toros' convincing 7–1 victory certainly did not hurt the team's efforts to reward the fans support. Two days later another 15,127 came through the turnstiles to witness the Toros drop a 5–2 decision to the Houston Aeros which featured Gordie Howe and his two sons, former Toronto Marlboros players. Upstarts or not, the Toros were filling the house with fans anxious to see some of the game's finest players. There was nothing minor league about completing against teams with the Howe's or Bobby Hull.

Bassett tasked Peter McAskile with helping sell tickets for Toro home games. The visit by Bobby Hull created such a clamor for seats at Maple Leaf Gardens that thousands of fans milled in the streets around the revered arena. "It was a cold, cold night," McAskile said of the early April evening. "We had been working on advance tickets, but the advance had not been great. But the walk-up was phenomenal. We could have had another 7,000 but they could not get tickets. People were lined up out on Carlton Street."[4]

The games against the Jets and Aeros were the final games of the regular season for the Toros. The Toros made the playoffs for the second year in a row while the Leafs fell short and went home early to polish their skates. Bassett's team had the sports section of the major dailies all to themselves and stood on the precipice of legitimizing their quest to be Toronto's best professional hockey team. All they needed was a deep playoff run for the second year in a row. They did not get it, primarily due to their lackluster defense.

The Toros match-up with the San Diego Mariners was a difficult draw. The Mariners were just as high-powered on offense as the Toros. Aided greatly by Andre Lecroix's professional record 106 assists, the Mariners scored a total of 326 goals. San Diego also knew how to play defense, evidenced by the fact they gave up almost 40 goals less than the Toros. This was the key to the series which the Mariners won four games to two. Compounding the relative mismatch was the fact San Diego held home-ice advantage in the series, necessitating a cross-continent trip by Toronto to open the series. Playing away from Toronto would not have been a big deal if the Toros had played better. Unfortunately, Toronto dropped the first two games, digging a hole that was difficult to climb out of. The lag time between home dates and their desultory performance scuttled a great deal of the attendance momentum Toronto had gained.

The Toros did battle back to even the series at Maple Leaf Gardens but only 9,135 attended Game Three and 10,197 came for Game Four. The totals were a far cry from the near-capacity crowds at the end of the regular season. At least those in attendance were passionate. After a few Toro players were doused with beer and accosted by Mariner fans at the San Diego Sports Arena in Game One, Toronto fans returned the favor in Game Three, pelting San Diego players with eggs and other debris.[5] Say what one will about hooliganism, it did prove a Toros game was livelier than the Leafs. The series returned to Toronto for Game Six with the

Toros facing elimination after a 4–3 loss in Game Five. Only 8,830 came to the Gardens despite their team's do or die situation. They saw the Toros lose 6–4. The loss meant Bassett's brief April window of Toronto hockey exclusivity slammed shut. It never opened again.

Youthful Mistakes of an Exuberant Maverick

Bassett's successful offseason run of 1974 was just a fleeting memory one year later. Nearly half of the original investment group departed. They were frustrated by a second straight year in which the Toros lost copious amounts of money. After losing an estimated one million dollars in year one, the Toros lost an estimated $1.5 million in year two.[6] With an annual rent of $750,000 and a season ticket base of only 4,000, the margin of error for Bassett was razor thin. Despite the sobering numbers, he remained steadfast in his belief that Toronto could support two hockey teams and fully intended to tilt at the windmill one more season. "I am not even going to entertain thoughts of folding the team. I refuse to talk about that possibility," Bassett told the press.[7]

With little revenue being generated during the season, Bassett agreed to a unique pre-season arrangement. Former Toros coach Bill Harris talked Bassett into holding the team's training camp in Sweden. For Bassett, the move to Sweden made economic sense. The cost of running a training camp could easily exceed $50,000. Swedish officials not only paid for the Toros camp but had sold out nine exhibition games in and around Sweden and Finland.[8] "This was the first time a team trained in Europe," said former Toros executive Gilles Leger. Leger recalled many problems arising during the exhibition season due to the Europeans not being used to the punishing style of North American hockey: "The police would have to come out on the ice when fights began and in one game a referee was knocked out. We thought we were the toughest team in the WHA, but it turned out we were only tough in Sweden because no one ever hit back. There hasn't been a training camp like that since."[9]

The training camp ended up being the Toros' highlight for the year. Leading the Toros was new head coach Bobby Baun. Bassett viewed the hiring of Baun as both a marketing move, and another dig at Ballard's Leafs. Baun had been a star defenseman for the Leafs during their Stanley Cup glory years. Known for hard-hitting defense and toughness, Baun scored one of the most famous goals in Maple Leaf history. In Game Six of the 1964 Stanley Cup Finals against the Detroit Red Wings, Baun broke his leg but continued to skate in overtime, scoring the game-winning goal and spurring the Leafs onto their third straight championship. Bassett viewed Baun as a perfect combination. Baun was beloved by Leafs's fans and possessed a passion for defense that Bassett hoped would shore up the Toros' largest weakness. Unfortunately, Baun's expertise did not have the desired effect. The Toros were even worse on defense in 1975-1976 than they were in 1974-1975. The Toros gave up a staggering 398 goals, an average of almost five goals a game. The year before the offense was able to offset such a deficiency but that was not in the cards this time. The Toros scored 335 goals with Vaclav Nedomansky leading the way with 56. A minus 63 goal differential was just too much to overcome, however, and the Toros fell like a stone, finishing with a 24–52–5 record, second-worst in the WHA to the Denver Spurs, a team which had folded midway through the season.[10] "We used to joke that a team of the owners could skate through our defense," said Bassett friend and hockey partner Peter Eby.[11]

It was Baun's first coaching job. A fan of Green Bay Packers coach Vince Lombardi, Baun installed strict rules, grueling practices, and a no-excuses policy reminiscent of the Green Bay Packers' legend. Baun even incorporated "Lombardi Time," requiring players to set their watches ahead so that someone arriving at 8:00 a.m. for an 8:00 a.m. meeting was actually ten minutes late.[12] This eye for punctuality and accountability did not translate to victories as the Toros suffered one excruciatingly bad loss after another. The most extreme of Toronto's many losses was eye-popping. The Toros travelled to Cleveland on November 30 for a match-up with the Crusaders. The Toros led the game 8–2 just before the end of the second period. This seemingly insurmountable lead quickly dissipated as the Crusaders scored eight goals in just over twenty minutes to take the game 10–9. In a particularly rough stretch, the Crusaders scored three goals in just 45 seconds.[13] The horrible season was arguably the most trying time in sports for Johnny F. Bassett. As it wound down, his inexperience as an owner showed and he committed the worst mistake a team owner can make.

The losses took a toll on Baun and the players, driving a major wedge between them. Baun was a stern disciplinarian, known to lash out at players both verbally and financially. As the losses mounted, so did the punitive actions from Baun. Following the epic collapse against the Crusaders, Baun drew the ire of his players by fining each one $500 for what he considered lack of effort. "That is only the start," the coach said about the fines. "I'm truly ashamed to have been a part of this game tonight. We were disgraced. I could have vomited."[14]

Things got worse before turning truly bizarre in mid–December. Following a 5–3 loss to Calgary at the Gardens on December 19,

Bassett stated that Baun expressed a desire to resign. Bassett took him at his word and dispatched general manager Gilles Leger to accompany the Toros to Edmonton for a game against the Oilers. "(Bobby) said he wanted to quit," Bassett told reporters. "He's very frustrated. What happens now? We wait until Leger gets back and then the three of us will sit down and talk."[15] Soon thereafter Baun's wife told the press her husband had told Bassett no such thing. She said her husband simply vented his frustrations and that Bassett took Baun's words out of context. The confusion was compounded when Baun returned to the bench as head coach of the Toros on December 27, a 5–0 loss at Cleveland. Bassett's public statements and behind-the-scenes actions created an unsettled organization and left Baun, the players, media members, and fans confused. Instead of clarifying the situation, Bassett, in his inexperience and desperation to save the season, acted rashly with horrible consequences.

The final episode of Baun's tumultuous tenure came following what should have been a joyous night. The Toros upset the powerful, Gordie Howe–led Aeros, 7–5 in Houston. Immediately after the game the Toros left for Phoenix to play the Roadrunners. Some of the players stayed out too late while having dinner and were fined $200 apiece by Baun. The players complained to Bassett, who rescinded the fines.[16] Bassett may have felt justified in negating the fines to keep his players' morale up in what he hoped would be another second-half charge, but by rescinding the fines, Bassett undercut the authority of his coach. Once an owner sides with the players against a coach, the credibility of the coach is gone. Under such a circumstance the team will no longer respect the authority of the coach and performance will suffer. Bassett's actions granted the inmates control of the asylum. Sadly, the gesture did not rally the troops at all. The Toros players got their money back but they did not reward Bassett for his loyalty by upping their game. In fact, the Toros got worse, going winless over the course of 17 consecutive games.

During the streak Bassett relieved Baun of his coaching duties. During his final press conference Baun let it be known that while he liked Bassett, the coach felt his former boss had some lessons to learn. Baun had been brought on board to instill discipline in the defensive end, yet Bassett had undercut him. If Bassett had truly wanted a taskmaster, then he should have allowed Baun to do what he saw fit. Baun felt Bassett's lack of commitment to his coaching was because the owner did not seem to have an operating principle other than having fun. "There have been misunderstandings from day one," Baun said. "Hockey is a business. It's not just a game. It has to be worked at. Johnny's trouble is that he wants to be a good guy, be a friend to everybody. An owner can't be like that with players. An owner almost has to be the arch-enemy of the player and can never be a friend."[17]

Baun's repudiation of Bassett at his departing press conference was part of a larger wave of bad news for the young owner. His Toros finished with a losing record, almost 30 games under .500. They also lost an additional $1.5 million for Bassett and his few remaining investors.[18] The financial hit put a major dent in Bassett's personal wealth. It also forced him to confront the fact that neither public nor private entities in Toronto had any interest in helping the Toros find a home of their own. Bassett could see that his Toros were not going to be able to put enough of a dent into the Maple Leafs juggernaut to make staying in Toronto economically viable. Facing the reality of the situation, Bassett conceded that the financial dynamics were not there to make a go of it. "Even if John had sold out every game, he couldn't have made money," former Toros goalie John Garrett told author Ed Willes. "He had players making phone calls to sell tickets!"[19]

"Johnny had always felt that if properly marketed, Toronto could support two teams," Gilles Leger said. "But we were charged so much for rent we could never break even. He certainly didn't fall short for lack of trying. He always attempted to put a team on the ice the city could enjoy. In the end he also received a good financial offer to relocate he couldn't refuse."[20]

The question became where could Bassett relocate? The WHA had several teams scattered throughout alleged "second-tier" markets across the United States and Canada. Bassett also needed to consider the impact of a move on his family. Johnny was married to college sweetheart Sue Carling and the couple had four children: John C., Vicky, Carling, and Heidi. The demands of his sports teams kept Bassett away from home a great deal and his son recalls that even when his father was home, he was working. "He would be in his den setting up sports ideas," John C. Bassett said. "There was a lot of road time. He was away more than he was home."[21] John C. was also not home a great deal. He attended boarding school like his father, but he did appreciate the time and memories they shared because of his father's efforts to be involved. Bassett maintained a presence in the lives of his children while Sue bore most of the child-rearing responsibility when he was away. That presence often manifested itself through sports. "When he was there, he would get up and have breakfast with the children and drive them to school," said the former Sue Carling, now Sue Bassett-Klauber. "He would play with the children when he wasn't working. Whether it was throwing footballs or flooding a rink in our back garden so they could play hockey. He would be up all night flooding that garden. He was constantly on the go."[22]

John C. played hockey with his dad and raced go-karts. Vicky loved playing hockey and her girls' team got to play at Maple Leaf Gardens between periods of Toros' games. Vicky also played tennis with her father, as did Carling and Heidi. Carling became quite proficient at tennis, although she admitted horses were her passion. Carling was a self-described tomboy and enjoyed playing baseball with her father. "My father threw the ball around with me," Carling said. "I loved anything with a ball."[23] Vicky recalls her father gathering the four children in the family room to watch television. A popular 1970s program depicted a lifestyle Bassett wanted for his family, but one that Vicky quickly

Bassett had a more traditional workday in the 1960s. This is a photograph of him and oldest son John C (left) and oldest daughter Vicky (right) in the mid–1960s while he worked for CFTO and the *Toronto Telegram* (courtesy the Bassett family).

realized her father was not temperamentally capable of attaining. "He would turn on *Little House on the Prairie* and scream out, 'Kids, I want you to watch this with me,'" Vicky Bassett said. "He said, 'This is how we are going to live.' He had tears in his eyes. He had the idea, but it just was not who he was."[24]

If Bassett intended to preside over a traditional nuclear family in the manner of pioneer patriarch Charles Ingalls, it was going to take place in a different country. Bassett stunned the family and his associates by announcing the Toros were moving to Birmingham, Alabama, for the 1976-1977 season. Birmingham was a moderate-sized media market far from the radar of any professional hockey executives. Johnny F. Bassett knew of the city because one of his peers in another sports endeavor had found a great deal of commercial and athletic success in the city. Bassett came to grow very fond of the Deep South.

Bassett's 1970s sporting life kept him on the road a great deal, but he maximized the time he could spend with his children. He had a knack for participating in their pastimes including (from left) Carling's tennis and love of film, John's go-karts and hockey, Vicky's tennis and hockey, and Heidi's photography (courtesy Anne Dowie).

In the next decade he located three of his franchises in the region. Two of the franchises were football teams. The first of those football teams was started in Toronto and, like the Toros, were eventually relocated, but not before Bassett shook up the NFL, the CFL, and Parliament in his quest to bring a new level of showmanship to sports in his hometown.

FIVE

IIIIIIIIIIIIIIIIIIIIIIIIIIIIIIIIIIIIII

No, Canada

The WFL Northmen and Canadian Anti-Americanism

The tidal wave of televised professional football in the 1960s and 1970s swept up tens of millions of sports fans on both sides of the 49th parallel, including Johnny F. Bassett. The international border proved quite permeable to football broadcasts. Broadcasts of NFL games carried by Cleveland and Buffalo television stations reached Toronto, exporting the action of the Browns and Bills, respectively. The Canadian Broadcasting Company (CBC) carried regular NFL *Game of the Week* telecasts, much to the chagrin of the Canadian Football League (CFL). This allowed Canadians from the Maritimes to Vancouver to become fans of the Rams, Packers, Cowboys, or any NFL team involved in these select games at the expense of the Edmonton Eskimos, Saskatchewan Roughriders, Hamilton Tiger-Cats, and the six other CFL teams. There is conjecture on which NFL team Bassett adopted as his own. Former Cleveland wide receiver Paul Warfield claimed Bassett was a Browns fan, while John C. Bassett stated his father was not beholden to any one team.[1] Bassett's passion for professional football is not in doubt, however.

A consequence of Lamar Hunt's successful challenge of the NFL and the resulting creation of the Super Bowl was the spectacle of professional football becoming unlike anything in sport at the time. CBS, NBC, and ABC paid the newly enlarged NFL a total of $58.5 million per year to televise games starting in 1973, and the ratings for all contests were high, particularly the weekly *Monday Night Football* telecasts.[2] On-field triumphs including the Miami Dolphins' undefeated 1972 season and O.J. Simpson's 2,003 rushing yards in 1973 made for great television. So did personalities such as New York Jets quarterback "Broadway" Joe Namath, a gifted passer known for his flair on and

45

off the field, a man equally remembered for being the first quarterback to throw for more than 4,000 yards in a single season and for wearing Beauty Mist panty hose in a 1974 national advertisement.[3] The appeal of the NFL was so great that dozens of cities across the United States clamored for the two expansion teams which were to be announced in 1974. Ultimately Tampa and Seattle were chosen, with the owners of those teams charged $16 million apiece in expansion fees.[4]

Bassett viewed this boom south of the border from afar and dreamt of bringing American professional football to Toronto. He received his opportunity when a new professional football league was formed in late 1973. Bassett's decision to bring an American-style football franchise to the largest media market in Canada permanently defined him as a maverick whose ambitions and dreams were too iconoclastic for the country of his birth. The resulting political theater it invoked captivated the sports fans of the nation, stirred passions about the meaning of Canadianism, and eventually forced Bassett to say good-bye to his hometown.

The World Football League

The World Football League granted Bassett a Toronto franchise in 1973. The WFL was the brainchild of Gary Davidson, who previously founded the American Basketball Association (ABA) and the World Hockey Association, of which Bassett's Toros were a member. Davidson was a sporting pied piper of sorts, who strongly believed professional sports to be an industry artificially limited in size. He was good at bringing others to this point of view, and the relative, fitful success of his basketball and hockey leagues gave Davidson's pitch some credibility. He felt there was an unfilled appetite for professional football throughout North America despite the 26 franchises in the NFL. Davidson also felt the sport could grow across the globe. Davidson announced the formation of the WFL on October 2, 1973. The name of the league hinted at its grandiose mission of growing the sport of professional football on multiple continents. Davidson did not just want teams in Los Angeles and New York; he wanted them in "Osaka, London, Tokyo and Mexico City."[5]

The method of play in the WFL was designed to differentiate the new league as much as possible from the NFL while still maintaining a recognizable version of the game. While the pro game was massively popular, it was also in the throes of a style-crisis. The AFL had been a pass-happy league, featuring wide-open offenses led by matinee quarterbacks such as Joe Namath, Len Dawson, and Daryle Lamonica. The high-risk, high-reward concept attracted fans and, when the New

York Jets' Joe Namath became the first quarterback to surpass 4,000 yards in a season, it seemed the era of Vince Lombardi's effective but stultifying "Run to Daylight" offense was passé. This new era of open offense proved to be a mirage. Statistics in the first few seasons following the 1970 merger made it appear that the AFL teams absorbed by the NFL left their offensive souls behind. In the years 1970–1973, only two passers eclipsed the 3,000-yard mark while 22 running backs surpassed 1,000 yards rushing.[6] The NFL was still popular, but a trend of fan apathy had begun, culminating with a 1977 Harris poll which found fans viewed professional football as dull, predictable, and only slightly more exciting than baseball.[7] Professional football needed a personality adjustment and the WFL seemed just the thing.

"We're going to try to loosen everybody up with a bright new look to the sport," Davidson said.[8] In order to do this, Davidson needed investors willing to pony up the franchise fees required to establish the league. Davidson's track record in establishing new leagues was solid but controversial. The ABA and WHA were legitimate leagues with proven results. Although both featured the usual gamut of relocations and folded franchises, both leagues kept playing and benefited from some truly high-profile stars and solid, well-supported teams in hitherto underserved markets. In the ABA, examples of stars included Julius "Dr. J" Erving, Connie Hawkins, and George Gervin; its better markets included Salt Lake City, Indianapolis, Louisville, and San Antonio. The WHA had a similar pattern: stars included Bobby Hull and the Howes, good markets included Winnipeg, Hartford, and Quebec City. Davidson had, in other words, proved that existing leagues did not fully tap out the basketball and hockey markets either in terms of talent or fans. The WFL aimed to do the same with football, but an unusual business practice Davidson instituted in the new gridiron league appeared shady. Gary Davidson's asking price for a WFL franchise was far cheaper than the NFL's expansion fees, but sill steep for 1973. In order to be granted a franchise, a prospective owner was required to pay a $600,000 "founder's fee."[9] Davidson required that the "founder's fees" go to him directly, giving off a vibe to many that he was a con man.[10] Bassett felt comfortable with Davidson, however, and was satisfied with his experience in the WHA fulfilling Davidson's mission of providing jobs and better wages to hockey players across the United States and Canada.

Over the course of the Toros' first two seasons under his stewardship, Bassett and Davidson became convivial due to their shared belief that professional sports were mired in innovative and artistic mediocrity due to a lack of competition. The founder of the WHA was an avid tennis player and, while not in Bassett's class, he enjoyed playing the Toros' owner.[11] Their in-match discussions led to serious talk of a Toronto entry in the WFL. When Bassett learned of Davidson's WFL he was excited. Bassett knew there was a large population of Torontonians eager for the chance to watch American football in their hometown. Bassett possessed experience with professional football and its Toronto fans, albeit football of a different variety. John W.H. Bassett owned a large stake in the CFL's Toronto Argonauts. The CFL was a nine-team league which grew out of its rugby roots, and blended rivals from the east and west. Toronto's franchise was a keystone to the league's well-being. Bassett's father invited his son to sit on the Argonauts' Board of Directors. It was not an honorary title. Johnny F. Bassett helped his father with the Argonauts by performing duties as important as making hiring decisions.[12] The younger Bassett believed he could use his CFL connections to build a new type of Toronto sports spectacle. Bassett in the WFL was a natural. Davidson needed a team in Canada's largest market to assist his quest to have a truly "World" league and he had faith in Bassett after seeing his commitment to the WHA. At the same time Bassett had a passion for football spectacle and trusted Davidson after dealing with him in hockey. With the stars seemingly aligned, and strong familiarity with Davidson already thanks to the WHA, Bassett agreed to start a franchise in Toronto, a decision the CFL viewed as an act of war.

The Canadian Football League and Canadian Anti-Americanism

Johnny F. Bassett was now the proud owner of a professional football team which he christened the Toronto Northmen. The entrepreneur hit the ground running and began to structure the organization, focusing first on settling the nagging issue which his Toros never could: finding a place to play. The Northmen quickly found a home base of operations thanks to Bassett's deep connections to one CFL team. Displaying true support for his son's sporting ambitions, John W.H. Bassett, in his role as owner of the Toronto Argonauts, foreswore his territorial rights to the city. This was not a small concession as the elder Bassett had exercised his prerogative the year before when he vetoed a proposed expansion team that would have provided a second Toronto CFL team. In addition to sharing his territorial rights with his son's WFL team, John W.H. Bassett also agreed to share the use of Exhibition Stadium with the Northmen. Compared to the machinations required to simply get his Toronto Toros a practice rink, Bassett's early days as owner of the Northmen were quite easy.

While Bassett was merrily putting his team together, trouble was brewing across the Provinces. Owners of franchises in the Canadian Football League and several members of Parliament expressed concern about the Northmen and rumblings of fighting Bassett were heard. The trouble that came made Harold Ballard's extortion-like rent payments pale in comparison. "The poor guy (Bassett) ran into the federal government on that one," said family friend John Eaton, recalling the drama that ensued.[13]

The Canadian Football League as an organization was a mere adolescent in the early 1970s. Operating nine franchises throughout the country, the CFL was only sixteen years old when Bassett announced the birth of the Toronto Northmen, although its championship game, the Grey Cup, dated back to 1909, giving the league some plausible claim to venerable status. The CFL started in 1958, but its roots in Canada ran much deeper. There had been organized football of some form or fashion in Canada since the 1860s.[14] Before the advent of the CFL, the professional game was governed by the Canadian Rugby Union (CRU).[15] The name alone hinted at the differences between the Canadian game of football and that played south of the border in the United States. The CRU/CFL developed a style of game that was distinctly Canadian over decades. The CFL game consisted of three downs instead of four as in America. The field was significantly larger than an American field: 110-yards by 65-yards with a pair of 25-yard end zones. A Canadian team had 12 players on a side instead of 11 and a single point, or rouge, was awarded to a team when it successfully kicked the ball into the end zone without it being returned by the opponent.[16] These rules were also followed by Canadian collegiate teams. Of course, despite the differences, the essence of the game remained similar to the American variant and there was player movement into the CFL from the United States. This resulted in the CFL limiting the number of American players per team. The result was that while Americans often dominated the skill positions such as wide receivers, there was plenty of room on CFL rosters for Canadian players, too.

Another traditional aspect of the CRU/CFL was worrying about the impact of "creeping Americanization" on their brand of football. When American teams embraced the forward pass as an offensive weapon in the 1920s, the CRU banned the play as "another baneful influence from the United States."[17] As overwrought as the phrase Americanization might sound to American ears, the notion that Canada was under threat from massive American influence never disappeared from Canadian nationalist circles. It was prevalent during those times as a leftover from the days when Britain and the United States were rivals, and it morphed into a David vs. Goliath complex as the United States grew richer, stronger, and more vibrant. The CRU continued to fight against American-style play until the 1940s.[18] This stance led to a schism between western rugby teams, which wanted to embrace American players and coaches, and the eastern teams, which worried such an embrace would cost Canadians jobs and opportunities.[19]

The rapid growth of the NFL in the 1960s also fed the CFL attitude of paranoia regarding American football. For years, there had been a rough parity between the CFL and NFL in terms of quality of play, and even prominence. The two divided the continent rather politely, but the AFL-NFL merger of 1966 provided American football explosive growth while the CFL maintained its relatively limited presence. As NFL revenue grew exponentially in the 1970s, broadening its presence on television and entrenching itself as "big time entertainment," the CFL was mired in mostly small towns, relegated to weekly contests between small-town teams from Saskatchewan and Calgary on national television. The CBC carried NFL games on Sunday afternoons, outdrawing the ratings of CFL telecasts, while CFL games did not appear on American televisions.[20] This fed a feeling of hopelessness shared by CFL owners, who were trying to combat the creeping mindset that because the NFL was bigger than the CFL, it was better.[21] Whether or not the NFL was better is open to debate, but with innovations like *Monday Night Football* and the Super Bowl driving its television popularity to new heights, the NFL was certainly glitzier and more popular than the CFL.

The popularity of the NFL at the expense of the CFL is illustrative of the growing Americanization struggle occurring in Canada during the 1960s and 1970s. There was unease among leading Canadians about the pop cultural output of America overwhelming Canada. This unease was especially acute in the 1960s and 1970s as American programming began to appear more and more on Canadian television sets. American television shows were being sold to Canadian broadcasters for $2,000 per 30-minute episode, nearly ten times cheaper than a Canadian-made production.[22] Henry Conmor, president of the Association of Canadian Television and Radio Artists, lamented to his American peers, "My young son thinks he lives in the United States."[23] Government and industry officials worried that a generation of Canadians was growing up believing that the American programs they saw on their televisions represented Canadian mores and sensibilities. As one Canadian author wrote, "It is through this kind of engrossing, relaxing perhaps mindless programming that most viewers absorb the particular quirks and values of their culture."[24] The Canadian government granted significant tax breaks to citizens willing to produce content with a decidedly Canadian flavor in an attempt to counter the amount and influence of American pop culture crossing the border. Despite these efforts, more than 90 percent of television programs aired on Canadian stations were produced in America.[25]

Many modern North American scholars align Canada with the United States, largely because the nation is beset by American hegemonic popular culture.[26] Canadians are not happy about having their national identity intertwined with America. In fact, many Canadian citizens, particularly in Ontario, agitate against American influence and fight on many popular fronts to maintain a semblance of Canadianism.[27]

One of those fronts is sports. National identity was one of the largest issues of the 1968 Canadian federal election. Liberal Party candidate Pierre Trudeau, who knew how to stoke Canadian nationalist fears without overtly antagonizing his large southern neighbor, commissioned the Task Force on Sport to investigate the role of sport on national culture as part of his "Unity Through Sport" campaign. The report argued that "sport is an effective antidote to economic cultural domination by the United States." Once elected, Trudeau made promoting uniquely Canadian sports a pillar of his administration: "Sport has an important role to play in any government attempt to promote unity and a unique Canadian identity."[28] Trudeau's appeal for maintaining the sanctity of Canadian sports resonated, tapping into a growing sense of urgency to preserve the nation's unique culture and illustrating the growth of "Canadian anti–Americanism," which grew bolder in the 1970s. Canadian political historian Jack L. Granastein offered his definition of Canadian anti–Americanism in his 1996 book *Yankee Go Home?* (italics added):

> Canadian anti–Americanism is a distaste for and a fear of American military, political, *cultural*, and economic activities that, while widespread in the population, is usually benign unless and until it is exploited by *business, political, or cultural groups for their own ends*. Added to this is a snippet—and sometimes more—of envy at the greatness, wealth, and power of the Republic and its citizens, and a dash of discomfort at the excesses that mar American life.[29]

Into this patriotic/economic maelstrom stepped Johnny F. Bassett and his Toronto Northmen.

Sins of the Father

Johnny F. Bassett's earlier attempts to bring auto racing to Toronto's lakefront and secure an arena for the Toros had taught him valuable lessons. Even if one has the best of intentions, one needs the full support of local government to get a sporting endeavor off the ground and one needs to have a solid, secure base of operations from which to work. The first few steps of Bassett's founding of the Northmen were made easier by the actions of his father. John W.H. Bassett ceding his territorial rights to the WFL when he had not done so for the CFL was huge, as his son did not have to worry about a Harold Ballard-esque competitor in the Argonauts.[30] So was handing his son the keys to CNE Stadium. The elder Bassett did something else that was quite unorthodox, he became a stockholder in the Northmen. The elder Bassett explained that he wanted financial protection if the Northmen put a dent in the value of the Argonauts. "As an insurance policy, we will take a small stake in the new club," W.H. Bassett said. "But our holding will be less than 15%."[31]

The leaders of Toronto were excited by the prospect of an American football team coming to their city and they were committed to helping. Paul Godfrey, Chairman of Metropolitan Toronto from 1973 to 1984, was also laying the groundwork for attracting a Major League Baseball team to the city and was firmly in Bassett's camp. "We shared a common interest in improving the sports life of Toronto," Godfrey said.[32]

Mr. Godfrey was not acquainted with Bassett at the time of his attempt to bring auto racing to the lakefront. Lack of support from all corners of Toronto's large governing structure had scuttled Bassett's racing dreams. Mr. Godfrey's recollections of the size of Toronto government in the early 1970s provides context for how much bureaucracy needed to be navigated, but also how much local support Bassett had in bringing forth a WFL franchise. "The structure has changed, but Toronto had a regional government then," Godfrey explained. "There were six municipalities which made up Metropolitan Toronto. There was the downtown core, which was the city of Toronto. There was also East York, Scarborough, North York, Etobicoke and York. Each municipality had its own council and own mayor. They realized in the 1950s it would be silly to have six police departments, six welfare offices, and six road departments. They set up a metropolitan council with senior representatives of each municipality. Over the top of that municipality they had a position called the Metropolitan Toronto Chairman."[33] Toronto's consolidation as well as an increasingly diverse immigrant population radically transformed the city once known as "Hogtown" into a dynamic metropolis.[34] That change lay years ahead, however. For now, Bassett was rattling cages in a city not known for enjoying high-profile change.

With John W.H. Bassett and Paul Godfrey on his side, Johnny F. Bassett enjoyed more local support than in any of his previous Toronto sports projects. Unfortunately, in the months ahead, he discovered that no amount of local allies could offset a national organization fighting for survival and relevance. Bassett severely underestimated the amount of angst, jealousy, and bitterness he was engendering as he blithely built and marketed the Northmen. This blind spot ended up costing his father a football team and forced the younger Bassett to budget far more money than he had planned in start-up costs.

The CFL had an axe to grind with the Bassett family, particularly John W.H. Bassett. They viewed John W.H. Bassett's ceding of Toronto territorial rights to his son as equivalent to Benedict Arnold's actions at West Point in the American Revolution. Many feared the Northmen would establish a beachhead for the introduction of more American football teams in Canada and John W.H. Bassett's treasonous action had eased that process. Jim Hole, then president of the Edmonton Eskimos, voiced the opinion of many in the CFL. "The Argos will have to decide which side of the fence they are on, the CFL or WFL," Hole said. "The WFL has to be considered competition for us, both in higher contracts for players and the availability of players. There is enough competition now for the CFL with the NFL. I personally view the WFL as unhealthy for us."[35]

Hole's comment about contracts and player availability got to the heart of the CFL argument. In the 1950s the CFL and NFL had been on similar financial footing making the Canadian game a viable alternative for NFL players unhappy with their contract situation. Players under contract to American professional teams could sign a "futures" contract to "jump" to the CFL when their current contract expired. Because the CFL and NFL were separate entities, the player in question was not bound by the reserve clause which required him to play one season without a contract with his original team before he could move to another NFL team. Therefore, the player was free to leave, and the NFL team received no compensation. As the 1950s progressed and the NFL gained in popularity, a financial disparity began to arise between the two leagues and the NFL started to strike back. When the NFL's Chicago Cardinals signed Montreal Alouette star quarterback Sam "The Rifle" Etcheverry to a contract, the CFL team had to match it in order to keep their marquee player in Quebec. When the Hamilton Tiger-Cats signed two members of the Chicago Bears to future contracts, Bears owner George Halas sued for $150,000 in damages. Shortly after the suit, the NFL and CFL agreed to cease their cross-border raids, which lowered player costs.[36]

The CFL still occasionally provided an alternative to American college football players. A handful of American college stars had been convinced to sign with teams north of the border. Notable signings were

Notre Dame's quarterback Joe Theismann, interestingly a member of the Argonauts, and Nebraska's Heisman Trophy-winning running back Johnny Rodgers of the Montreal Alouettes. For the most part, however, the CFL was losing the talent war with the NFL in the early 1970s and the idea of another American professional football league, with a team in Canada no less, only meant the Canadian league would lose out on more potential star power. It also meant the CFL's unique revenue-sharing plan was at risk.

The NFL truly took off as an entity when Pete Rozelle convinced the owners of all clubs to equally share their revenue in 1961. This pooling of revenue allowed small market teams like Green Bay, Wisconsin, to compete on equal footing with New York, Chicago, and Los Angeles. The CFL also looked to provide a sense of balance between large and small market teams, but their approach to sharing was stricter than their American counterparts. The five western teams: Edmonton Eskimos, Saskatchewan Roughriders (Regina), British Columbia Lions (Vancouver), Calgary Stampeders, and Winnipeg Blue Bombers, were all community-owned, not-for-profit entities. To provide these teams with an equal financial footing compared to their eastern counterparts, the CFL instituted a policy called gate equalization. In this format, the four eastern teams, Toronto Argonauts, Montreal Alouettes, Hamilton Tiger-Cats, and Ottawa Rough Riders, shared their profits rather than just the revenue. This gnawed at John W.H. Bassett's business sensibilities. "It's clear what the CFL's basic problem is," W.H. Bassett said. "There's no community of basic interest between the eastern teams, which belong to businessmen and are run as businesses, and the western teams, which are publicly owned and operated in the manner you might expect."[37]

John W.H. Bassett felt the best way for the CFL to survive was for the western teams to go private.[38] John W.H. Bassett's contempt for the western teams was high and his feelings were returned in force by those western owners. The thought circling around the media was that the western CFL teams were using the pretext of John W.H. Bassett's affiliation with his son's Northmen and concerns over Americanization as excuses to settle old scores about gate equalization. In a *Regina Leader-Post* column, Bob Hughes argued the stance of maintaining that the CFL was purely Canadian football was hypocritical. "Only two of the nine CFL general managers are Canadian," Hughes wrote. "Every CFL head coach is an American, the most important positions, including all nine starting quarterbacks are American. The only thing Canadian about the CFL is they play our national anthem, and sometimes that is done by an American band! You get the feeling there are no more than just a handful of CFL brass anxious to get John (W.H.) Bassett out of the Toronto Argonauts."[39]

No matter how flawed their logic, the elder Bassett's stake in the Northmen gave his opponents an opening and they took advantage. Knowing full well that Toronto was the most lucrative market in the league, the owners stated that John W.H. Bassett's actions towards the Northmen were a blatant conflict of interest.[40] The presence of a professional football team from a rival league would naturally mean less revenue for the Argonauts. If the Argonauts received less revenue, the western teams would be subjected to a decrease in their gate equalization payments. As a shareholder of the Northmen, the elder Bassett was set to profit off the very entity that would lower the value of his CFL team and, by association, the western CFL franchises. The western owners argued that could not be allowed to stand.

A motion was put forth at the annual CFL owner's meeting that John W.H. Bassett should have his ownership of the Argonauts rescinded due to the conflict of interest his minority share in the Northmen represented. The motion carried 7–2 with only Montreal and Toronto voting against. The elder Bassett was reported to have responded to the vote with a string of profanities. With more comportment later in the day, W.H. Bassett told the press, "If my Eastern Conference colleagues are unhappy with me as a partner, and if they believe that I'm harmful to the Canadian Football League, I don't want to stay. If they're unhappy with me, I'll sell the Argonauts to the league for $4 million."[41] Thus ended the reign of John W.H. Bassett as owner of the Toronto Argonauts. Shortly after the owner's meeting, John W.H. Bassett also sold his shares in the Toronto Northmen. Whatever joy the CFL may have experienced in ousting someone they viewed with disdain was tempered by the fact that Johnny F. Bassett was continuing to build his WFL franchise.

Amazingly, despite the CFL's shabby treatment of his father, Johnny F. Bassett attempted a conciliation effort that bordered on the extraordinary. Bassett had no desire to destroy the Canadian Football League. He grew up playing the Canadian version of the game and helped run the Argonauts. He also did not want his father forced out of the CFL, but he had no intentions of giving up his Northmen either. In an attempt at smoothing the matter over, Johnny F. Bassett resigned his post with the Argonauts and worked out an arrangement with the WFL that he thought would assuage the legitimate fears of CFL owners. Bassett acquired WFL territorial rights for the entire country. By doing so, Bassett had final say on any future WFL franchises in Canada and he was willing to transfer the veto power to the CFL, giving the Canadian league the power to prevent any further WFL encroachment into Canada.[42]

In an interview, Bassett gamely tried to explain that he was a fan of both American football and the CFL. He did not want to be seen as the agent of the CFL's demise. In his estimation, his ownership of the Northmen allowed him to be in control of the inevitable growth of the American game while also protecting Canada's home game. Bassett spelled out plainly that the WFL had planned to come to Toronto or Montreal whether he owned the team or not, but in having acquired veto power, Bassett could protect CFL owners. "I feel two teams can exist in Toronto without hurting the Argonauts, but somewhere else could be a different matter," Bassett said. "If the worst were to happen and the CFL is to go down the tubes, I'd like to be in a position to tell someone who wants to put a team in say, Montreal, that he must include (Alouettes owner) Mr. Sam Berger."[43] His father seconded his son's views, arguing the CFL would not have to worry about further WFL incursions. "In my view, Johnny has a deal that has a helluva protection for the CFL. He holds a national veto. He has to approve any other Canadian entry into the WFL."[44]

CFL Commissioner Jake Gaudaur was not overly thrilled with the Northmen encroachment, but he chose to withhold judgment on the issue because of the veto power Bassett presented to the league. "I don't think it's the most desirable position," Gaudaur said. "But I don't see any specific undesirable manifestations at this point in time."[45] Gaudaur may have felt more comfortable due to the comments by the WFL's legal counsel, Donald Regan, who publicly stated Bassett's demand for a veto over future WFL teams in Canada was meant to offer protection for the Canadian game. "Johnny is a very circumspect businessman," Regan said. "He knows the World Football League is a reality and he wants to work out something that protects the Canadian League."[46]

In addition to granting the CFL complete veto power over the possibility of a future WFL team in Canada, Bassett provided the western teams with an insurance policy. Realizing how important the gate equalization revenues generated by the Argonauts were to the teams out west, Bassett guaranteed to personally make up the difference. Using the Argonauts' 1973 equalization payments of $48,000 per team as his base, Bassett agreed to make up any shortfall caused by the Northmen.[47] For example, if the Argonauts' gate allowed for a payment of only $35,000 per team, Bassett would pay the difference of $13,000 per team. Despite these efforts, the mere existence of the Northmen continued to be an issue for the western CFL owners. The Toronto Argonauts were considered the "strongest link in the CFL chain."[48] Even a minor loss of prestige to a cross-town rival by the Argonauts could trigger financial upheaval throughout the CFL. Bassett's foray into the WFL meant only one thing to the CFL. Johnny F. Bassett had to go by any means necessary.

Six

IIIIIIIIIIIIIIIIIIIIIIIIIIIIIIIIIIIIII

Bassett Becomes
a Political Football

The Canadian Football League found a powerful ally in their battle with Johnny F. Bassett: the Canadian federal government. Traditionally, Canada's provincial governments have a great deal of devolved power, but Trudeau was in the mold of prime ministers who aggressively sought to maximize the federal government's profile and power as a unifying factor in a somewhat decentralized, hybridized nation. Trudeau's vision was that Ottawa, seat of the federal government, could put forth policies that would both differentiate Canada from the United States and give Canadians their own cultural institutions around which to rally and upon which to build a more robust sense of nationhood.[1] Two examples were the national health insurance plan and close diplomatic relations with Fidel Castro's Cuba, both of which frustrated American officials. A third would be Canadian football. One national politician particularly carried the banner for upholding Canadian football at the expense of Bassett: Marc Lalonde. Lalonde was the Liberal government's Minister of National Health and Welfare in 1973. Like many Canadian politicians and leaders of the time, Lalonde viewed the increasing "Americanization" of his country's culture with a wary eye. "If one defines culture very widely as being the identity of a country, then for many Canadians the real competition should be between Canadian teams," Lalonde said recently. "You can say that the fact there is a Canadian Football League constituted of Canadian teams is important to the many citizens who follow this. It is the only professional sport which is exclusively Canadian with its own unique set of rules."[2]

Lalonde and others viewed the WFL encroachment on the CFL as an invasion. "I was responsible for sports and frankly Canadian football is something I didn't know much about, but it was close to many people's hearts," Lalonde said. "They felt if an American team came to Toronto it

57

would be the end of the Argonauts. Eventually, Montreal would also get a team and then other markets would suffer. Hamilton, Winnipeg, Saskatoon, Edmonton, Calgary, and Vancouver were too small to sustain the league. The concern was the disappearance of the CFL."[3]

The Canadian Gridiron War

Buoyed by CFL owners who were arguably more worried about the WFL's impact on their bottom lines than culture, Lalonde issued what came to be known as the "Regina Manifesto" on February 21, 1974. In an address delivered to the Regina Rotary and Kiwanis Club luncheon at the Hotel Saskatchewan, Lalonde declared that it was a priority of the Liberal government to prevent a WFL team from beginning play in Toronto. "The federal government views with disfavor any move to expand the World Football League into Canada," Lalonde said at the address. "I intend to be in touch with provincial and municipal officials in Ontario within the next few days to see what action we should take."[4]

One of the provincial officials Lalonde spoke with was Paul Godfrey, Chairman of Metropolitan Toronto. Godfrey and several other local politicians were firmly on the side of the Northmen and told Lalonde so. Unfortunately, according to Godfrey, their arguments to Lalonde fell on deaf ears. "When Johnny was trying to bring the Northmen to Toronto, I spent the better part of two evenings trying to convince the federal government they would not hurt the CFL," Godfrey said. "I also argued it would help expand interest in football, but to no avail."[5]

Godfrey and Metro Council voted 24–2 in favor of the Northmen playing at CNE, but this did nothing to sway Marc Lalonde.[6] Lalonde's major point of contention was what he viewed as the Bassett's disdain for the CFL. The Minister cited John W.H. Bassett's veto of a proposed expansion team for Toronto that would have provided the nation's largest market two teams. This veto, Lalonde argued, was indicative of the Bassett's contempt for the CFL. Lalonde's comments were quite strong, intimating the Bassett's were nothing more than hucksters. "The most recent application for a Toronto area franchise was vetoed last fall by the same people who own the present Toronto team," Lalonde said.

> So, while the CFL marks time, unable to expand, another threat to Canadian football has appeared—this time the World Football League. The new league has issued a franchise in Toronto, apparently with the silent assent if not the blessing of the same CFL owners who adamantly refused to consider a second CFL team in

Toronto only a few months ago. The future of the CFL is too important to be left to the tender mercies of a few entrepreneurs out for a fast buck.[7]

This salvo wounded Bassett. He felt he had taken on a tremendous financial risk in liquidating his Baton Broadcasting assets to bring a WFL franchise to his hometown. Once the team was established, Bassett had acted in good faith, gaining the support of Toronto politicians and the blessing of the CFL franchise which held the city's territorial rights. One could argue that John W.H. Bassett was motivated by a father's love in giving the blessing, but the blessing had been given fairly and legally. Any measures to stymie the younger Bassett would thus smack of *ex post facto* maneuvering. Furthermore, Bassett was establishing a model professional football franchise. The football operations were being run by a well-respected icon of Canadian football, Leo Cahill, the team was drafting star American college players, and Bassett had just hired an up-and-coming head coach, John McVay. These were not the actions of a mere entrepreneur out to make a few bucks. These were the actions of a maverick sportsman out to implement his vision of what a professional sports team could be in Toronto. Bassett wasted little time firing back at Lalonde.

"His reference to me as an entrepreneur out for a fast buck is libel," in view of what our family has put into sport over the years," Bassett told the press.

I played tennis for my country; I represented Canada in the Pan Am Games; I played on Canada's cricket team; our family sponsored the Telegram Indoor Track and Field Games; we've had interests in the Toronto Argonauts; the Toronto Maple Leafs; the Toronto Toros, and even the Montreal Canadiens, and we didn't get rich off one of them. Nobody is going to malign my family's contributions to Canadianism inside and outside sport.[8]

Libel or not, the insult had staying power because it spoke to such a distinctive American stereotype, the fast-talking business hustler. Glad-handing aggressive entrepreneurialism was more associated with American business culture than with the conservative Toronto style.

"All I want Lalonde to do is confront me and tell me what law I've broken," Bassett continued. "We've already spent $350,000 just establishing a legal business. We're committed to honor more than 20 contracts worth another $500,000. We've already signed a three-year radio contract. We've signed a stadium lease. If I was forced to get out now, it would cost me another $1 million to pay all my bills."[9]

The press conference was Bassett's last subtle move in fighting for his right to establish a football team in Toronto. As the calendar turned to spring, the snow and ice began to melt in Ontario while the battle between Bassett and Marc Lalonde heated up. By the time it ended both men made headlines for daring strategies. Bassett single-handedly pulled off a coup that effectively ended an NFL dynasty and sent CFL owners into paroxysms of terror. Marc Lalonde responded with the political equivalent of a nuclear device.

Oh, Canada: Johnny F. Bassett's Coup

The CFL and the Canadian government had legitimate reasons to be wary of the WFL's encroachment, but the two entities' heavy-handed response in the face of Johnny F. Bassett's multiple olive branches showed an underestimation of his prowess and tenacity. It also betrayed their conscious decision to use football as a nationalist pitch for political purposes. To be fair, there was little in Bassett's background to cause either the CFL or the Canadian government to quake with fear. Bassett's track record so far in sports had been lackluster at best: a failed auto race and a financially struggling WHA hockey team. This may have colored the perception of him in the eyes of his foes. Bassett permanently laid to rest all these perceptions with three strokes of his pen in March 1974, and in so doing altered the fortunes of professional football for the rest of the decade.

Larry Csonka, Jim Kiick, and Paul Warfield were as dissatisfied as three men who played for a perfect team could be. The three players were major contributors to the Miami Dolphins' historic 1972 season in which they finished 17–0, the only NFL team of the modern era to complete an entire season undefeated. That season culminated with a 14–7 victory over the Washington Redskins in Super Bowl VII. The following year the Dolphins finished with a 15–2 record and a second Super Bowl title. These three players should have been on top of the world, but the economics of the NFL had them feeling unappreciated. "I think the entire NFL was growing a little frustrated," Larry Csonka said. "The NFL was making more money than ever before and the ratio of profit to labor was the age-old question that goes on in our society constantly."[10]

Csonka had been the Dolphins' top draft choice in 1968 out of Syracuse. A bruising fullback, Csonka had once drawn an unnecessary roughness penalty *while running with the ball.* His running style demoralized opponents and that was never more apparent than in Super Bowl VIII. Csonka carried the ball 33 times for 145 yards and two touchdowns while wearing down the Minnesota Vikings. The performance earned Csonka Most Valuable Player honors in the 24–7 Dolphins victory. Csonka was All-Pro three straight seasons and was unquestionably the Dolphins' chief offensive weapon.

Jim Kiick was Csonka's running mate in the Dolphins backfield. A Pro Bowl-caliber back and fifth-round draft choice out of Wyoming, Kiick joined Miami the same year as Csonka. Kiick and Csonka became best friends and their exploits both on and off the field earned the pair the nickname "Butch Cassidy and the Sundance Kid." A shiftier runner than Csonka, Kiick provided the Dolphins a versatile threat. During the Dolphins' perfect season, it was Kiick who scored the game-winning touchdowns against Cleveland and Pittsburgh in the playoffs.

Paul Warfield was a ten-year veteran with a track record of excellence. A first-round draft choice out of Ohio State by the Cleveland Browns in 1964, Warfield played flanker and terrorized cornerbacks for six seasons along the shore of Lake Erie. The Browns won an NFL title his rookie season and played for the NFL championship three other times. Warfield earned All-Pro and Pro Bowl honors in three separate seasons. The Browns traded Warfield to the Dolphins in 1970 for Miami's number one draft choice so Cleveland could take quarterback Mike Phipps. Phipps never panned out while Warfield continued to shine in Miami, continuing to average a staggering 20 yards per catch despite playing on a run-dominated team.

For the astounding production generated by this triumvirate of players the Miami Dolphins paid the average sum of roughly $65,000 per player per year.[11] Granted this was a very good salary in 1973, but compared to the revenues reaped by Dolphins owner Joe Robbie and the rest of his fellow owners, it was borderline parsimony. Just getting those salaries had required a lot of angst. In a sensational for its time joint autobiography titled *Always on the Run*, Csonka and Kiick openly shared their ongoing battles with owner Joe Robbie, team president Joe Thomas, and head coach Don Shula. Following the 1970 season in which the Dolphins reached the playoffs for the first time, the contracts of Csonka and Kiick expired. Each player was earning roughly $30,000 per season. At the advice of Paul Warfield, Csonka and Kiick hired International Management as their representative. Believing that two were stronger than one, the duo also took the unusual step of using one agent, Ed Keating, to negotiate both of their contracts at the same time, a package deal for "Butch and Sundance." The Dolphins offered raises to $40,000 annually. Unsatisfied, both players elected to hold out of training camp. After two weeks the pair signed three-year contracts worth an estimated $60,000 per season.[12] Csonka appreciated that he made a good living but chafed at the monopolistic nature of the NFL. "It was obvious the salaries were getting better," Csonka said. "But the pay scales were staying the same. Since there was no competition, there was no chance to get an outside bid. I've always liked the free market, and the NFL at that time wasn't."[13]

Paul Warfield had also been through numerous contract battles with both the Browns and Dolphins. A thoughtful, eloquent man, Warfield recounted in an interview that negotiations were always laborious affairs that highlighted generational differences between the owners and their employees. "The ownership was pretty much Depression-era and World War II-era," Warfield said. "So, they were individuals who were tough-minded and guarded about monetary interests. It was a chore to negotiate contracts."[14] Following his trade from the Browns in 1970, Warfield had also engaged in a lengthy battle with the Dolphins when the contract he brought over from the Browns expired. Lacking a partnership with a fellow player, Warfield went it alone while being represented by Ed Keating. Warfield's view of the process illuminates the sour feelings that can emanate from a contract battle.

"Speaking only for myself, I was not particularly happy with some of the agreements made," Warfield admitted.

> I was not happy with the one and only contract I had with the Miami Dolphins. It was a royal battle and it lasted for several months to the point where I had to withhold my services during training camp. Ed Keating urged me to sign it and I certainly didn't want to. I wasn't asking for all the money in the world, I just wanted what was fair. I always tried to take the position of being fair to the employer and fair to myself. I was committed to the contract, I worked hard for it, but I wasn't happy for it.[15]

The contracts of Csonka, Kiick, and Warfield were set to expire at the same time, following an option year in 1974. One did not have to be an NFL insider or investigative journalist to figure out the trio was dissatisfied. Just checking out *Always on the Run* from the library would have accomplished this. But with the NFL reserve clause in place, no other NFL team was going to dare sign them. Bassett in his role as WFL owner was under no such restriction.

Bassett learned through an emissary in December 1973 that Ed Keating felt his three clients could be swayed to join the WFL if enough money was offered. The figure Keating came up with was $2.7 million split among the three players.[16] Less than a month later, Keating and Bassett were holed up in a suite at the Sutton Place Hotel in Toronto negotiating a heretofore unfathomable contract. Keating was accompanied to Toronto by Csonka, Kiick, and Warfield. The players and their agent were under the impression this was simply an exploratory meeting. Over the course of the weekend they expected to get to know Bassett, learn more about the city of Toronto, and be able to return to Miami with a viable alternative to increase their bargaining power against Joe

Robbie. "With a new kid on the block, so to speak, Johnny Bassett represented an alternative," Csonka admitted. "And I appreciated the fact we could use the Northmen as leverage to better our situation."[17]

What the group of Dolphins did not count on was the creativity and daring of Johnny F. Bassett. He had a marketing vision for his football enterprise similar to that of his hockey team: stealing fans away from his rival's team by using the weaknesses of his rival's business practices against them. Bassett signed several former star Leaf players away from the miserly Harold Ballard, capturing disenchanted Leaf fans for the Toros. Bassett repeated the ploy with the Northmen, but on a much grander scale. Bassett felt the economics of the NFL made enticing players to jump to the WFL possible and he intended to prove it by going after the stars of the most recognizable team in professional football: the defending back-to-back champion Miami Dolphins.

Bassett read the same sports pages as everyone else. Csonka, Kiick, and Warfield were on record as feeling they were getting less than market value from the Dolphins. With a lack of viable alternatives in the NFL and uncertainty over the validity of the WFL, however, their comments had to be taken with a grain of salt because most players felt underpaid. Once Bassett learned from Keating that players of their magnitude could be convinced to leave the Super Bowl champions if the price was right, he put his experience as a showman and promoter into overdrive. This was not going to be a passive meeting; Bassett was going to pull out all the stops. The three players were registered to stay in one of the fanciest hotels in Toronto, invited to eat at the finest restaurants, scheduled to have personally tailored suits made, and set up with a tour of the town all on Bassett's dime. Bassett intended to sell himself as much as the Northmen and make the appeal of playing in the WFL irresistible.

It was a daring plan that required a lot of things to go right to pull off. If Bassett was feeling a great deal of apprehension over his weekend meeting, he did not betray it. The three players and their agent met briefly with Bassett on Saturday morning. Paul Warfield was duly impressed with Bassett's demeanor, which was so different than what he had observed in other owners. "I found him to be an upbeat and jovial guy," Warfield said. "A lot younger than the owners I was accustomed to being in the presence of. I felt very comfortable in his presence and liked him immediately as an individual."[18]

Pleasant personality aside, when the three players departed to let Keating and Bassett talk financials, none of them expected anything other than a typically onerous negotiation. After all, they were asking for close to one million dollars apiece, which far outpaced the average salary in football. "I thought there was no way in the world Bassett would agree based on my previous experiences," Warfield said. "When we left Keating and Bassett, we walked around Toronto and visited a tailor. I had a suit made for myself, not necessarily meaning I was going to sign. When we returned three-and-a-half hours later we were on pins and needles. We expected to hear from Ed, 'You guys are asking for too much money.' Instead he told us, 'I want you to know he gave you everything you asked for.' I couldn't believe it!"[19] No one could, especially Ed Keating.

The agent and Bassett were having a difficult time coming to agreement on the length of the contracts. Naturally, the players wanted more security given the tenuous nature of the WFL and Bassett did not want to commit to guaranteed, long-term deals. Around noon the two men repaired to separate rooms to refresh. Keating felt the negotiations were in trouble. What the agent did not realize was that Bassett was in the other room engaging in a bit of soul-searching. Signing the three stars of the two-time defending NFL champions was Bassett's chance to, in his words, "make the club and the league."[20] This was also the chance for him to establish his place in sports. A signing coup of this nature would put Bassett into the same class of bold owners as Sonny Werblin of the New York Jets. When Werblin was negotiating with Joe Namath in 1965, he knew that signing the quarterback from Alabama would not just burnish the Jets, but the American Football League as well. According to Namath, Werblin told him point blank, "I don't want to quibble over money. This is what I'm going to offer you and you are going to take it."[21] That $427,000 contract was the richest in football at the time and cemented the AFL as a league to be reckoned with. This was Bassett's chance at a "Sonny Werblin moment" and he embraced it.

Bassett was joined in the room by Herb Solway. Solway was an original investor of the Northmen and acted as the team's Chairman. Solway recalls expressing his doubt that the three Dolphins were serious about moving to Toronto. "Keating presented us with a binder full of requests," Solway said.

> It is fifteen pages of terms and conditions. I thought they had no intention of coming to Toronto. It is just a bargaining tool to get more money from Miami. I said, "Johnny, there is no way we are going to sign these guys." Johnny said, "There is one way to get them. Suppose we just say yes?" I said, "Yes? These are some weird things they're asking for." Johnny said, "I know, I know. But I'm just going to say yes."[22]

Bassett walked into Keating's room, shuffled some papers on the table, looked up and said, "Ed, you've got a deal."[23]

The deal was eye-popping. The total of all three contracts came to $3 million with the following breakdowns: Larry Csonka, $1.4 million over three years, Jim Kiick, $700,000 over three years and Paul

Warfield, $900,000 over three years. The contracts were "futures contracts," which would not go into effect until 1975, the year after the Dolphin contracts expired at the conclusion of the 1974 season. In addition to the salaries, Bassett also agreed to provide the players with a luxury car and cover their rent while living in Toronto.[24] Keating's initial reaction was shock and the agent began sputtering. "Johnny came into the room and asked Keating, 'This is your request? I don't think you're serious about signing. I think if we gave you all this stuff you wouldn't come,'" Herb Solway recounted. "Keating said, 'Absolutely we would come.' Johnny says, 'Then you've got a deal!' It looked like Keating was struck by a thunderbolt!"[25]

As recipients of this largesse, the three Dolphins were beside themselves with glee. After years of fighting for every penny, they were pleased with the money, naturally, but also shocked at the unexpected positive atmosphere of the negotiations and Bassett's attitude toward player satisfaction. "I couldn't believe it," Paul Warfield said. "For the first time someone agreed we were of value. It was unbelievable. Mr. Bassett believed I had proven myself, so he was willing to compensate me for my ability. That was a new experience for me."[26] Csonka added, "When he put that kind of money on the table, it got my attention."[27] If the players had a hard time believing the contracts, imagine the reaction of the Miami Dolphins.

To be fair to their current employer, Csonka, Kiick, and Warfield verbally agreed to the contracts but did not sign, wanting to give the Dolphins an opportunity to match. Csonka felt it was the right thing to do out of respect for Don Shula. Reluctantly, Bassett agreed. "The offer was so outlandish the only thing I wanted to do was have the chance to talk to Don Shula and Joe Robbie before it hit the paper," Larry Csonka said.[28] The players sensed the enormity of the weekend. If they signed their names to the contracts, they would significantly weaken the Dolphins at the expense of their coach and teammates, dramatically upgrade the credibility of the WFL, and fundamentally change the economics of professional football forever. Bassett understood this as well, but he was not going to be completely sanguine about the situation. The three players could reach out to the Dolphins, but if they did not sign the contract the next day, he would pull the deal off the table. The players certainly knew where Bassett was coming from when he made that ultimatum. "He knew this was going to be a significant deal and he wanted it to happen in a big way," Paul Warfield said. "Larry Csonka said we had to at least inform the Dolphins and see if they wanted to retain our interests. Bassett was fearful he would lose us to the Dolphins overnight."[29] Csonka respected both Bassett's position and the need for the ultimatum. "Bassett wanted the impact (of the contracts) to be as immense as he could make it," Csonka said. "If we walked away from that table, we walked away from that offer."[30]

Bassett sent the players out to enjoy the evening, springing for their dinner at Bigliardi's Steakhouse. In addition to the meal, Bassett was also paying for their accommodations in the $400 a night Prime Minister's suite at the Sutton Place.[31] While they dined, Bassett was left to ponder the evening's proceedings. Bassett was on the verge of making a name for himself as a new type of football owner. Whether that name would be synonymous with daring or eccentricity was out of his control. As a Northmen employee close to the negotiations commented, "Would it be good publicity to bring these guys up here and strike out? I'd call that lousy publicity which we don't need."[32]

According to Csonka and Kiick, Bassett was legitimately concerned that the Miami Dolphins would spare no expense to keep their roster intact. Bassett could not fathom a situation where Joe Robbie would allow his stars to leave. They recounted the conversation they had with Bassett before departing Saturday evening in their joint autobiography. Bassett believed Joe Robbie would be hopping on the next flight to Toronto to match the offer. The players explained that Bassett did not know Joe Robbie. "Joe Robbie won't be here," Jim Kiick said. Bassett was stunned, responding to Kiick, "He's got to. I know if I owned the Dolphins and you three were signing with another team, I'd be on the plane."[33]

It was this mindset that endeared Bassett to the three Dolphins. Having just struck the most monumental deal in football history, Bassett was acceding to the trio's need to give the Dolphins the chance to match. He was also continuing to be a gracious host even though he was doubtful of the outcome. "Mr. Bassett was a great sportsman," Paul Warfield said.[34] Clearly, what attracted the three Dolphin stars was not just Bassett's lucre, but his heart-on-the-sleeve style. They knew he craved their talents *and* cared about their fates.

Bassett's evening of trepidation was rewarded the next day. When Sunday afternoon came around there was no corresponding offer from the Miami Dolphins. Just as the three players had predicted, Dolphins owner Joe Robbie did not fly to Toronto. Refusing to negotiate over the telephone, Robbie told Keating he had believed the group only flew to Canada to hear an offer from Bassett, not "to be spirited off and held for ransom."[35] With no offer from Miami, Larry Csonka, Jim Kiick, and Paul Warfield signed their Toronto Northmen contracts on March 31, 1974. Contract is a polite way of describing the original agreement document. As Johnny Bassett later admitted, the contracts were "written in ink on yellow foolscap paper."[36]

News of the signings hit the newsstands on April 1, 1974. The sign-ings were viewed as anything but an April Fool's Day joke. This was a tectonic shift in the landscape of professional football. The Miami Dol-phins dynasty was severely weakened, the cost of doing business in the NFL had just gone up substantially, and the prestige of the Northmen and WFL had just blossomed. *Time* magazine called it "the deal that astonished sports," and in publications around the United States the name Johnny F. Bassett was prominent.[37] "Howard Cosell put Johnny and the three players on his television show," Herb Solway said.[38]

Larry Csonka uttered a phrase during the press conference announcing the signings that reverberated across professional sports. The standard player-owner relationship in which the player was to come to the owner with hat in hand was ending. Offering less than market-value contracts and viewing negotiations as trench war-fare could no longer work. Labor negotiations and court settlements throughout sports were bringing true free agency closer and closer with each passing year. In addition to money, owners who wanted to

Bassett (far left) and Toronto Northmen general manager Leo Cahill (back row) with (from left) Paul Warfield, Jim Kiick, and Larry Csonka. The three former Miami Dolphins signed with Bassett's Northmen for a combined $3 million in 1974. The franchise was forced to relocate to Memphis because of the threat of Canadian legislation. The three only played part of one sea-son (1975) before the WFL folded. Unlike the majority of WFL owners, Bas-sett honored his contracts and the three players (and all others) received full pay (Getty Images).

sign quality players also had to prove that they ran quality organizations which treated players with common courtesy and decency. "There's a new psychology being used in the signing of players," Csonka said of Bassett. "Frankly, I was impressed with the Northmen owner. They have already established a good rapport with us."[39]

Forty years later Larry Csonka stood by his mindset about Bassett being advanced in his thinking towards the value of players as more than just a spot on a roster. "I knew Bassett represented a new era for players," Csonka said.

> To pay three players that amount wasn't a smart economic move from the standpoint of a fledgling league, but the impact it had on the general public was where Bassett was coming from. It was more than paying for labor for a series of games over three years. It was the fact he was pulling off a coup, signing three players from the Super Bowl champions. In that scenario we were worth a lot more money. You're worth "X" in the NFL under these conditions, but in the WFL you are worth "Y" because you are quality players who can attract other players to the WFL.[40]

Paul Warfield echoed that sentiment, stating that Bassett pioneered a new aesthetic of ownership. "For the first time I was dealing with an individual who appreciated what I could bring to a ballclub or organization," Warfield said. "When one is talking about dollars and cents, certainly I think they want value. But there is the thought that it is nice to know that they appreciate what one can contribute. That was the first time I experienced that. Johnny Bassett was part of the new breed. I think Johnny Bassett was right in touch with the owners of today."[41]

Bassett could no longer be viewed as a wealthy eccentric. His daring and courageous signing of the heart of the Miami Dolphins made him the face of the WFL and removed any doubt he may have harbored over his future in sports. For the rest of his life Bassett's confidence, vision, and daring in sports only grew. One can pinpoint the date March 31, 1974, as the day Johnny F. Bassett became sports ownership's most dynamic maverick.

The only thing that could stop Bassett's Northmen from taking Canada by storm would be an act of Parliament. Ironically, that is just what happened.

The Canadian Football Act

From coast to coast in both the United States and Canada there was buzz about the signings. Fans in Toronto were legitimately excited about the Northmen. Bona fide American football stars from the NFL's best team were going to play in their city. To the pleasant surprise of many

Canadians who sometimes harbored feelings of inferiority about their football, *the players were excited about the move!* "I'd prefer to play in Toronto," Csonka was asked when queried for his opinion on the battle the Northmen were engaged in with the CFL.[42]

Before the ink was even dry on the contracts, the Minister of National Health and Welfare cropped back up. Marc Lalonde's interference was especially nettlesome for Bassett. At what should have been his shining moment, he was forced to deal yet again with a politician out to put a stop to his sports business. It was shades of Lakeshore Racing all over again. "I think Johnny felt he had everything set to play in Toronto and then out of the blue comes Mark Lalonde, who I don't think set foot in Toronto five times in his life," Bassett's friend Peter Eby said. "Lalonde takes the position that the Northmen are anti–Canadian and will hurt the CFL and the rest of the country."[43]

Like a veritable wet blanket, Lalonde put a damper on the celebratory mood by announcing in no uncertain terms that the Canadian government would never allow the three Miami Dolphins to play a down on Canadian soil. The official went so far as to paint the signings as nothing more than a desperate attempt by Bassett to con the fans out of their "right" to CFL football. Lalonde also seemed to take the signings as a personal affront. "The signings are proof positive that a lot of investors are willing to put a lot of money into making a lot of money even if it means killing Canadian football," Lalonde said. "If this is meant as a squeeze on Parliament then it will be counter-productive. Parliamentarians will not take kindly to this kind of pressure on this kind of stage."[44] Taken alone, Lalonde's position was ridiculous. There was no way in which exposure to three of the best athletes in their sport would harm Toronto sports fans, unless improving the quality of the sports product was itself problematic. But Lalonde was a politician operating with an eye on larger concerns: saving a uniquely Canadian institution.

Within a week Lalonde introduced Bill C-22: The Canadian Football Act: An Act Representing Canadian Professional Football. The title was more than a mouthful, but the gist of the act was simple: grant the Canadian Football League a monopoly on professional football in the country backed with the full protection of the Canadian government. The preamble of the bill took indirect aim at Johnny F. Bassett (italics added): "Whereas Canadian football developed for itself a unique national institution contributing to the strengthening of the bonds of nationhood, it is in the national and public interests to protect this institution from the encroachment of *foreign-sponsored enterprises extending into Canada.*"[45]

Lalonde was assailed by some critics who felt the Canadian

government had better things to do than be involved in professional football. Others feared the "big-brother" aspect of the legislation which was setting a precedent for the Canadian government to pick winners and losers rather than allowing the free market to determine what style of football could be played in the nation. An anonymous Montreal critic lambasted Lalonde, "If Marc Lalonde has his way, the people of Toronto and Montreal will be compelled by law forever to accept an inferior brand of football simply because people living in smaller cities can't afford big-league entertainment."[46]

The argument of the critic particularly galled Lalonde and the minister's response indicated he was taking this cause personally. "The basic assumption here seems to be that, if it is Canadian, it is inferior," Lalonde retorted. "That is an assumption that I for one am not prepared to accept. We all know that football itself is not a life and death issue, or even a bread and butter issue. It is an emotional issue, a gut issue if you like, and it obviously stirs up deep feeling in a great many Canadians."[47]

Today Lalonde looks at the back-and-forth with Bassett and the WFL as just one of many challenges confronting him in the early 1970s. He conceded that out of all these challenges, Canadian football was the least important. "I did have much more pressing matters than football," Lalonde said. "We were dealing with major reforms in health and social security. I was responsible for the status of women also, which was a very lively issue at the time. I had about one-third of the federal budget under my supervision, so the CFL was not a major priority. But I thought the CFL's argument was a valid one."[48]

As Parliament began debating the merits of the proposed legislation, Bassett continued to build his ball club by day and engage in political debates by night. Bassett scored another coup when he signed Arizona State quarterback Danny White to a contract. White had been a third-round draft choice of the Dallas Cowboys, "America's Team," and a much sought-after player. Bassett also induced University of Oklahoma defensive lineman Lucious Selmon to forgo the NFL. An All-American, Selmon was the older brother of fellow Sooner linemen Lee Roy and Dewey Selmon, a trio that had been terrorizing college teams in America's heartland. In addition to Selmon, Bassett brought in Notre Dame's Heisman Trophy-winning quarterback John Huarte. It had been a decade since Huarte's salad days, but his name recognition and veteran experience would help Bassett sell tickets while the coaching staff groomed Danny White. The Northmen were shaping up to be the best team in the WFL by far.

In mid–April, Bassett appeared in a televised debate with Norm Cafik, a Member of Parliament from Ontario. Cafik, who was eventually appointed to a cabinet position by Pierre Trudeau, upheld the Liberal government's view that the WFL franchise would irreparably damage the CFL. Bassett, a third generation Conservative, countered that no matter what Parliament may think of the WFL and the Toronto Northmen, they were a legitimate business that simply wanted to put a good product on the field for the benefit of Torontonians. "My reaction to the bill is no different now than before," Bassett said. "I feel we have a legal right to set up a business here to operate a football club. We haven't broken any laws and until this bill becomes law, if it does, we are willing to go ahead with our plans."[49]

When Cafik pointed out that Bassett knew the position of the Trudeau government all along had been to protect the sanctity of the Canadian Football League, the entrepreneur pounced. "If we knew of it in August 1973, there would have been no necessity for us to take a franchise," Bassett said. "If there was a policy then it must have contained such little substance that no one thought enough to mention it to us sometime between August and the end of last year. No one—not my father, Lalonde, Gaudaur, or Hamilton Tiger-Cat president Ralph Sazio—who was in on our original negotiations said anything to us about such a policy."[50]

The debate over the place of the WFL in Canada continued for weeks and weeks. In the interim, the CFL became Bassett's unintended victim. Bassett's signing of Csonka, Kiick, and Warfield was done to create publicity for his team and league at the expense of the NFL, a fat and happy league which was grossly underpaying for labor. Like the Dolphins trio, many NFL players signed "futures contracts," promises to report to their WFL club the minute their NFL contract expired. While this meant delayed gratification for the WFL, it was instant panic for the NFL as they saw star players such as Ken Stabler, Bill Bergey, Joe Gilliam, Daryle Lamonica, Curley Culp, Ted Kwalick, and Calvin Hill sign with the new league.[51] Sadly, the Canadian Football League was not immune to player wanderlust as a not insignificant group of CFL players also signed on with WFL clubs. All-Star running back Johnny Musso of the BC-Lions jumped at the chance to return to Alabama as a member of the Birmingham Americans. Calgary running back Jesse Mims, who had scored the game-winning touchdown for the Stampeders in the 1971 Grey Cup, signed with Detroit. Another Grey Cup hero, Ottawa quarterback Rick Cassata left for the WFL as did Saskatchewan wide receiver Rick Eber and Toronto Argonauts quarterback Greg Barton. These names may not have had the cache of Stabler and Csonka, but they were major losses for the CFL nevertheless.

Appalled at the injury he inflicted on his native league and trying to stem the political tide going against him, Bassett offered to mediate an end to the WFL policy of signing CFL players to future contracts. Bassett stated the NFL and CFL had entered into an agreement not to sign each other's players to futures contracts and he would be willing to promise the same thing if the government would allow the Northmen to play in Toronto. "If we remain in Canada we are prepared to urge upon our associates the adoption of the same policy against the signing of 'futures,'" Bassett said. "Since our associates are anxious to have a team in Canada, we would expect them to adopt this suggestion. If the signing of 'futures' is permitted to continue, we would expect that fully 30–70 percent of the 'name' players in the CFL will not be playing in the CFL next year."[52]

Not wanting to come across as a blackmailer, Bassett also offered an additional incentive for allowing his Northmen to remain in Toronto unimpeded by governmental whims. The Northmen would only seek a local television contract with a Toronto station and would forgo being shown on Canadian national television. Bassett also offered to have his Northmen play an annual exhibition game against a team of CFL all-stars with the Canadian Football League taking home the bulk of revenues such a game would generate. "We believe the concessions we are prepared to make should satisfy every argument that has been made," Bassett said. "The CFL would be in a much better position if we stayed in Toronto with these assurances—no raids, guarantees of equalization payments, an all-star game—then if we moved elsewhere and the assurances did not exist."[53]

Reportedly the Bassett offer swayed the minds of some CFL owners and the national legislature. Otto Jelinek, a Member of the House of Commons put forth a proposal to allow American football on Canadian soil with strict limitations, almost identical to what Bassett offered.[54] Word leaked that Marc Lalonde was considering the proposal but the Minister vehemently denied the story when it appeared in print.[55] Lalonde was going to see his proposal though to the floor of Parliament.

Lalonde's intransigence put Bassett in a real bind. He had a legitimate argument against the actions of Lalonde and had made several attempts to provide reparations for the damage he had caused the CFL. Local public opinion stood squarely on his side, much of it fueled by the excitement over the prospect of seeing Csonka, Kiick, and Warfield play at Exhibition Stadium. Having the right argument and favorable public opinion was not going to help him put his team on the field, no matter how much talent he acquired if the government voted against him. If Bill C-22 passed, the Northmen would literally be a team without a country. Bassett had to find a back-up plan and he had to find it fast.

In a maverick move intended to both find a ready-made audience and tweak the bigger NFL, Bassett chose a scorned city as his possible landing zone.

The AFL and NFL had announced as part of their merger deal plans to expand from 26 to 28 franchises in the mid–1970s. The league held numerous meetings over late spring/early summer 1974, winnowing down a list of possible expansion sites. There were four finalists: Seattle, Tampa, Phoenix, and Memphis. Of the four Seattle was poised as the most obvious given it was the last region of the United States not to have a professional football team. Of the three remaining possibilities Phoenix was deemed the weakest due to a lack of an NFL-caliber stadium. That left Tampa and Memphis, two cities with similar selling points. Both cities were growing Southern metropolises with a history of rabid support for college football. The two cities had also hosted well-attended NFL exhibition games in the past at stadiums which were in the process of being expanded. Tampa Stadium was being brought to a capacity of 72,000 as was Memphis Memorial Stadium. Tampa was reported to be favored by the NFL, specifically by influential Los Angeles Ram owner Carroll Rosenbloom. When he owned the Colts, Rosenbloom hosted training camp in Tampa and felt the region was NFL ready.[56]

Bassett was able to read these tea leaves. Realizing the NFL was leaning towards Tampa, he approached the city leaders of Memphis to inquire about relocating the Northmen. Memphis mayor Wyeth Chandler and members of the Memphis Parks Commission received Bassett warmly. Being so close to an NFL expansion franchise, the city of Memphis was also looking to hedge its bets. They proposed to Bassett a non-exclusive lease to Memorial Stadium that would allow his WFL team to play while also accommodating an NFL tenant.[57] Bassett was agreeable to the conditions. The possibility of joint occupancy became moot when the NFL announced that it was expanding to Tampa. This left Memphis available to Bassett. With the city looking at an empty expanded stadium, they offered Bassett a very lucrative lease that provided him multiple sources of revenue including a 50 percent share in the sale of beer and other concessions.[58]

Bassett returned to Toronto and found the political climate had not changed significantly. Lalonde's proposed act was still being given serious consideration on the floor of Parliament. The clock was ticking down to the July WFL season opener in Toronto. Bassett was faced with the cold reality that he was going to have to bid farewell to his country if he wanted to run his football team. Even with all his assurances and past commitments, Bassett was viewed with suspicion and fear by the CFL, Parliament, and some influential voices in the media. In Memphis,

Bassett found a warm and welcoming city eager to purchase the product he was offering. The choice was simple.

"If Memphis wants us, we would be proud to move our team," Bassett announced in early May. "This is a great city with a great stadium and we would be proud to have our team here."[59] Shortly after the announcement Bassett and the city of Memphis agreed to a five-year lease for the use of Memorial Stadium.[60] The Toronto Northmen were no more; enter the Memphis Southmen.

Queried by the press, Bassett let his frustration and anger with Lalonde and other politicians show, immaturely burning bridges on the way. "The gloves are off now," Bassett said. "Lalonde went to every extent to protect the CFL, but as far as I am concerned that game is over. I would never return this team to Canada. The Northmen now belong to the people of Memphis. If an election is called, I hope the people of Toronto will remember that Lalonde denied them football of a superior quality," Bassett concluded.[61]

Ironically as Bassett loaded the moving vans, Lalonde's legislation died an agonizingly slow death. The legislation was raked over the coals during debate. One MP stated the proposed bill was "was bad legislation garbed in Canadian nationalism." As for protecting the CFL, another MP scoffed: "It is misleading to suggest the CFL possesses a Canadian identity so distinctive as to be a place of priority when protecting Canadian culture." Perhaps the most damning comments came from Toronto politician Andrew Brewin. Brewin's statement got to the heart of the matter and spoke for many Toronto sports fans. "Canadian culture and unity do not depend on which two types of football are played or watched in Canada," Brewin said. "If the CFL is symbolic of Canadian nationalism, then Canadian nationalism is pretty sick."[62]

"In the end we never needed to pass it," Laldone said recently about the bill. "We introduced the bill as a warning shot and in the end, Mr. Bassett felt the threat of legislation was enough to move the team to the United States."[63]

The proposed legislation never went to a vote by Parliament. This left Toronto open to Bassett to remain in Toronto. His reference to the WFL as superior, implying the inferiority of the CFL irked many and no doubt would have led to many awkward press conferences. More than pride and ego led Bassett to continue to Memphis. He realized what the NFL did not. The Tennessee city was desperate for professional football of any kind. In just four short weeks his team sold 5,000 season tickets.[64] Tennessee civic officials had provided him everything Canadian officials did not, and he was unmoved by the political shift. "It's too late," Bassett said. "We've already gone to Memphis and gotten a lease there. We're moving the franchise the moment the lease is formally signed."[65]

The anger Bassett felt over the political shenanigans of Lalonde and others never dissipated. "He never forgave the situation created by the Canadian government," said his widow, Sue Bassett-Klauber.[66] Just like the modern Lakeshore Raceway, which came about following Bassett's 1986 death, American football in Toronto was an idea twenty years too early. The popularity of American football continued to grow to the point that Toronto hosted pre-season NFL games in the 1990s and regular season NFL games in the early 2010s, when the Buffalo Bills agreed to play one home game a season at the Rogers Centre. Almost 40 years after the attempted launch of the Toronto Northmen, Johnny F. Bassett's vision of American football in Toronto is slowly coming to fruition. "If Johnny could have gotten an NFL team in Toronto, there would be a statue of him somewhere downtown," conceded his friend Peter Eby.[67]

One thing that worked against Bassett in the mid–1970s was his early reputation. In the words of one writer, "Johnny Bassett has been thought of as arrogant, tough, mean, and a spoiled lazy punk. It's part of the price rich and highly-visible sons of rich and highly-visible sons pay."[68] This perception began to change as a result of his battle against Parliament. Many started to view Johnny F. Bassett as the idealistic sports maverick he was. Interestingly, one of those who held Bassett in high esteem was his political foe Marc Lalonde. "To me he appeared to be a very decent man young man who wanted to make a name for himself," Lalonde said. "In that sense he was very ambitious and desiring of being known as something other than John W.H. Bassett's son. He wanted a business venture that would carry his own imprint and that is only natural."[69]

Ironically, the same Johnny F. Bassett who national politicians decried as anti–Canadian was feted at an awards banquet in 1974 for his pro–Canadian activities. The B'nai B'rith Sportsmen Lodge of Toronto named Bassett their Celebrity of the Year in 1974, singling out his efforts to create new hockey and football teams for Toronto. "Johnny Bassett is an excellent example of a young Canadian who, having attained numerous goals by dint of sheer ability, business acumen and personal effort, has never spared himself in promoting a truly Canadian image," read the ceremony program.[70] It seemed many in Canada were starting to come around to Bassett, but it was too late for Toronto. Memphis was now the place to be.

SEVEN

The Best of a Bad League

The Memphis Southmen lost resoundingly to the Birmingham Americans in the third game of the inaugural WFL season. The 58–33 defeat on July 24, 1974, was the football equivalent of Sisyphus incessantly pushing his boulder up a hill in Hades. The Southmen were down by three touchdowns early and every time they clawed their way back, the Americans rolled the boulder back down over them. Bassett stood on the sideline of Birmingham's Legion Field in a state of cognitive dissonance. On the one hand, the competitor side of Bassett reeled at the sight of his team being outclassed on the field. The promoter in Bassett, however, was thrilled by the 61,319 Birmingham fans who purchased tickets for the game. The Americans were the first team in the WFL to secure a stadium lease and establish a marketing campaign.[1] The Americans had also enticed a high-profile NFL star to agree to switch leagues. Oakland Raiders star quarterback Ken Stabler, a graduate of Alabama, was committed to joining the WFL in 1976.[2] In the interim, the Americans had former NFL quarterback George Mira leading an offense which included former NFL running back Charlie Harraway and future NFL star receiver Alfred Jenkins. Given Birmingham's proximity to Memphis, Bassett viewed the Americans as his chief rival and saw the city's passion for the team as an exemplar of what the WFL could be.

The WFL fell far short of Bassett's ideals in the end. The Southmen had an excellent season at the box office and on the field, although they fell short of a championship. The Birmingham Americans finished the season as champions, but like the rest of the WFL they suffered huge financial losses. In fact, Birmingham's World Bowl title celebration was cut short when IRS agents and sheriff's deputies stormed their locker room to repossess the shirts off their backs due to lack of payment on multiple debts.[3] The WFL was victimized by a poor business model and a ham-handed response to an accounting scandal which blew out of proportion in the heated journalistic era of Watergate. These errors were exacerbated by the NFL's stranglehold on network television and, ironically, a series of management setbacks in labor lawsuits which raised the salary of athletes and led owners attempting to follow Bassett's example down the primrose path to insolvency. Bassett's responses to the league's collapse fluctuated between altruism and self-aggrandizement, but he ended his WFL tenure with a reputation for probity unmatched by his peers. That reputation came at high cost, the near exhaustion of Bassett's personal wealth.

Who Wants to Be a Football Owner?

Gary Davidson's business model for the WFL was ill-conceived and ill-timed. Davidson admitted in a 2001 documentary on the WFL that when it came to the vetting of prospective owners for his football teams, his methods were more psychological than fiscal:

> We created a concept and then sold parts of it (franchises). We sold a dream. A guy like (Jacksonville Sharks owner) Francis Monaco doesn't want to be a brassiere manufacturer, he wants to be known as the owner of a sports franchise.... I had an advance guy and he would call the newspapers and say, "We're interested in putting a franchise in (your town) and we think that John Doe who owns the biggest brick factory would be interested." Now John Doe doesn't know anything about this. So, then we would call John Doe and say, "John, are you interested in buying a franchise?" He would say, "No, I don't want a football franchise." Then we would call the paper and say, "John Doe is not interested." The paper would then call John Doe and say, "Aren't you interested?" John would say, "I might be," because he had never been called by a sports department before. Then I would go see him and talk to him. I'd say, "In the press conferences, be sure you watch the cameras and find one reporter to talk to." Now John Doe is buying into the concept. Well that concept didn't exist a week before. In America we love sports, so we packaged it and sold it. We had people from all over the country call us and now they are trying to find out about the league.[4]

The problem with Davidson's process is that it only gauged interest and not fiscal commitment or business savvy. This became an issue for first-time owners, particularly those who felt they needed to make a Johnny F. Bassett-type splash with expensive player signings. This may not have been an issue in 1967 and 1971 when the ABA and WHA were founded, respectively. In 1974, however, the cost of players was going up due to long-awaited recognition of player rights and a general economic downturn which impacted even the owners of monopolies in the NFL. The year of 1974 coincided with Watergate, uncertainty in the markets, and the ill-starred "Whip Inflation Now" campaign of Gerald Ford. It was not the best time to launch a sports venture that would need plenty of luck to succeed.

The two words most hated by professional athletes in 1974 were "reserve clause." The reserve clause was a proviso in the standard players contract which automatically extended a player's contract for one year when the player and team could not reach a settlement on a new deal.[5] The player had the option to play under the extension or re-sign. This essentially bound the player to his team for life as few players were willing to lose the security that a multi-year contract provided. Additionally, owners maintained a gentleman's agreement in which they would not poach players from other teams to keep salaries down.

NFL players had success in getting the reserve clause weakened through the courts. The 1957 Supreme Court ruling *Radovich v National Football League* held that Congress could force the NFL to do away with the reserve clause.[6] Congress granted the NFL limited exemptions in the realm of television, such as the 1961 Sports Broadcasting Act, but opted to allow contract language such as the reserve clause to be collectively bargained.[7] The end of the NFL reserve clause began in the early 1970s. The Supreme Court decision *Mackey v NFL* allowed players to freely negotiate with other teams after playing out their option. The decision was not finalized until 1976, so the reserve clause remained in place in 1974. The likelihood of the NFL's defeat, however, gave the threat of playing out an option validity as leverage, as did the slow strengthening of the NFL Players Association, which was threatening a strike over the reserve clause in 1974.[8]

These legal developments placed the WFL in an odd situation. Traditionally, upstart professional sports leagues benefited from the depressed salaries of the NFL. The All-American Football Conference (AAFC, 1946–1949) and AFL were able to sign NFL drafted players to reasonable contracts. This had been a mutually beneficial relationship. The AAFC and AFL could sign marquee names for reasonable amounts, while NFL players staying behind benefited from the leverage of a new league willing to pay slightly more money through increased salaries.[9] With free agency becoming a distinct possibility, NFL players were not as willing to jump to the WFL unless presented with an eye-popping amount in the neighborhood of Csonka, Kiick, and Morris. "We're looking after these offers as businessman," said NFL linebacker Ted Hendricks, echoing the sentiment of many players who viewed the new league as an option for leverage.[10] Not all WFL owners were happy with the amount of money Bassett had spent, arguing it was self-defeating for the new league to attempt to engage in a spending war with the NFL as player salaries were on the precipice of exploding. "It is crazy, insane, idiotic," exclaimed Chicago owner Tom Origer of the signings. "We don't have to throw away millions of dollars to get players."[11] Sadly for Origer and other owners advocating for common-sense finances, many owners followed Bassett's lead. Teams in the WFL inked deals with quarterbacks Ken Stabler (Birmingham) and Craig Morton (Houston); defensive stars L.C. Greenwood (Birmingham) and Bill Bergey (Florida); and running backs Calvin Hill (Hawaii) and Harmon Wages (Jacksonville). Few of the announced contracts provided specific details, such as the dollar amount. Many owners played coy, such as Jacksonville Sharks owner Fran Monaco, who only said the deals were "guaranteed."[12] In professional football parlance, that was a magic word, because NFL players who are released for any reason are not guaranteed the entirety of their contract.

It should be noted that the economic conditions of the United States of this era was not the best time for a start-up either. A recession which economists labeled the worst slowdown since the Great Depression began in November 1973 and ran until March 1975. A wave of high unemployment followed by a period of inflation was exacerbated by an oil embargo by the Organization of Arab Petroleum Exporting Countries (OPEC).[13] The effects of the recession were far-reaching, even impacting owners of the monopolistic NFL. The Tampa Bay Buccaneers expansion franchise was awarded to Philadelphia construction magnate Tom McCloskey, whose company had built Washington's RFK Stadium, home of the NFL Redskins, and the Sam Rayburn Office Building, site of the U.S. Senate's office space. Shortly after taking ownership of the team, McCloskey defaulted on his initial installment of the $16 million franchise fee, citing the economic downturn and the loss of revenue for his company.[14] New England Patriots owner Billy Sullivan leveraged his franchise to help fund a relocation from Boston to Foxborough, Massachusetts, in 1971. When the bills came due in 1973 and 1974, the overburdened owner was forced to divest of a good share of his team's stock, retaining the bare minimum level required by the NFL to still be considered the team's primary owner.[15]

The impact of these economic developments on the WFL became clear as the inaugural season grew closer. Concerns that some WFL ownership groups were not as financially stable as they claimed to be transitioned from rumor to fact. The Detroit Wheels were owned by a massive and unwieldy conglomerate of 33 individuals, with no single authority figure. Despite the size, nobody in that group could secure a better playing venue than Rynearson Stadium on Eastern Michigan's campus in Ypsilanti, almost a 40-mile drive from Detroit.[16] Things were even more chaotic in Oregon. The Portland Storm's first owner, Bruce Gelker, did not even make it to opening day before financial difficulties forced him to turn the team over to Robert Harris in much the same manner that Tom McCloskey had to walk away from an NFL team in Tampa.[17]

WFL financial concerns stopped at the Memphis city limits. Bassett was determined to build a stable franchise and a winner. The Southmen became a veritable amalgamation of NFL, CFL, and NCAA all-star teams. Head coach John McVay was a happy beneficiary. "We had a lot of good players," McVay said. "We were blessed to have a really good team. We signed a lot of top players out of the CFL including our linemen Wally Highsmith, Charlie Bray, and Ron Mikoljaczyk. Dick Thornton was a big star in the CFL at defensive back and was one of our captains and was one of our top dogs on the defensive team."[18] While Csonka, Kiick, and Warfield were still a season away from being eligible to play for the Southmen, Memphis had a bevy of talent at the skill positions courtesy of Leo Cahill's scouting work and Bassett's willingness to pay. "J.J. Jennings was a very strong and stable presence for us at running back," McVay said.

> We had to trade him the next year because of Csonka and Kiick. Our tight end was a man named Gary Shirk who went on to play a long time with the New York Giants. We had a really good wide receiver in Ed Marshall. We had John Huarte and Danny White, who went on to quarterback the Dallas Cowboys, so we had not one, but two very good quarterbacks. The secret of our success was that Johnny gave us the money and allowed us to sign a lot of good players.[19]

That talent was on display for the season-opener at Memphis Memorial Stadium on July 10, 1974. A crowd of 30,122 saw the Southmen whip the Detroit Wheels 34–15. The following week, Memphis doubled up the Portland Storm, 16–8, before another 31,088 in Memorial Stadium. The two victories came against a pair of the WFL's more dysfunctional teams. As the year wore on it became clear that the Southmen were an elite franchise on more than one level. From a talent standpoint, the Southmen were arguably the best in the league. An eleven-game winning streak led many to fear that Memphis could do to the WFL what the Cleveland Browns had done to the All-American Football Conference. The Browns were so dominant in winning four straight AAFC championships that the league grew stale and folded. From a financial commitment standpoint, no other owner in the WFL was near Bassett's class. Ultimately, the disparity between Bassett's business integrity and that of his fellow WFL owners, rather than the talent on the field, doomed the league.

Papergate

Financial concerns about the WFL were everywhere, and plagued every team, except Bassett's organization. The league entered into a television contract with TVS, a syndicated network not available in all markets. The TVS contract called for a WFL *Game of the Week* to be broadcast each Thursday evening. Seeking to piggyback off the three-man booth ABC employed on *Monday Night Football*, TVS hired veteran broadcaster Merle Harmon to do play-by-play, former NFL running back Alex Hawkins to provide color commentary, and a rotating band of celebrities to bring a dash of pizzazz. Among the celebrity commentators were actors Burt Reynolds and McLean Stevenson, and author George Plimpton.[20] The TVS deal promised the WFL some exposure and revenue, but not on par with the millions the NFL got from its arrangements with ABC, NBC, and CBS. Teams in the WFL entered 1974 realizing that ticket sales would provide the bulk of their revenue.

The Southmen earned respectable gate figures. Memphis attracted 30,122 fans for their first game against the Detroit Wheels. The following week 31,088 came to Memphis Memorial Stadium to watch the Southmen defeat the Portland Storm. The week after their big loss to Birmingham, the Southmen returned to Memphis and 25,176 came out to see a 25–15 victory over the Southern California Sun. The attendance figures were solid but paled in comparison to the number of fans that turned out to see games in Philadelphia and Jacksonville. The numbers reported from Philadelphia and Jacksonville impressed many and were the talk of the national sports press for a few days. But these attendance figures proved to be dishonest. Bassett had worked hard to secure his solid fan base and assumed others in the WFL had done so as well. Here, he fell victim to wishful thinking. In an embarrassing move that proved fatal to league credibility, Philadelphia, Jacksonville, and other WFL clubs fudged their attendance figures and "papered the house." The resulting scandal dragged down the league despite Bassett's best efforts to save it.

The Philadelphia Bell played in massive and venerable John F. Kennedy Stadium, frequent home to the Army-Navy game. The facility had a capacity of 90,000 and the Bell played before stellar crowds of 55,534 and 64,719 during their first two home games.[21] At the same time the Jacksonville Sharks reported crowds of 59,112 and 46,780 at the Gator Bowl.[22] In addition to Philadelphia and Jacksonville, the four other teams hosting games reported an average attendance of almost 36,000 spectators. Altogether, the opening week of WFL action drew 258,624 fans.[23] These massive crowds were the talk of sports during the dog days of summer. Commissioner Gary Davidson crowed to the press: "We're off to a super start. At almost every city, we are going well ahead of what anybody would predict."[24] Writers in cities without franchises took note of the WFL's apparent and surprising strong start. The weekend between games one and two of the WFL season continued to bring good news. Buoyed by the fan response, TVS president Eddie Einhorn announced that national advertisers purchased more than eighty percent of the network's commercial space for the remainder of the season.[25]

Additional and sobering news from the NFL became a boon for the WFL. The National Football League Players Association (NFLPA) went on strike on July 1, weeks before the start of the WFL season. Players called the strike to protest the lack of free agency and stagnant wages. Star players refused to report to camp, leaving rookies and unknown free agents to play in televised exhibition games.[26] This meant the WFL's chief rival would be fielding teams with less star power than the upstart league and might have to carry that talent into the regular season. Television partners NBC and CBS, worried about not having a marketable product for Sunday afternoons, reached out to TVS about purchasing select WFL games to broadcast.[27] NFL players on strike began looking at employment in the WFL as more than a bargaining chip in their battle with owners, they viewed it as an up and coming league which appeared to have struck a chord with fans. The future of the WFL as a viable, uncontroversial alternative to the fracturing NFL looked bright, but this fair forecast proved illusory; clouds formed quickly.

The unexpectedly high attendance figures around the WFL on opening week led some skeptical journalists to question the validity of the opening tallies. Buddy Martin, a Florida sportswriter who covered the Jacksonville Sharks, hinted at rumors of "wallpapered" attendance figures, particularly the then WFL-record of 59,112 who attended Jacksonville's nationally televised contest with New York.[28] Papering a venue is a standard practice in entertainment, including sports. Free passes are often given away to fill seats so "that paying members of the audience impressed by a well filled house may start the rumor that the theatre was crowded."[29] In the television age, a full stadium could also pay dividends to a home audience, which would see the crowd and assume the event was "big league" and popular. The extent to which some WFL teams went to paper the house and the WFL's ham-handed attempt to hide the truth from the press, however, soured many on the upstarts.

The first major discrepancy was noticed when the Bell filed their business taxes. With an average ticket price of $7.50, the Bell should have generated revenue of $900,000. When they reported the income, the Bell claimed only 20,000 tickets had been sold.[30] The other 100,000 tickets had been given away to "paper" the crowd and fill the stadium. *Philadelphia Inquirer* sportswriter Frank Dolson broke the story when he learned of the discrepancy. The revelation, essentially an accounting trick, shone an unfavorable light on Bell executive vice president Barry

Lieb. Lieb had promoted the crowds as proof the WFL team had mass appeal, but when it came time to file taxes, Lieb had to admit there was little interest from the ticket-buying public in the Bell. As one reporter put it, "Lieb either had to say he lied to the public or to the IRS. You don't go to jail for lying to the public."[31]

Lieb's response was blunt and sadly symptomatic of what was occurring in other WFL cities. "What can I say?" Lieb asked rhetorically. "I lied. I never thought those figures would come out. I admit I lied to reporters. I never regarded a reporter as a priest."[32] When asked why he had felt compelled to give away nearly 100,000 free tickets to the team's games and then lie about it, Lieb conceded that he was trying to make the Bell and the WFL look good on national television. The games had been broadcast on TVS as the *WFL Game of the Week* and the prospect of 80,000 empty seats did not appeal to Lieb. "We just had to do it, or we would have been a joke," Lieb said. "I admit we lied to everyone."[33] While lying to reporters would not land him in jail, Lieb and the WFL came to learn that the sporting press and public could be unforgiving.

When the news from Philadelphia broke nationally, reporters in WFL cities from coast to coast turned an investigative eye on the attendance figures put forth by their local teams. Starting in Jacksonville, local reporters discovered the Sharks gave away 44,000 of the 100,000 tickets used for their first two games. Jacksonville vice president Danny Bridges seemed shocked at the interest the media were showing in the topic: "I can't really understand why people are so interested in the number of free tickets we gave away."[34] Bridges' dismissive attitude when the story was already hot and growing more so was indicative of a severe disconnect about the negative perception the WFL was generating over the giveaway. Even Bassett, whose Southmen were found to have not papered their figures, defended the practice. Bassett's Toros had papered the gate by offering free tickets or radically discounted tickets on more than one occasion. Bassett had an answer for those who questioned his wisdom. "What's wrong with it?" Bassett asked of detractors of the practice from the *Toronto Star.* "When a soap company sends out thousands of boxes of soap, nobody says anything. It's merely a sample thing."[35]

That may have been true for the small number of tickets the Toros gave out, but the level of giveaways granted by some of the WFL franchises and the declaration of strong attendance as an indicator of the league's viability was an extreme misrepresentation of performance. All told, five WFL teams, representing nearly half of the league's franchises, gave away 158,000 tickets.[36]

The scandal came to be known as "Papergate." The "gate" suffix came from the Watergate scandal which reached its climax at the same time the WFL ticket fiasco came to light. The term was the brainchild of sportswriter Frank Dolson. The *Philadelphia Inquirer* columnist equated the phonying of attendance figures with the high crimes and misdemeanors of the Nixon administration. Dolson's term is one of the first uses of the suffix –gate to describe a scandal.[37] "Washington has its Watergate. Now Philadelphia has its Papergate," Dolson wrote. "The impact is hardly the same, but the actions of the high officials involved are strikingly similar. Announcing absurdly phony paid figures to the press in an attempt to make the public think that one of the least desirable tickets in town is actually one of the most desirable is indefensible."[38] Interestingly, Philadelphia Bell president John B. Kelly, Jr., resigned his position as a result of the imbroglio with his franchise on August 8, 1974, the exact same day that Richard M. Nixon announced his resignation as President of the United States over the Watergate scandal.

Watergate brought down Nixon and cemented the reputation of the *Washington Post*. Papergate fatally damaged WFL credibility at a crucial early stage and alienated the reporters the league needed to spread their product. The new league never bounced back from Papergate. It did not help that Gary Davidson employed a poorly considered method of damage control. Davidson issued a heavy-handed directive to all owners in the days after Dolson's coining of the term Papergate. The directive was almost Nixonian: "Your position is that this (ticket giveaways) will not be released."[39] Requests for ticket sale information by reporters in WFL cities across the country were mostly met with silence. "We have been informed we cannot give out any of that information," said Detroit Wheels ticket director Carolyn Mosko, a quote nearly mirrored by Birmingham Americans ticket director Alan Gack, "We're not allowed to give out any such figures."[40] Dolson viewed the actions of the WFL as indicative of an organization attempting to hide something. In Dolson's opinion, WFL and Bell officials chose to obfuscate and stonewall when confronted with proof of lying rather than admitting they did so, a tactic that was currently embroiling the resident of 1600 Pennsylvania Avenue. "There's nothing wrong with giving away tickets," Dolson wrote. "But there is something wrong with misleading the public, and the Bell (and WFL) was guilty of doing that."[41] The demise of the league may have been foreshadowed in August of 1974, but for the time being it was business as usual in Memphis. The Southmen had avoided the taint of Papergate insofar as their reported attendance accurately reflected tickets sold.

"We work on a cash basis only," general manager Leo Cahill said

when asked about the Southmen policy on freebies. "The only complimentary tickets we give away fall into the category of people that have
to get them."[42] The Southmen averaged a legitimate 30,000 for their first
two home games, which placed them in the upper echelon of the league.
The Birmingham Americans, who averaged 43,000 over their time in
the WFL, were the premier team as far as drawing power.[43] As the season wore on however, the Americans struggled with finances like most
other WFL teams. The exception to the rule was Memphis and Johnny F.
Bassett. What the fans at Memphis Memorial Stadium saw was a dominant franchise run by a savvy businessman and confident showman.
Whether it would be enough to prolong the show beyond one season
remained to be seen.

Bassett Puts on a Show: On and Off the Field

The Southmen were humiliated in Philadelphia, losing 46–15 at
John F. Kennedy Stadium before a sparse crowd of 12,396 in the first
game following John B. Kelly's resignation. Memphis quickly put the
loss behind them. The Southmen travelled to Ypsilanti, Michigan, the
following week and dismantled the Detroit Wheels 37–7. The game was
the start of an eleven-game winning streak which helped the Southmen
claim the best record in the entire league. Memphis finished the season 17–3 and qualified for home-field advantage throughout the playoffs, finishing two games ahead of their chief rival Birmingham.

The talent that Leo Cahill had brought on board was ably coached
by John McVay. The Southmen had the WFL's most prolific offense to
go along with an opportunistic defense. The Southmen led the league
with 629 points scored and 79 touchdowns. Memphis also tallied 396
first downs, 3,852 yards rushing and an amazing 15.7 yards per pass
completion. All totals led the WFL. Wide receiver Ed Marshall led the
league in scoring with 144 points, including a best in the league nine-
teen touchdown receptions. Tim Beamer had the best average kickoff
return yardage with 28.7. Out of the backfield, J.J Jennings finished second in yardage with 1,524. His backfield mates, John Harvey and Willie Spencer, were high performers as well. Harvey finished second in
average yards per carry with 4.9 while Spencer led the WFL in rushing
touchdowns with 15. Not to be outdone, the defense led the league with
38 interceptions, including a league-leading ten by cornerback David
Thomas and nine by safety/cornerback Seth Miller. Safety Dick Thornton also contributed an impressive five more interceptions.[44]

The Southmen were also the class of the league when it came to fan appreciation and entertainment. Bassett was provided the opportunity to build his ideal football operation and he did so in Bassett style. One of the chief fans of the Southmen was none other than Elvis Presley. Memorial Stadium was just a short drive from Graceland for "The King," and he made the trek on multiple occasions. Elvis became such a fan that he once asked Bassett for his autograph rather than the other way around.[45] Bassett's widow explained that Elvis was just one of many notable celebrities Bassett invited to Southmen games to offer fans a little something extra for their ticket purchase. "Elvis sang one of our opening national anthems," Sue Bassett-Klauber recalled. "So did notable football player and singer Rosey Grier. There was always surprise entertainment at the games. Elvis and his large entourage would sit with us high up in the press box."[46]

Bassett's close friend and musical star Gordon Lightfoot, the artist behind the songs "If You Could Read My Mind" and "The Wreck of the Edmund Fitzgerald," whom Bassett helped promote in the 1960s, attended many Southmen games as both a guest and performer. Given his own professional experiences, Lightfoot was impressed at what his friend and neighbor was doing in Tennessee. "I was becoming more and more amazed," Lightfoot said. "I was always thinking how is he doing

Bassett (right) and longtime friend Gordon Lightfoot (left) aboard Bassett's boat. The Canadian singer/songwriter was one of many celebrities Bassett befriended and invited to perform at various Bulls, Toros, Southmen, and Bandit games. The normally clean-shaven Bassett joked that one could tell his current business prospects by his appearance: "My hair is short when I'm raising money and long when I'm spending it" (courtesy Andrew Chisholm).

this? I would just sit back and watch. It was amazing. First, he shang-haied those three (Miami) Dolphins to come over. Then he's got Elvis Presley and Isaac Hayes coming to the games."[47] Lightfoot recalled that Bassett was so polite and professional in how he treated the celebrities who came to games, that it was never viewed as a chore or job, but as a pleasant way to spend an afternoon or evening. "I was never encroached upon by Johnny," Lightfoot said. "My time was respected. Johnny never took advantage."[48] Fans of the Southmen were so enthralled by the action on and off the field that many treated Bassett and his family like rock stars themselves. "Those were the days when a police motorcade would pick us up in our rented townhouse and escort us to the stadium. Talk about 'Southern Hospitality!'" Sue Bassett-Klauber said.[49] It helped that Memphis was a football hotbed with long-simmering aspirations for a professional team to call its own and fans embraced the Southmen with real enthusiasm.

Csonka, Kiick, and Warfield were still in Miami, preparing as best they could for the 1974 NFL season during the strike. They had time to read the papers and watch the news and felt a sense of bemused wonder at the organization they were primed to join. Warfield was especially excited by the promotions that Bassett ran to make fans feel appreciated. One that stuck with Warfield was a simple gesture Bassett arranged to thank fans who came to the ballpark each week. "He had promotions that were kind of interesting," Warfield said. "Mr. Bassett had a promotion that after a ball game, you could show your ticket at any Burger King and they would give you a Whopper and a drink for free."[50] One of the few promotions that did not work out as planned involved the Southmen's live bear cub mascot. The Southmen had a bear logo on their helmet which led many people to refer to the club as the "Grizzlies." The bear cub got to chewing on electrical wires during one game and suffered mild electrocution which resulted in a short that knocked out the stadium scoreboard for ten minutes.[51]

Paying veterinarian bills for bear cubs and buying hamburgers for up to 25,000 people were no small financial contributions, but they were in line with the image Bassett wanted for his Memphis Southmen. Unlike the NFL and its belief that fans simply paid to see a game in which the home team better win, Bassett envisioned a Southmen game as a celebratory event regardless of the score. He put a lot of money into player salaries to make sure the Southmen were on the right side of the scoreboard more often than not, but Bassett also believed the fans who made the trip to the stadium deserved to be pampered by the staff and given music and spectacle as part of the admission price. Bassett wanted the organization to be first-class at every level and he issued that mission statement to all his employees, whether player, coach, or equipment manager. As the season wore on, it became apparent that Bassett was a breed apart from the other WFL owners not just because of his eye for organization and promotion, but because he was willing to finance the effort fully. "He told us what he wanted us to do and more importantly he gave us the wherewithal to accomplish those goals," head coach John McVay said. "It's too bad all of the owners weren't as committed as Johnny."[52] Here, McVay touched upon the heart of what was Bassett's virtue and the WFL's vice. Bassett was a well-intentioned and imaginative owner who understood that for his enterprise to succeed, he needed to operate in a professional and engaging manner. He succeeded in Memphis, by all accounts, but a league needs more than one solid team to flourish. Despite his success in their own market, the Southmen depended upon other franchises to ensure a WFL future.

Eight

Too Good for the WFL, Not Enough for the NFL

Johnny F. Bassett was a cheerleader for the WFL, but he was not blind to the root cause of the league's trouble. There were too many owners who had not been properly vetted by Gary Davidson to see if they had the money to back up their big talk. That became readily apparent when Bassett learned of the 33-man syndicate which owned the Detroit Wheels. Bassett's initial ownership group of the Toronto Toros had included 22 people, so Bassett did not have an issue with the group's size. A key differentiator between the Toros and Wheels, however, was that Bassett's Toronto group had real money and it was fast becoming apparent Detroit's did not. Thirty-three undercapitalized minority owners did not make for a stable team. "I don't know the situation up in Detroit," Bassett said before his team pummeled the Wheels 37–7. "They tell me 33 men got together and put in 15 cents to buy the club. I don't know if they have any money up there."[1]

The Wheels, and Other Teams, Come Off

Reports of missed paychecks were confirmed throughout the WFL. Such reports are like bank runs during a financial panic: they generate nervousness and focus grim attention on the crisis. Players for the Florida Blazers went more than a month without being paid. The fact that players kept performing at an excellent level reminds us that WFL athletes had more to be proud of than league executives did. Things were getting so bad for the Orlando-based team that they could not afford to process game-film. The Blazers also depended on opponents to help them with laundry bills so the team could have clean uniforms come game time. Players even ate meals at the homes of the team's booster club so they would not go hungry. It was only when the WFL forwarded checks to the team that players were able to breathe a sigh of financial relief.[2] While the Blazers' case was extreme, there were other tales of hardship in the WFL. The Southern California Sun and Portland Storm also missed payroll. Storm players were so incensed that they initiated a boycott that was only resolved when general manager Ron Mix promised that team owner Robert Harris was on the way with payment. Things got so bad for the Houston Texans and New York Stars that both teams had to take the unusual step of relocating to a different city *in the middle of the season.* The Texans relocated to Shreveport, Louisiana, and were rechristened the Steamer. The Stars moved to Charlotte, North Carolina, where they retained the moniker Stars for one game before rebranding as the Charlotte Hornets. The confusing and itinerant natures of the Texans/Steamer and the Stars/Hornets led one *Sporting News* writer to quip, "When they asked me to predict where the WFL teams would finish the season, I didn't know that meant geographically!"[3] It does not take a marketing degree to realize that a mid-season departure—or arrival—makes for horrendous public relations.

Things were worse in Detroit and Jacksonville. The Wheels collapsed under the weight of their oversized and underfunded conglomerate and suspended operations with six weeks left in the season. Players, fans, and opponents were left in the lurch. The Wheels declared bankruptcy with vendors claiming $1.4 million in unpaid bills.[4] Jacksonville, still suffering from their part in "Papergate," also suspended operations with six games to play. In an episode so bizarre it strains credulity, Sharks owner Fran Monaco borrowed $27,000 from head coach Bud Asher and then fired Asher the next day![5] Stories like this circulated and contributed to widespread belief that the WFL was foundering and about to go under.

As founder and president of the WFL, Gary Davidson was looked upon to provide leadership and at this, he proved lacking. Many of the league's issues came to a head in mid–October. With Detroit and Jacksonville suspending operations, numerous open dates began to appear on team schedules. With other teams struggling to meet payroll, Davidson altered team schedules requiring some teams to play on the road despite having a previously scheduled home game. Also, the checks the WFL had presented to the Florida Blazers to make up for six lost game checks had stop payments placed on them because Davidson did not want to violate an injunction filed by the Blazers' former owner.[6] These actions, and the abysmal confusion, did not endear Davidson to either owners or players. Davidson ultimately resigned on October 29, 1974, leaving even more of a leadership void than before.

Bassett stepped in to fill that void, becoming the *de facto* league spokesman and commissioner through his role as head of the WFL executive committee. His first order of business was to calm the waters surrounding Davidson's departure and pave the way for Donald Regan, Davidson's successor, to begin his job. Bassett stated that Gary Davidson did not resign as part of a coup, but instead left for personal reasons, a viewpoint verified by Davidson himself. Bassett placed the blame for the WFL's woes on the underfunded owners and not the man who did a poor job of vetting. "I think there were a number of franchises awarded to individuals or groups that never should have been awarded," Bassett conceded. "That was the cause of the problems. And those problems cost Gary his credibility with investors, much of the media and the public. We've absolutely got to do something about that."[7]

It was only natural that Bassett take a more visible role within the WFL. Besides being arguably the most solvent owner, Bassett had displayed a league-first attitude while trying to build a dominant team. The maverick from Ontario turned out to be the WFL's only owner who put league well-being alongside his own team's fortunes. One of Bassett's first gestures of good will had been to pay for the Florida Blazers' airfare to and from Memphis for an October game at Memorial Stadium. The game was played on October 16 and came on the heels of the Blazer players getting their first paychecks in six weeks from the WFL. The Southmen won the game 25–15, their eleventh consecutive victory. Such acts were overshadowed, however, by Bassett's misfires in strategy and actions which some in the WFL construed as self-serving considering the fiscal misfortunes visited upon many players, coaches, and owners.

Shortly after succeeding Davidson as president, Donald Regan and Bassett attempted to make the best of a bad situation when two near-bankrupt teams were set to face each other in the final weeks of the season. The Florida Blazers were scheduled to play at Portland against the Storm on November 6, but Storm owner Robert Harris was struggling to cover payroll and rent for the team's stadium. An ownership group interested in taking the Blazers off the league's hands said they would not follow through on the purchase unless the game was rescheduled for Orlando. Regan and Bassett, desperate to keep a viable team in Florida, announced the game would be moved from Portland to Orlando to appease the prospective Blazer owners.

The move was not popular with Portland players, who did not fancy embarking on a cross-country flight to play in a game for which they were not guaranteed to be paid. When Portland quarterback Greg Barton asked Bassett why the Storm should be inconvenienced, the

Southmen owner bluntly stated, "The $3 million deal of new ownership is contingent on moving the game."[8] Such reasoning made sense from a corporate perspective, but Bassett overlooked the competitive disadvantage faced by Portland players. The Storm was a viable playoff contender despite their owner's history of missed paychecks. They took pride in winning. Forcing them to fly across country on short notice and to play without their usual preparation regimen before a crowd of strangers would put them at a distinct disadvantage, not to mention leave fans in Portland out in the cold. The Storm lost the game to Florida, ending any hopes of the post-season, proving the validity of their fears. Worse, Storm general manager Ron Mix left Orlando empty-handed as Harris' paychecks did not come through again. Worse for Regan and Bassett, the new Florida ownership group did not make good on their guarantee to buy the Blazers, meaning the gambit put Portland and Florida players at risk of injury for no fiscal gain.[9]

Bassett was in a quandary when the final week of the season arrived with playoff seeding at stake. His Southmen had finished with the best record and had home field advantage for the playoffs, but the playoff itself was at risk. Due to the financial straits of some teams, a movement was afoot to cancel the playoffs and simply declare the Southmen champions. The call was sounded by Southern California Sun general manager Curly Morrison, whose team had qualified for the playoffs but had also missed some payrolls. Morrison had an ally in Chicago Fire owner Tom Origer, who had forfeited his team's season finale against Philadelphia. Because the Fire was not in playoff contention, Origer termed the game "meaningless" and forfeited.[10] Morrison's view was not as extreme as Origer's, but it made no sense to him to pay for playoff games if the team could not afford regular season games. "It is ridiculous to continue when we know the playoffs are going to lose money," Morrison said.[11]

Bassett and the Southmen would have been best served from a marketing and competitive standpoint to simply claim the championship, but Bassett had no intention of claiming his first championship as an owner that way. First off, Bassett's nature alone prevented him from accepting a championship by concession. A former Davis Cup competitor, Bassett wanted the thrill of the sudden-death nature of playoffs. Bassett also believed his players, coaches, and fans deserved the thrill of hosting a playoff game. Lastly, Bassett believed that the WFL would lose all credibility if its playoff games were cancelled and a champion was not declared on the field.

Bassett tried proposing a watered-down playoff to appease those who wished the season to end as soon as possible. Bassett's proposal would have the three teams who finished with the best records,

Memphis, Birmingham, and Florida, in the postseason. Birmingham would host Florida in one playoff game while Memphis, as a reward for achieving the best record, would enjoy a bye and host the winner the following week for the WFL title. This proposal angered owners of teams which had won their divisions, but ended up with lesser records than Memphis, Birmingham, and Florida. Curly Morrison, despite not wanting to have a playoff, argued that if the WFL went forward, it made no sense to exclude division winners. "If you're going to have three teams, at least have the three division winners."[12] Owners disregarded Bassett's compromise, stating that he did not speak for the league.[13] Instead of Bassett's proposal, WFL owners agreed to put on a playoff tournament involving six teams, two of which, the Hawaiians and Philadelphia Bell, had losing records. The first round of the playoffs came and went with little notice nationally. The Florida Blazers defeated the Philadelphia Bell and were rewarded with a trip to Memphis. The Blazers then made Bassett rue his decision to advocate for the playoffs.

No Blaze of Glory

The Florida Blazers could not have been more different from the Southmen in terms of financial stability and operational methods. The Southmen had been paid on time every week. The Southmen travelled in style, with multiple players reporting the quality of the organization as on par with the NFL. Bassett rewarded his fans with a winning team and a pleasant in-game experience. When the possibility to claim a title without a post-season presented itself, Bassett demurred, endearing himself further to his team. "Johnny wanted to have that championship game in Memphis," John McVay said. "In fact, he paid the airfare for Florida to bring them up to the game."[14]

The Florida Blazers were angry. They were angry at their owner, David L. Williams, an underfunded executive who failed to honor game checks for almost the entire season. They were angry at general manager Rommie Loudd, who was so oblivious to the team's needs that head coach Jack Pardee was forced to purchase office supplies and toilet paper for the team.[15] They were angry at Bassett, who forced them into a game against Portland to appease an ownership group which ultimately failed to pay the Blazers for their game. They were also angry at Bassett for being the driving force behind a playoff that few players wanted and for which the Blazers felt would again leave them unpaid. "The WFL has tried to ruin the Blazers since their inception," Florida quarterback Bob Davis said before the game. "We're mad now. The majority feels we're never going to get paid. But we're going to finish out the season because of pride."[16]

Proving that no good deed goes unpunished, the Blazers played with pride, shocking Memphis 18–15, behind running back Tommy Reamon's 125 yards and a stifling defensive performance that shut Memphis out for three quarters. The loss was devastating to Bassett and the WFL. As a result of the defeat, Memphis lost out on hosting a title game and the WFL was forced to market a game between two bankrupt teams. The Blazers advanced to the World Bowl against the Birmingham Americans. Despite the Americans' league-leading attendance figures, the team posted $1 million in losses due to the exorbitant signing bonuses they had paid out on futures contracts to Kenny Stabler and others. The Americans won the game 22–21, but their locker room celebration was interrupted by law enforcement officials who repossessed all team equipment including the uniforms the players wore.[17] Bassett could only hope the league made it to 1975 when his team would be bolstered by the eagerly anticipated arrival of Larry Csonka, Jim Kiick, and Paul Warfield.

The trio of players kept their eyes on the news emanating from their future employer as they started the 1974 season, which resulted in a fifth-straight playoff appearance and a 28–26 loss to Oakland in the famous "Sea of Hands" game. Csonka was pleased to see Memphis doing so well but he also viewed the viability of the WFL with a pragmatic eye when Papergate hit the news and word of missed paychecks and bankrupt teams suspending operations became regular. Csonka was not concerned about getting paid because Bassett had set minds at ease by paying a good deal of the contract up front. "There was enough front money put down that whatever happened would happen," Csonka said. "I wasn't worried. If it all went down the pipes, I'd be fine financially and I'd stay in Miami."[18] One of the reasons Csonka and his two teammates could feel so secure was they had something few others in the WFL could bank on: The word of Johnny F. Bassett. "Johnny shook my hand and guaranteed the contract," Csonka said, alluding to the fact that he never doubted Bassett.[19] Too bad so many other WFL players did not receive the same feeling of security from their owners.

Out with a Whimper

WFL version 2.0 kicked off in 1975 with a new commissioner and a radically different salary structure. Chris Hemmeter, former owner of the Hawaiians, was installed as commissioner and instituted a financial policy called "the Hemmeter Plan." The plan was a profit-sharing salary system for the players. In it, the players split a percentage of the net income earned by each owner. If no net income was earned, the players would receive a minimum salary of $500 per game. Many of the players on the Southmen, including Csonka, Kiick, and Warfield, were excluded from the plan because they had personal services contracts with Bassett.[20] The Hemmeter Plan was designed to help the WFL navigate a financially troublesome sea caused by the pullout of TVS as a broadcaster. The Papergate scandal had soured TVS on broadcasting WFL games. In the words of TVS chief Eddie Einhorn, even though TVS had finished in the black on its contract in 1974, he was having a hard time finding advertisers willing to sponsor what they considered to be a morally suspect league. "The first thing that got the credibility of the league in trouble was the phonying of attendance," Einhorn told *Sports Illustrated.* "From that day on we never got another nickel's worth of business. At the end of the year no one is getting paid and this was in the paper everyday. By the time we got to the World Bowl, we went from about an eight rating to a two." Einhorn went on to explain that while the Hemmeter Plan may have made financial sense, it also made the World League look inferior to advertisers. "We couldn't sell a thing," Einhorn said. "In the final analysis the league had mediocrity written all over it. It had $250-$500 players written all over it."[21]

To Bassett's credit, he did not let the state of the WFL alter his commitment. He had set out to create a first-class professional football operation and he continued to do so no matter how bush league the rest of the WFL became. In media profiles of the team, the Southmen were credited with having "NFL-quality food, lodging, equipment, medication and transportation."[22] These trappings engendered loyalty and devotion from Bassett's players, especially the former Dolphins, who to a man said the Memphis Southmen style was comparable to what they had experienced in the NFL. "My experience with Mr. Bassett and his organization in Memphis is that it functioned on a parallel with other organizations I performed for in the NFL," Paul Warfield said. "He was a professional and a great owner."[23] Larry Csonka concurred, "Having money on hand to do things the correct way and in a prestigious way is a trademark of the NFL. If that is the comparison, the Memphis Southmen were of that caliber."[24]

The former Miami Dolphins returned the favor, reporting to training camp in Mississippi on time and not requesting any kind of special accommodation. According to their head coach, the three players were just as advertised, even better. "They had great attitudes," John McVay said. "They had obviously been in the NFL so when they came into the

WFL it was a different atmosphere from what they were used to. They came in and embraced the opportunity and practiced well and blended in with the team."[25] Although Larry Csonka got injured and missed a few games, the Southmen got off to a hot start. With Danny White taking most snaps, Memphis sprinted to a 7–2 record. Jim Kiick had nine rushing touchdowns and gained more yards than Csonka on the ground. Warfield averaged close to 17 yards a reception and things seemed to be going smoothly until back-to-back losses to the newly renamed Birmingham Vulcans knocked Memphis into second place. "It was a good season," Csonka said. "Things kind of all came together. The team had more money to work with, so they were a little more competitive."[26] Unfortunately, the Southmen did not get the chance to take the field again following their 21–0 loss to Birmingham on October 19, 1975.

For weeks heading into October, ugly but familiar stories about missed paychecks and unpaid bills began to pile up for the second straight year. Despite the WFL's austerity measures under the Hemmeter Plan, the league was hemorrhaging money and failing to attract crowds. The Chicago Winds folded in September just days after losing 31–7 to Memphis. In Hawaii, former NFL star running back Calvin Hill sued his club because they cut his pay in half when he was injured and unable to finish the season. In October, the San Antonio Wings had to take pay cuts of up to 40 percent.[27] In a sign of just how little grip the WFL had on the sporting public, a game between Philadelphia and Southern California was pre-empted by a test pattern. The game ran long and the local Philadelphia station covering the contest chose to go off the air at midnight as usual rather than continuing to cover the game. No one phoned in to complain.[28]

On October 22, 1975, the WFL announced it was disbanding. Larry Csonka remembers being informed by Leo Cahill that the Southmen would no longer play that season. "We had a general manager who sent a memo to the locker room," Csonka said. "I never had a chance to talk to Johnny. Johnny spoke to my agent who advised us to pack up and go home. I wasn't too quick to do that, but after I spoke with my agent, I packed my car."[29] Bassett, seeing his league collapsing around him and filled with uncertainty about his beloved football club, could only laugh. "If you want to look at the WFL optimistically, you can make a hell of a story," Bassett said. "If you want to look at the situation pessimistically, you can make a hell of a story. If you want to look at things realistically, you've got a problem."[30]

Bassett had attempted to look at his situation with a combination of optimism and reality. He had a financially viable and athletically gifted team which he could see as a competitive NFL franchise. The downfall of the WFL could be just an irritating speed bump in Bassett's quest to craft a team in his image if he could convince the NFL that Tennessee was ready for them. Bassett tried to find a place for Memphis in the NFL over the next several years. Bassett's vision of an NFL team in Tennessee was accurate, but his belief that the NFL would invite someone who had crippled the league's flagship franchise was shockingly naïve.

Mid–South Grizzlies v National Football League

The AFL had succeeded in forcing the NFL to merge because it had generated league-wide television revenues which were comparable to its older counterpart. Those revenues made the AFL a financially viable entity, so the NFL chose to join forces when it became apparent the older league could not beat them. The WFL had not come anywhere close to matching the AFL, but in Bassett's opinion, the Memphis franchise successfully created a quality football organization which was comparable to NFL teams and therefore ready to join the league. In fact, Bassett's point was buttressed by the fact that the senior league was readying for expansion by two teams, meaning that the league was in growth mode. Bassett met with Oakland Raiders managing partner Al Davis to propose a merger in the summer of 1975. Al Davis had experience in battling the NFL and was a key driver of the tactics that forced the NFL to absorb all ten AFL teams in the mid–1960s.

Bassett and Davis discussed the cost of the NFL absorbing one or more WFL franchises. The two men agreed that a WFL team would need to pay a $12 million entrance fee to join the NFL.[31] Davis liked what Bassett was proposing and took it to the NFL owners meeting in 1975. Davis told his fellow owners the NFL could get millions from the absorption of WFL franchises into the NFL and was promptly laughed out of the room.[32] While Bassett's proposal did not fly, it did show that during the demise of the WFL, he was looking for ways to keep his beloved Southmen alive. Bassett felt preserving the Southmen would be a salve for the hurt he felt over having his sterling reputation for probity associated with a now disreputable league. "It's like a brand new car," Bassett said of the WFL's loss of credibility and its impact on his. "Once you've wrecked it, no matter how well it's fixed up, it's never the same."[33]

Bassett's credibility was spared because of his efforts to sustain the Southmen, but also because he honored all his financial commitments at great cost. If anything, the name Johnny F. Bassett gained stature for being the most straight and honest man in football. The first prong of the strategy was to help any employee on the Southmen find another job in the NFL. The second prong was to get his team in the NFL. Bassett had a whole lot more luck with the former job than the latter.

Bassett vehemently believed his Memphis Southmen were an NFL-ready franchise, but he was realistic. Bassett knew that with the Tampa and Seattle franchises set to come online in 1976, he faced an uphill battle to join the NFL for the upcoming season. As such, he was not going to hold back any of his employees from attempting to join the NFL. Ironically, the NFL did the holding up. "The NFL blocked us from returning that season," Larry Csonka said. "It was kind of a shock. They said it was to protect the integrity of the league and quality of play because teams would be in disarray with so many players running around on the open market."[34] This meant that Csonka, Kiick, Warfield, and any other players from the Southmen who wanted to join the NFL had to head home and wait for 1976. This also meant that Bassett had to pay these players for not playing, as he had signed them to personal services contracts. To his credit, Bassett did not bat an eye and kept signing the checks.

"He fulfilled the contract," Larry Csonka said. "Several people were of the opinion that we didn't get the money. Even Shula, he was surprised when I told him I got it. Johnny lived up to everything he said. That was the measure of what I thought made a great owner. He'd make a great NFL owner. He'd make a great President."[35] Paul Warfield seconded Csonka, "My comment is that Mr. Bassett fulfilled his obligation. I was very happy. I was very satisfied with the financial inducement."[36] Head coach John McVay was also going to have his contract fulfilled, but McVay did not hold Bassett to his commitment. The coach walked away from his salary as a sign of thanks to Bassett for helping McVay land a job with the New York Giants. "I know when the league finally shut down Johnny came to me and said, 'What do I owe you?'" McVay said. "I thanked him for the opportunity and told him he didn't owe me any money. He was very influential in my getting hired by the New York Giants. I had signed a contract for three years, but the league lasted a year and half. I said, 'We're okay, you don't owe me anything because you're a good and decent man.' I do know he was a very legitimate owner who took care of his people and paid his bills."[37]

While Bassett's effort to get Memphis in the NFL would have been aided by having a roster that included Csonka, Kiick, and Warfield, he did not stand in their way when they opted to rejoin the NFL. Jim Kiick signed with the Denver Broncos, Paul Warfield reunited with the Cleveland Browns, and Larry Csonka followed John McVay to the New York Giants. In full disclosure it is fair to point out that Bassett did benefit financially from the return of the three players to the NFL as the way

he had structured their contracts allowed him to cut some of his losses. "There were stipulations in the contract that if anything happened, it was understood the contract would pay off in accordance with how far along we had gotten," Larry Csonka explained. "What he hadn't paid off I got from the New York Giants. Joe Robbie had laughed saying no NFL team would accept that obligation. We went to New York and the Maras said, 'Yeah, we'll talk.' New York picked up exactly what I didn't get from the WFL. Johnny was my biggest fan when I went back to the NFL."[38]
The WFL experience for Csonka, Kiick, and Warfield was a mixed bag. The trio had received their full payment and had struck a blow for equitable compensation in relation to revenues generated. They also had the unique experience of joining a new league on the ground floor in an attempt to help build something from scratch. Also, they had the chance to work with Johnny F. Bassett. All of this added up to an enjoyable experience that they do not regret.

"In building something new there is always good and bad," Paul Warfield said.

> While we were all hopeful the league would have the opportunity to grow like the AFL had, other owners and individuals didn't have the clout of Mr. Bassett. When I look at today and see that most contract negotiations are not long and drawn out tug of wars with holdouts and fines, I think Mr. Bassett was right in touch with owners of today. I saw that with Miami. The Dolphins learned how valuable their players were and called them in to re-work contracts. The club was forced to do something they had not done before.[39]

Csonka agreed up to a point, stating the sting of hurting Don Shula never left him, but that he was happy to have been an employee of Bassett. "Given a Monday morning quarterback situation, there might be some things I would have done differently," Csonka admitted. "I didn't like leaving overnight and I would have liked to have gone back and talked to Shula. It was a pretty big shock to Shula and Dolphins fans. But Johnny Bassett had respect for money and power. But he respected intelligence more than the other two. Having known the Robbies, the Maras, and the Rooneys, the Southmen were a great group of people."[40]

With his head coach and star players joining the NFL, Bassett rolled up his sleeves and went about promoting Memphis as an NFL city and the Southmen as an NFL team. Bassett sought to gain entry to the NFL as an existing club. Language used by the expansion committee piqued Bassett's maverick tendencies. Bassett planned to use the NFL's habit of pitting expansion sites against each other to ramp up expansion fees and stadium expenditures to his own advantage. It was a long shot, but Bassett planned to use past positive comments about Memphis' viability as an expansion site as the crux of his argument as to why the Southmen should be admitted to the NFL for the upcoming 1976 season. Some of the quotes came from the NFL's most powerful men: "Memphis has a high level of interest from a majority of owners," Kansas City Chiefs owner Lamar Hunt told the press during the 1974 expansion process. "By majority I mean 14 or more."[41] Hunt was one of the most influential owners in the NFL, so his words carried weight. Another owner, Leonard Tose of the Philadelphia Eagles, was less influential, but he was much more adamant in his belief that the NFL should move into Tennessee. "My feeling is that I definitely think we should expand and that we should go with Memphis," Tose was quoted as saying in the same article in which Hunt's comments appeared. "We should go in 1975 or 1976."[42]

Bassett reasoned that if so many owners of the NFL viewed Memphis as a hot prospect for expansion in 1974, the commercial and athletic success of the Memphis Southmen should only have bolstered the city's appeal. Bassett pointed out that Memphis Memorial Stadium was being expanded, tickets were being sold, and they expected a total of 40,000 subscribers. Additionally, players were being scouted and signed, and all employees were continuing to be paid. The question was: Did the NFL want Johnny F. Bassett? The answer was an unequivocal no.

Bassett trumpeted the financial commitments being made by Memphis football fans to all who would listen. These were commitments which he had worked tirelessly to obtain. "The NFL has to be impressed with the Memphis application," Bassett said. "We have money from 46,000 applicants for season tickets along with written requests for 8,000 more. That's at $10 per ticket. There are 1,200 box seats at $15 that are sold. We have sold the most season tickets in history for a team that doesn't have anyone to play against."[43] Despite "coming on strong," in the words of Dallas Cowboys president Tex Schramm, the Memphis bid to join the NFL was voted down 25–3 at the league's annual meeting in 1976.[44] Certainly, part of the rejection was the NFL's determination to maintain its own control over who could join their league, and when, and how. But Bassett was extremely disappointed. He had put $4.5 million into the Memphis Southmen and the city of Memphis had rallied around him.[45] To Bassett the NFL's move not only defied logic, it was rude. "This is a tremendous rejection to the people of Memphis who have demonstrated their ability to support a team," Bassett said.[46]

Bassett responded by filing a lawsuit alleging the NFL had violated the Sherman Anti-Trust Act. According to Bassett, the NFL conspired to boycott his admission into the NFL despite the fact he and Memphis met all reasonable requirements for admission. This was an anti-competitive stance in Bassett's estimation. The case, *Mid-South Grizzlies v NFL*, was dismissed at the district court level and upheld on appeal. The decision read, "The exclusion was pro-competitive since it left Memphis available as a site for a future franchise."[47] Memphis just was not a site for a franchise now. Memphis never did become home to an NFL team with the frustrating exception of 1997 when it hosted the Tennessee Oilers for one year while their stadium was constructed 200 miles away in Nashville. After all their years of staking civic hopes on gaining an NFL team, Memphis wound up as a way station for a team headed to the other side of the state. In the end, it was through professional basketball that Memphis finally achieved coveted big-league status, when the Grizzlies relocated from Vancouver in 2001. The Oilers were rebranded as Titans in 1999, and their twenty-plus year existence offers current proof of Bassett's belief in Tennessee as a viable NFL market.

Frustrated in his attempt to bring the Southmen to the NFL, Bassett tried to buy his way into the NFL by focusing on a team in distress, the San Diego Chargers. The Chargers were a pathetic franchise in 1976. The team had not posted a winning season during the decade and were embroiled in an embarrassing drug scandal. If the intrigue of the team doctor passing out illegal steroids wasn't salacious enough, team owner Gene Klein was being sued by the minority partners to oust him from his position running the franchise.[48] The Chargers' dysfunction was a complete opposite of the Southmen organization, but Bassett viewed it as the perfect opportunity. "When the expansion committee seemed negative about our application, I went back to Memphis and said if they don't want to give us an expansion club, let's see if we can buy an established club," Bassett explained. "Since the Chargers had the worst attendance and the worst record, I had my attorney call Gene Klein."[49] Klein confirmed he was approached by Bassett's lawyer about a purchase that would involve moving the Chargers to Tennessee.[50] While tempted, Klein chose to not sell and did eventually enjoy the Chargers' run to AFC West supremacy under Don Coryell.

With all his options played out Bassett reluctantly terminated the Memphis football operation. In the eyes of one of his friends, the NFL's decision to not admit Bassett into their fraternity set them back for more than a decade from a marketing standpoint. "Johnny was so smart," Steve Ehrhart said. "He would have fit in very well. He knew when to stir things up. Had he been an owner in the NFL they would have appreciated him. He was the forerunner of the Jerry Jones–style owner. Johnny would have been good for the NFL and would have been a terrific NFL owner. I often thought Johnny was the predecessor to Jerry Jones."[51]

Jones is the respected and somewhat controversial owner of the Dallas Cowboys, a figure known for audacious promotions and challenges of the orthodoxy. The comparison is apt, but in 1976 Bassett had more problems than just NFL rejection. The Southmen had cost him millions as had the Toros. The ownership group of the Toros diminished almost as fast as his funds, leaving him alone to face a new reality. His once significant personal fortune was next to nothing and creditors for his hockey team were not patient. Bassett elected to throw one last Hail Mary to stave off both bankruptcy and the need to abandon sports. If one bright spot came out of the WFL for Bassett, it was that he discovered a heretofore hidden hotbed for professional sports. One that did not seem fit for hockey until Bassett proved it possible.

NINE

||||||||||||||||||||||||||||||||||||||||

Selling Hockey in Alabama

Money was rapidly becoming an issue for Johnny F. Bassett. After pumping $4.5 million into the Memphis Southmen, he no longer had a team to show for it. Bassett lost close to an additional $6 million on the Toronto Toros before he reluctantly relocated to Birmingham.[1] All of this time, effort, and money did not come out of an endless bank account. His enthusiasm, idealism, and passion led to extreme highs and lows emotionally, and this up-and-down personality was reflected in the extreme nature of his sports decisions. Successes and failures colored his mood and Bassett knew it took a toll on his wife and four children as well as upon his emotional well-being. He was not merely in it for the investment, nor for mild amusement. Bassett cared, and his family felt the effects. "The good thing about being an entrepreneur is you have your independence," Bassett told *Sports Illustrated.* "But it is tough on the family. I am sure Susan would rather I have a regular job. I don't know what I'll be doing six months from now, much less two years from now. Hopefully, we won't be broke."[2]

The same *Sports Illustrated* profile detailed some of Bassett's highs and lows, but also pointed out that Sue Bassett was ably equipped to either pick him back up or give him a swift kick in the pants, depending upon his needs. One story recounted a breakfast incident during the folding of the Memphis Southmen and relocation of the Toros. Susan had made Johnny breakfast and the eggs were not to his liking. In frustration, he threw the eggs against the refrigerator and demanded Sue clean it up as he stormed out of the house. Instead, Sue left the mess where it stayed for days, and of course it hardened into an unsightly mess. Guests to the house could see the mess, but Sue never mentioned it. Finally, after the egg monstrosity became the talk of their social circle, Bassett, properly chagrined, was seen with a scraper in the kitchen cleaning the mess he had made.[3] Sue drew a boundary line, which Johnny knew he had crossed, and refused to enable his tantrum. He

John Bassett married his college sweetheart, the former Sue Carling, on June 11, 1960, at St. Paul's Cathedral in London, Ontario. Bassett never found a more dependable partner or friend than Sue in all his years in sports and promotion (courtesy the Bassett family).

accepted and needed this limit at home, but in the sports world, Sue had no counterpart.

Cancer

A shocking new emotional dilemma befell Bassett and Sue as his sports teams were slowly falling apart: cancer. The 37-year-old Bassett took a fishing trip in 1976 to relieve stress. The Toros team doctor and Frank Falkenberg, a partner in the hockey team, noticed something odd about Bassett's back when the owner removed his shirt during the outing. "Johnny had his shirt off and Gordon (Robinson), the team doctor, saw a mole on the shoulder and said, 'You need to come see me quick, that looks really angry,'" Falkenberg recounted.[4] The diagnosis was melanoma and the malignant, metastasized tumor required major surgery. Within six months, Bassett underwent two procedures requiring multiple skin grafts and the removal of his lymph glands. "It was a sizeable and ugly procedure leaving a lasting scar on his back for a lifetime," explained Bassett's wife Sue Bassett-Klauber.[5] Bassett underplayed the cancer as much as he did his perilous finances. "When I knew I had cancer, I knew I was going to beat it because I'd had so many losers (teams) that I knew I was due for a winner."[6]

Bassett was given a clean bill of health but did an awful job following his post-operative regimen. His medical team's prescription included rigid adherence to a regularized, healthier, and less stressful life routine. Such was not Johnny's nature. Bassett threw himself into the day-to-day operations of his newly christened Birmingham Bulls, much to the dismay of his wife. "It did not really slow him down," Sue Bassett-Klauber said. "When an operation was over, he would just keep moving forward. I had to change his dressings and bandages, and he would still defy the odds. He was very strong-willed and determined that nothing would prevent him from moving forward. I remember thinking, 'What is he doing to himself?'"[7] Motivated by souring finances and recognition that the WHA would soon go the way of the WFL, yet also probably suppressing his medical worries in the excitement of a world he knew and loved, Bassett set about positioning his Bulls as a legitimate candidate to be absorbed into the NHL. To do that he needed to prove the viability of a Deep South city as a hockey market, a seemingly Herculean task. The first method Bassett used to accomplish this goal was the construction of a unique hockey environment. The second method introduced a brutal playing style to the league. Sadly, the former method came too close on the heels of a dark chapter in American history and put Bassett in an uncomfortable situation. The latter so angered the WHA and NHL that his team was not seriously considered for the merged leagues.

Birmingham as a Hockey Market

Birmingham, Alabama, was at first glance an odd choice for a professional hockey team. Locating an ice hockey team in a medium-sized city in the American Deep South known for heat, humidity, college football, and, tragically, one of the worst episodes in the sorry history of American racial violence, the 16th Street Baptist Church bombing, was a head-scratcher, particularly to Bassett's director of marketing. "I said, 'Are you nuts?'" recalled Pete McAskile. "He said, 'No, you should see the fans, they are so passionate.' I said, 'Passionate for football. This is hockey. They've never even seen a game!'"[8] McAskile was correct, but narrowly. Bassett knew something his marketing director did not. Birmingham had a significant corporate presence eager to throw off the shackles of Jim Crow, and to transform the image of the city from one of backwoods violence to one that matched its regional rival Atlanta. Birmingham had been losing economic and cultural ground to Atlantans for decades and was heartily tired of it. The cities had been nearly identical in size before the Second World War, but in the thirty years since, Atlanta grew to double Birmingham's size. Atlanta's relatively progressive stance on civil rights—it was home to Martin Luther King, Jr., and had been W.E.B DuBois' base for many years—compared favorably to Birmingham's lurid spectacle of fire hoses, police dogs, and bombings. Many companies located their offices in a city whose motto is "The City too Busy to Hate" instead of the one nicknamed "Bombingham."[9]

Among the companies locating to Georgia's capital were professional sports franchises in all four major leagues: Atlanta Falcons (NFL, 1966), Atlanta Braves (MLB, 1966), Atlanta Hawks (NBA, 1968) and Atlanta Flames (NHL, 1972). In their quest to keep pace with Atlanta, Birmingham built a modern sports arena in 1976, the Birmingham-Jefferson Civic Center. An arena was the one thing Bassett lacked in Toronto and he leapt at the chance to move in. Frank Falkenburg, one of the men behind the construction of the arena, recalled the marriage between Bassett and Birmingham being a natural. "I met Johnny on (one of his) trips down here," Falkenburg said. "We had just built a state-of-the-art arena with wonderful sightlines, but we had no idea if we could get a team. We listened to Johnny's pitch, and 35 very prominent businessmen bought into the idea."[10] Bassett now had an arena and Birmingham now had a team. The new team was christened the Birmingham Bulls. The alliterative nature of Toronto Toros carried on with Birmingham Bulls as did the nickname's bovine theme. Bassett also benefited financially with the name change. "He didn't need to spend money on new uniforms," John C. Bassett recalled with a laugh.[11] Following the first season, however, it was apparent fans in the city were not buying the new Bulls.

Bassett had moved into a market hungry for major league status but hazy on hockey knowledge. The Bulls drew average audiences of 8,000, which was neither impressive nor embarrassing, but rather mediocre.[12] "We drew about what I thought we would," said Peter

Bassett standing outside the family's Alabama row house following the relocation of the Toronto Toros to Birmingham, Alabama, in 1976. Notice that the sleeves of the jersey read Toros. The franchise kept the same jerseys but just changed the wording. According to John C. Bassett, the team being rechristened the Birmingham Bulls meant continuing alliteration, but also his father saved money by not needing new uniforms (courtesy the Bassett family).

McAskile. "We had put up a phone number, 251-BULL. The phone calls were impressive because no one wanted to be left without a ticket. We sold 7,500 season tickets, but no one knew what they were buying. When we sent an invoice, they realized there weren't 13 games like in football, but 40 or so. It dropped from 7,500 to 2,500 and we'd get another 4,000 to 5,000 per game."[13] The fans started to make their way to the arena more regularly as the season wore on and word-of-mouth had its effect. This had something to do with the Alabama Crimson Tide football team concluding their season, but it was also the result of Bassett's tireless efforts to educate the local population on the intricacies of hockey.

Bassett's general manager, Gilles Leger, noticed that the local papers showed marked improvement in their game coverage over the course of the season. Were scribes learning the new game? Leger found out the truth. "It turned out Johnny was writing the stuff and turning it in," Leger said.[14] Peter Eby, Bassett's friend and partner in the Toros/ Bulls, had stuck by the owner's side on the move south and recalled the strange marriage between the Bulls and Birmingham. "We all hung in there and moved to Birmingham," Eby said. "It was great fun, but it was evident at the time the fans had no idea what was going on. They weren't used to hockey."[15] Things got so bad that Bassett and his marketing director joined the faculty of the local university to bring prospective fans up to speed on the new game in town. "We taught a course at the University of Alabama–Birmingham on hockey to explain the action on the ice," said Peter McAskile.[16]

The turnout for the first season had been solid. Given a few years, Bassett might be able to turn Birmingham into a legitimate hockey town. Unfortunately, Bassett realized that, due to larger forces at work in the hockey and sports worlds, he might not have a few years with the Bulls.

WHA/NHL Merger Talks

The WHA and NHL were both losing money and shedding franchises hand over fist during the mid–1970s. The inter-league hockey war drove up salaries and depleted team bank accounts. The game was simultaneously overextended and underfinanced, and the hockey war cried out for settlement. With 32 teams between them, both leagues discovered there was a dearth of talent available and the financially weaker clubs were unable to compete. This was not limited to the newer league: the NHL itself had trouble starting and maintaining franchises in markets such as Cleveland, Kansas City, and Denver. "There is more of a pool of good football players than a pool of good hockey players," Peter Eby said in explaining the problem. "Football is a game of courage, desire and will. In hockey, you've got to have some innate skills: skating and handling the stick while on skates. It's not as easy as it looks. At that time, the U.S colleges weren't producing the hockey players they are today. It hadn't really caught on at that time in the States."[17] Without a pipeline of talent, the NHL and WHA were left to put players on the ice who were not of major league quality and both leagues suffered as a consequence. "If you don't have some guys who can score or stick handle through the other team at a high level, it doesn't work," Eby continued. "Some of it was boring."[18]

The hockey glut led WHA teams to fold in Minnesota, Chicago, Denver, Cleveland, Baltimore, San Diego, Calgary, and Phoenix. Heading into the 1977-1978 season, the WHA was left with only eight franchises. The more established NHL was not immune from contraction. Besides relocations, the Kansas City Scouts and California Golden Seals went under, casualties of the war with the upstart league. As is often the case when a new league comes on the scene, the WHA attempted to seek legal redress against the NHL in the early years of battle to lessen the established league's monopolistic grip on professional hockey. The WHA filed a lawsuit against the NHL in the winter of 1974, contending the elder circuit was a monopoly. Seeking $50 million in damages, the WHA was granted a partial victory when the NHL agreed to settle the suit out of court. The settlement sum of $1.75 million was paltry, but the ramifications carried great weight, specifically prompting the resignation of NHL President Clarence Campbell, an avowed foe of the WHA.[19] With the stubborn Campbell's resignation, the mantle of power passed to John Ziegler, a rational thinker who knew the NHL and WHA were doomed to mediocrity or worse if they did not come to terms. Ziegler and many NHL and WHA owners met shortly after Ziegler's promotion in 1977 to discuss a merger.

From the start, Bassett's Birmingham Bulls were left out of the merger equation, and it was that equation which offered the peripatetic Canadian his best hope for redemption through major league status. With a poorly-drawing team in Atlanta, the NHL was not enamored with the thought of a second franchise in the Deep South. The irony, of course, is that Bassett's marketing in Birmingham proved more imaginative than anything the Flames tried in Atlanta. The first merger proposal put forth granted NHL status to six WHA franchises: Cincinnati, Edmonton, Houston, Winnipeg, New England, and Quebec. The NHL owners voted 12–6 in favor of the proposal, but the tally fell short of the three-quarters majority required.[20] Naturally, Toronto Maple Leaf owner and former Bassett foe Harold Ballard was one of those opposed. Like his former commissioner, the mulish Ballard simply refused to countenance a compromise with the upstarts. With the first serious merger proposal defeated, the WHA set out to start the 1977-1978 season with eight franchises and its eyes set on recalibrating their merger proposal. Bassett started the 1977-1978 season with a retooled Bulls lineup. Bassett wanted a roster which served the dual purpose of matching the culture of the Birmingham sports fan while, at the same time, showing the Bulls to be a team a merged league could not do without. What he created was arguably the most physically intimidating team ever put on ice. It was, in fact, a signature franchise not just in the WHA, but in professional hockey history. Bassett created a hockey team with a football mentality. Not just any football mentality, Bear Bryant's football mentality.

The Crimson Tide on Ice

"I remember my Dad saying after the first game in Birmingham, 'It is a football crowd going to a hockey game,'" recalled Bassett's son, John C. Bassett. "He had never seen fans in a hockey crowd holding a sign that read 'D–Fense!' like at a football game. Paul 'Bear' Bryant was still coaching at Alabama and they were huge."[21] Bassett knew the impact of Alabama football in the state. He knew that every child in Alabama grew up as a fan of either Alabama or Auburn, but mostly Alabama in Birmingham. He saw how Crimson Tide games affected attendance for the Birmingham Americans of the World Football League when Bassett owned the rival Memphis Southmen. The Americans attracted crowds of over 50,000 prior to the start of college football season. Once the colleges kicked off, Americans attendance plummeted to 20,000.[22] If they had to choose between their nationally renowned school team or a renegade professional outfit, fans followed the Crimson Tide's moveable feast of home games to Tuscaloosa or Birmingham or Montgomery every time. Alabama football seeped into all aspects of life in the state, prompting former Crimson Tide player and head coach Ray Perkins to quip, "Alabama is football; football is Alabama."[23] Bassett began studying the methods of Alabama's football team, attended Bear Bryant's coaching dinner, and picked the brains of those affiliated with the Crimson Tide. The research gave Bassett a schematic of how to transform his Bulls into an on-ice version of the Alabama football team.

Bassett wanted to market the Bulls as an Alabama institution, a hockey team which defied the conventional wisdom of Northerners that the Deep South could not appreciate hockey and that would defeat the Yankees at their own game the way the Crimson Tide did on the gridiron. Alabama football had been defeating Northern teams in intersectional games since the 1920s, winning multiple national championships, including titles under Bryant in 1961, 1964, and 1965. To pull off being an ice hockey version of Crimson Tide football, Bassett needed voices recognizable to Southerners who could speak the language of hockey. The team developed a plan to dominate the local radio waves. Bassett's marketing director was the point man on this strategy. Peter McAskile's job was to normalize the sport of hockey in Birmingham. McAskile hit the airwaves regularly extolling the virtues of the game, comparing it favorably to Alabama football, and championing the local business institutions which became corporate partners with the Bulls. McAskile's time on the air was so prevalent that he received angry phone calls from station executives. "I worked hard on the on-air media," said McAskile. "The morning deejay at the top rock station would come to practice.

We would let him get in goal and he actually became a decent goalie. Every morning he would discuss us on the air. I got a call from the station manager saying he needed the deejay to play more music!"[24] The Bulls also hired a play-by-play man with a voice known by Alabama fans, although the owner of the voice was a Yankee. Eli Gold was known as one of the radio voices of NASCAR, the auto racing circuit which was still primarily a Southern phenomenon in the 1970s. The recognizable sound of Gold's voice lent a semblance of Deep South normalcy to a Yankee sport. Ironically, the New York-born Gold eventually became the radio voice of Alabama Crimson Tide football.

The "Birmingham Bullies"

Bassett further attempted to add a "crimson hue" to his Bulls by changing the make-up of his roster. Bassett and the Bulls faced multiple quandaries with their hockey identity in Birmingham. One was the ethnicity of the players and the other was the team's playing style. Many of the Bulls players, while solid hockey players, had backgrounds and personalities that did not mesh with Birmingham's culture. Left winger Paul Henderson was a productive scorer for the Bulls and a national hero in Canada after scoring the winning goal in the epic 1972 Summit Series against the Soviet Union. In Birmingham, however, Henderson was just an anonymous Canadian, although he admitted a preference for being unknown. "I was happy to be in Birmingham because my family and I got away from all the national limelight in Canada," Henderson said.[25]

Vaclav Nedomansky, a forward known as "Big Red," defected to Canada from Czechoslovakia in 1974 for the chance to play professional hockey. Nedomansky's harrowing escape was assisted by Bassett, who helped him achieve Canadian citizenship thanks to a job with the Toronto Toros. The two remained close for decades, but in 1977 Birmingham, the Czech émigré was a strange-speaking former Communist who had more of a connection to Alberta than Alabama. Bassett and his team needed players the community could relate to. Unfortunately, there were not yet any Deep South hot beds of hockey training. This meant the Bulls could not lure local farm boys onto the ice the way Bear Bryant could to the gridiron. They could not tout the latest sensation from Andalusia, Clayhatchee, or South Vinemont. Instead, at the behest of Peter McAskile, Bassett and his executive team decided that if they could not attract players born and bred in Alabama, they would build a team of players suited to a style of play which would make the Bulls a skating version of the Crimson Tide.

"If you guys want me to sell hockey, we need to get more physical," McAskile told Bassett and general manger Gilles Leger. "We're not hitting enough, and this is what the crowd wants."[26] The Bulls marketers hit on a significant point. Bear Bryant's mantra to his recruiters included the expectation that his players be fast, strong, and mean. Within 24-hours, Bassett and Leger transformed the roster of the Bulls to meet these criteria, with an emphasis on mean. Shopping for intimidation and physicality, Bassett and Gilles Leger set out to hire as many notorious enforcers as they could find in all corners of hockey. Among the newcomers were Frank Beaton, Serge Beaudoin, Gilles Bilodeau, and Bobby Stephenson. The Bulls also made hockey history when they traded Nedomansky to the Detroit Red Wings, the first inter-league trade between the WHA and NHL, to acquire Steve Durbano and Dave Hanson.[27] Neither Durbano nor Hanson were known for prodigious offense; instead they were known for a skill set referred to as "goon" in hockey parlance.

A goon's job is to retaliate with extreme prejudice when an opponent physically harasses opposing star players. If an opponent slammed a team's player into the boards, the goon responded by trying to throw that opponent through the boards to "de-motivate" such behavior from happening again. The goon was also expected to get in the head of the opponent's star offensive player by employing taunts, hits, high-sticks, and other physical extracurricular activities. A great goon embraced the job with the flair of a professional wrestler, enjoying the chance to drop his gloves and engage in fisticuffs at a moment's notice. While the goon was a fan favorite in his home arena, he was undoubtedly the villain on the road. Either way, the goon made for great theater. Hockey sophisticates, and Europeans, whose grasp of the game did not include goons, found this tradition embarrassing or frustrating. There was no denying that North American fans moved the turnstiles to come in and see goons at work. For example, the NHL's Philadelphia Flyers won back-to-back Stanley Cups in 1974 and 1975 with a goon squad and became a beloved local institution affectionately known as the "Broad Street Bullies."[28]

Hockey franchises normally employ one to two goons on their roster so each shift on the ice consists of a protector and designated brawler. Bassett's Bulls increased the number of such players exponentially. The Bulls started entire lines made up of goons, making Birmingham the talk of hockey and earning the team a new nickname: "Birmingham Bullies." This was a real-life version of the fictional Charlestown Chiefs hockey team made famous in the 1977 cult classic film *Slap Shot*. In the film, a coach played by legendary actor Paul Newman realizes he needs to put a team of goons and enforcers on the ice to get fans to attend. The ploy works as the Chiefs become a box office hit and win a championship. Ironically, Bassett was facing a similar dilemma as the Paul Newman character. In a bizarre twist, two members of Bassett's franchise had direct ties to the film *Slap Shot*. Assistant coach John Brophy was a renowned fighter during his minor league playing days. As coach of the Long Island Cougars in the minors, Brophy had put together a tough unit that contended for titles in the North American Hockey League. His reputation as a fighter and coach were the inspiration for Paul Newman's character in *Slap Shot*.[29] In addition to Brophy, defenseman Dave Hanson had been a star in the film, playing one of the infamous Hanson Brothers. The role as an enforcer with a mean streak in the film was not a stretch for Hanson, who was well-known at different levels of hockey for his tough play. Hanson quickly became a Birmingham favorite, although he had plenty of competition for the role of most physical player.

It is important to realize the players Bassett brought in to play a style of hockey meant to appeal to Birmingham had no connection to the region. Hanson hailed from Wisconsin, Durbano from Toronto, Beaton from Antigonish, Nova Scotia, Bilodeau from Quebec, and Beaudoin from Montreal. Some of them were small-town products, some big city boys. Place of origin, however, was not as important as statement of purpose. The Bulls relished their role as a frozen extension of Alabama football. The WHA announced shortly before the advent of the "Bullies" that it would mete out severe punishment for thuggish play and brawling.[30] The fear was that the wide-open style of play the league prided itself on would be hamstrung by too many fights and hard contact. With a league office in the far-off North advocating for a clean style of play, the Bulls doubled down on their roughhouse tactics. The Bulls set a professional hockey record for most penalty minutes by one team in a single season (2,159). Steve Durbano led the team with 284 penalty minutes. Joining Durbano in the record-setting season were Frank Beaton (279), Gilles Bilodeau (258), Dave Hanson (241), and Serge Beaudoin (115).[31]

The season was rife with examples of Bulls gone wild. On November 24, 1977, the Bulls beat the Cincinnati Stingers 12–2 at the Jefferson County Civic Center. The number of goals scored by the Bulls was eye-catching, but it was another statistic that was eye-popping. The Bulls put a starting unit of enforcers Steve Durbano, Frank Beaton, Serge Beaudoin, Gilles Bilodeau, and Bobby Stephenson on the ice. Within a mere 24 seconds of the puck drop, game misconduct penalties were handed out to Birmingham as their players pounded the Cincinnati players unmercifully.[32] The tactic had the desired effect. The Stingers were intimidated and bludgeoned until they could put up scant resistance, allowing a whopping seven goals in the third period. The game came to be known as the "Thanksgiving Day Massacre." The team's marketing director knew something different was about to happen when he was approached by the Bulls head coach shortly before faceoff. "Glenn Sonmor came up to me and said, 'I don't want you to miss the faceoff tonight,'" Peter McAskile said. "I went to the press box and saw what Cincinnati put on the ice and what we had, and I said, 'Oh, no.' People went absolutely nuts."[33] In the words of one writer, the Birmingham Bulls resembled "Mongol hordes on skates."[34] An eyewitness to the "Thanksgiving Day Massacre" compared the Bulls to the German army in the Second World War. "It was like watching the German army invading Poland," the Cincinnati writer said. "Absolute carnage everywhere you looked."[35] These accounts were not fancy and the public relations rough-edged, but the attention was salutary and delighted the Bulls front office. What mattered is that fans reacted, and that the Bulls were a hot topic.

"They still talk about it today," said Frank Falkenburg. "There is not a Thanksgiving Day in Birmingham that does not go by where people [don't] still wish we had a hockey team, so we could have another massacre."[36] The "Thanksgiving Day Massacre" was just a harbinger of things to come. The Bulls took the violent show on the road, playing up their rebel image to the hilt. Durbano, Hanson, et al were about as Southern as an iceberg, but their willingness to fight for each other, fight on the ice, and fight against the convention of how hockey should be played won the hearts and minds of a region which valued such action.

Dave Hanson, the hockey player famous for playing himself in *Slap Shot*, became the public face of the Bulls rebel ways. Crazed on the ice and hardly calm off it, he recalled in his biography an incident with Hall of Famer Bobby Hull which highlighted how much glee Birmingham fans had in watching their rebel hockey team. Hull was a superstar, the "Golden Jet," a fast-skater and hard-hitter himself. Landing him helped the entire WHA with credibility, and even the most adamant NHL snob could not deny that Hull was one of the sport's greatest players. "I hit Bobby hard and got my elbows a little higher than he appreciated," Hanson wrote.

> Off went our gloves and we proceeded to exchange a flurry of lefts and rights. Suddenly, we both stopped, and Bobby looked much different to me. I then realized he was bald, and I was holding his hairpiece in my hand! The roar of the crowd turned from ear splitting to a deafening silence. I frantically threw his rug out toward the center of the ice and went directly into the penalty box without assistance or saying a word. Bobby then sheepishly skated over to pick up his toupee before going off to the locker room.[37]

The next time Bobby Hull and his Northern teammates came to a game in Birmingham, he was greeted with signs and cheers of "Hair Today, Gone Tomorrow." Hanson loved the response, stating that he enjoyed playing the role of on-ice rebel for his fans. "The fans loved it, and sure we needed to sell tickets down in Alabama. We wanted to keep our jobs and do what we were expected to do."[38]

Even the owner found himself subjected to the scorn of the league as he was punished financially in an attempt to tone down the rebelliousness of his team. Bassett did not receive any penalty minutes, but an unamused WHA fined him $24,000 for rough play.[39] Bassett paid the fine but enjoyed the increased interest by locals in the hockey team and the resulting revenue growth. Attendance rose throughout the season as the Bulls became a playoff contender. A prominent Bulls fan was none other than Bear Bryant. The Crimson Tide coach was a regular attendee and became a friend of Bassett. Bassett's son recalled with amusement that the normally taciturn coach came up to him following a particularly intense game and joked he was going to make an addition to the Alabama athletic department. "Bryant told me he was going to start a hockey program and give me a scholarship," said John C. Bassett.[40]

Going Too Far?

The Birmingham Bulls gave fans something to do once college football season ended. The long months of late winter were previously desolate on the Southern sporting calendar, with only basketball to relieve the tedium. No longer. If an almost cartoonish level of violence and rebellious actions were all Bassett authorized, then his efforts would be no different than teams like the Flyers. In addition to establishing an identity as a football team on ice, Bassett also attempted to make the Bulls more "Southern." Bassett went along with the playing of "Dixie" following the American and Canadian national anthems before games. Rebel yells, hearkening back to Confederate infantry charges of yore, resonated off the walls of the arena, interspersed with drawling chants of "In the crease" and "Icing!" Confederate battle flags of all shapes and sizes were seen flying in the stands, providing stark contrast to the Maple Leaf flag which hung from the rafters to represent the home country of Bassett and many Bulls players.[41]

There is a definite downside to Bassett's embrace of such aspects of Deep South culture when viewed through the prism of today's sensibilities. At best, it demonstrated a lack of sensitivity to some extremely fraught historical and cultural patterns, which surely merited a more deliberate approach. After all, the Crimson Tide was one of the last collegiate football teams to integrate, and Alabama politicians from William Brandon to Frank Boykin to George Wallace viewed the team's triumphs as gridiron proof of the supremacy of Alabamians in general and white Alabamians specifically.[42] Yet Bassett was not trying to raise cultural consciousness about anything except hockey. To this Canadian showman, the issue was finding a way to get the local fans interested in his project, into the arena, and willing to spend their money and emotions on his team. All else was either a distraction or a marketing opportunity. There is nothing in Bassett's background which leads to an assumption that he in any way agreed with the undertones of white supremacy evident of such activities. Bassett earned a reputation for fair dealing across a wide array of endeavors, earning accolades from men and women of multiple races and creeds, and was never labeled a racist. Southern history, with all its discontents, was not a part of the Ontarians cultural baggage. So, Bassett's intentions are not really in question, but one can and should question his approach with benefit of hindsight. Unfortunately, it is clear Bassett was either naïve or obtuse in okaying behaviors to sell hockey which some used to enable or promote racist causes. One unfortunate episode shows how ill-equipped he was to deal with certain ramifications. That these came as a surprise to him reveal the dangers of plunging into deep cultural waters without doing adequate preparatory work.

Bassett made waves in Birmingham when he signed Tony McKegney, an African-Canadian free agent, to a contract. Lamentably but predictably, many season ticket holders revolted, sending notices of cancellation and angry letters and telegrams to the Bulls' offices. The commotion was so intense that Bassett released McKegney so he could sign with the Buffalo Sabres of the NHL to get the young player out of the maelstrom. Gilles Leger recalled that Bassett ultimately bowed down but not before engaging in several heated phone calls with season ticket holders. "Bassett was getting all these calls," Leger said. "My office was next to his, and I kept hearing him go, 'Same to you, buddy!' and he would slam down the phone."[43] Bassett's acquiescence to bigotry is arguably the most uncomfortable example of how his marketing choices were not always enlightened and were based on naïve assumptions. Bassett expressed his anger and disappointment in his fan base in a statement to the press. "It showed me a side of Birmingham I did not know was here anymore," Bassett said. "It's very discouraging."[44] McKegney enjoyed a successful professional career, putting the tumult of Birmingham behind him, but Bassett was briefly tarnished for having given in. He did, in fact, cross a moral line. One can see how his genial ignorance, accompanied by promotional zeal, led him to enthusiastically embrace a marketing strategy catering to cultural patterns he only dimly understood or considered. But submitting to a racially-based fan revolt against one of his own players placed Bassett on the wrong side of the racial divide. It was one of many examples of how, no matter how hard many try to avoid its centrality, race always resides at the heart of the Southern story. Despite this incident, which admittedly occurred as his efforts to maintain the team's viability grew increasingly frantic against an unstable league backdrop, Bassett ultimately prevailed in his determination to prove that the Southeast was a viable market for hockey. A series of extravaganzas orchestrated by Bassett and the Bulls helped to cement that reputation. Naturally, these events were designed with an eye towards appealing to Birmingham's unique sensibilities.

Promotional Wizardry

Thanksgiving Day hockey games in Birmingham became quite popular when Bassett embraced the culture of his new state, particularly in the year's following "The Thanksgiving Day Massacre." The owner traditionally celebrated Canadian Thanksgiving Day in October with his family, and just like in America, football was usually the sport of choice. In Alabama, Thanksgiving Day includes plenty of conversation about the upcoming "Iron Bowl," the annual clash between Alabama and Auburn University played the Saturday of the holiday weekend. Alabama and Auburn met annually in Birmingham from 1904 until 1988 at Legion Field. Taking advantage of the fact rural Alabamians descend regularly on Birmingham for the weekend of the Iron Bowl, whether they had tickets or not, Bassett and McAskile created Thanksgiving Day promotions that mixed ice hockey with turkey. None of the promotions were as bizarre as the fictional Mr. Carlson dropping turkeys from a helicopter in the infamous 1978 "Turkey's Away" episode of *WKRP in Cincinnati*, but they were close.[45] The annual Thanksgiving Day promotions evolved over time, from childish to outlandish. McAskile recounted that it was at this moment he became aware of Bassett's imagination.

"We conferred a lot," McAskile said. "He was always coming up with ideas, that is why it was fun to be around him. We had to get people in the building. We had a promotion on Thanksgiving where if you came dressed as a turkey, you got in for a buck. Johnny didn't think anyone would do that (so he wouldn't have to pay too much), but 100 people came dressed as turkeys!"[46] Dressing as a turkey was one thing, but Bassett gave fans a chance to literally bag a turkey at a Bulls game. Bassett authorized a turkey shoot, inviting spectators to test their skills. The best shooters were provided a free turkey. According to McAskile the event became the talk of Birmingham. "Maybe 1,000 came for the game, the rest came for the chance to win a turkey."[47]

The owner also realized that Birmingham had a civic rivalry with Atlanta, the city that over the past half-century had usurped the unofficial title of capital of the Confederacy. Bassett felt if he could show Birmingham off as a better sports town than Atlanta, he could do a great deal to burnish the city's pride. The Atlanta Flames struggled to attract fans and ultimately relocated to Calgary, setting in the minds of some that hockey in the Deep South was a fool's errand. Those engaged in that thought process overlooked Birmingham, where Bassett's gamble was paying off as attendance continually rose.[48] With one stroke of his marketing brilliance, Bassett not only proved his prescience on Deep South hockey, he provided Birmingham permanent bragging rights over Atlanta regarding hockey.

Bassett arranged with a local jewelry chain to sponsor a diamond giveaway. For weeks leading up to a Friday night game, the Bulls ran advertisements stating that fans would have a one-in-seventeen thousand chance to walk out of the arena with a diamond worth several hundred dollars. Bassett purchased one real diamond and thousands of fake diamonds and placed them on a large pillow in the arena and invited journalists and photographers to come and do stories on the promotion. On the night of the game, Bassett and Bulls staffers personally handed out one real diamond and the thousands of fakes to fans as they came into the arena. Bassett announced before the game that the fans needed to take their "diamond" to the local jeweler to have it appraised. The promotion was a rousing success according to Peter McAskile. "Obviously, the local jeweler got a lot of traffic and by the day of the game we had lines to get tickets," McAskile said. "The fire marshal came in and stopped us from selling more tickets; we could have sold another 5,000. The passion Johnny had foreseen showed up that night. We set a WHA attendance record with 17,500 that night."[49]

The night of the diamond giveaway was emblematic of the effect Bassett had on Birmingham. For the four seasons the Bulls were in the WHA, Birmingham was known for professional hockey. Sadly, Bassett's team could not erase the history of bombs, fire hoses, Jim Crow, and anything else to do with its sordid past. It also did nothing to change the mind of those negotiating a merger between the WHA and NHL.

TEN

‖‖‖‖‖‖‖‖‖‖‖‖‖‖‖‖‖‖‖‖‖‖‖‖‖‖‖‖‖‖‖

Emancipation of the Canadian Juniors

The hockey landscape changed yet again when the two leagues met in 1978 for the second round of merger talks. The NHL folded the Cleveland Barons, lowering their total number of teams to seventeen. The WHA total dropped to seven when the formerly formidable Houston Aeros disbanded. Losing Houston, the team with Gordie Howe and his sons, was a major blow. With an odd number of teams, the NHL pronounced itself willing to absorb three WHA franchises: Edmonton, Winnipeg, and New England.[1] Howard Ballard, ever the obstructionist, once again led a large enough contingent of NHL owners to prevent the three-quarter majority necessary to ratify the agreement, but the financial pressures on the entire system were ineluctable. Further talks were planned during both team's seasons. An agreement which came up during these talks called for the Quebec Nordiques to also be accepted, leaving Cincinnati, Indianapolis and Birmingham out of the merged league. "The NHL really didn't want any of us," said Howard Baldwin, owner of the Whalers during negotiations. "But they knew if they didn't take the three teams from Canada, there would be a huge hue and cry in Canada. The only franchise they took from the United States was mine because we were the most well-funded team and in a major market."[2]

For the second year in a row Johnny Bassett's Bulls were deemed unworthy. Birmingham's size and proximity to Atlanta had something to do with it, but so too did the staid NHL's reluctance to embrace the maverick who had alienated one of their signature franchises while he ran the Toronto Toros. As far as the NHL was concerned, Bassett was a rebellious troublemaker. Being frozen out did not entirely put Bassett out in the cold, however. A positive development in the negotiations was the possibility of the surviving WHA teams paying an indemnity to those forced to fold. Bassett, gritty and competitive as always, did not

119

fold his team and simply await a check. Instead, he undertook a third retrofit of his roster, this time with an emphasis on youth that changed hockey in his native country. Bassett's radical youth movement in 1978-1979 was just an intense continuation of a personnel philosophy he had started in Toronto. It was a philosophy that caused consternation in the NHL and may explain the lack of interest by the elder league to bring Bassett and his franchise on board.

The Feudal Canadian Junior System

Canadian Junior hockey, officially known as the Canadian Amateur Hockey Association, is a cultural phenomenon embraced by fans in that country. The junior leagues are populated by players between the ages of 16 and 20 with franchises that fall into different tiers of competition. Many teams have affiliations with NHL parent clubs, akin to the A, AA, and AAA levels of minor league baseball in the United States. One of the most successful junior teams was the former Toronto Marlboros (now the Guelph Storm), which was a feeder team for the Maple Leafs. The Marlboros, also known as the Marlies, won several Memorial Cups in their league and had a passionate fan base.

The Marlboros and other teams in the Canadian Juniors oper-ated under an agreement with the NHL that the major-league clubs would not sign any players on the junior rosters until they had reached 20 years of age. This was beneficial for both entities. The junior teams had the chance to develop stars and rosters which were easier to sell to the ticket-buying public, while the NHL was provided a regular supply of battle-tested hockey players who had already endured many grow-ing pains.[3] This was, in fact, a well-balanced arrangement. It was also a closed system that kept players from making choices, and which stood in dramatic contrast to the trend toward players' freedom of movement which was then shaking professional sports. Plugged into the currents of larger trends, Bassett looked at this arrangement and saw a blatant example of what was wrong with professional sports.

Bassett felt the young players were being treated like serfs in a mod-ern form of hockey feudalism, paid as little as $60 a week while they could be sold to an NHL club for millions.[4] Given his belief that play-ers should be treated as professionals and not assets, Bassett went to work on a strategy which freed many players, promoted his ideal of what professional hockey could look like, and strengthened the WHA at the NHL's expense. "My dad always thought outside of the box and that's sort of what made him endearing to some people," said John C. Bassett.

"Junior players were considered amateurs back then and they couldn't be drafted until they were 21. My dad thought it was unfair and was a way to challenge the NHL. These players could go to war and vote at age 18, but they couldn't make any money playing hockey? My dad thought, 'If the NHL doesn't want to sign them, it doesn't mean we can't.'"[5] By modern lights, he was entirely correct, and his position was vindicated by subsequent events. To the contemporary hockey powers, however, which was so accustomed to operating in a tightly controlled environment, Bassett's strategy was dangerous.

The seeds of Bassett's commitment to freeing junior players from the bonds of the NHL's gentleman's agreement were planted by the actions of a mother with a keen eye for detail. Colleen Howe, wife of hockey legend Gordie Howe and mother of Marlboros stars Mark and Marty Howe, realized a small stipend the junior team paid to her sons could be interpreted as a salary. When she gained a favorable legal opinion that her sons could be considered professional, word got to the WHA's Houston Aeros, who quickly chose both brothers in the 1973 Professional Player Draft.[6] The selection of the Howes opened the door for other juniors to be drafted, a door which Bassett burst through with conviction. Bassett learned another Toronto Marlboro star was interested in moving to the WHA but had fears of being blackballed. Bassett not only signed the player, but also promised to fund any legal battles that might result.[7]

Bassett shocked Toronto when he signed Toronto Marlboros star center Wayne Dillon to a contract in 1973. The NHL and Harold Ballard cried foul over Bassett's signing of the 18-year-old, citing the arrangement between the league and the junior ranks. Bassett replied that a gentlemen's agreement between the NHL and the juniors had no meaning to him because the agreement was a violation of free trade and therefore illegal. "I will continue to defy their laws until they start conforming with the laws of Canada," Bassett told the press. "These kids can go to jail and drink booze. I don't see how a little hockey could hurt them."[8] Here, Bassett appeared as a free-wheeling, goal-oriented entrepreneur, which was more of an American archetype than one appreciated in conservative, slow-moving Toronto.

"I think Johnny liked being a burr in the saddle," recalled Howard Baldwin. "He was a rebel and he liked going against the grain. Johnny knew what the hell he was doing and what entertainment was all about."[9] Wayne Dillon had moderate success as a member of the Toros, scoring 30 goals in 1973-1974 and 29 in 1974-1975. Dillon left for the New York Rangers of the NHL in 1975, but his performance gave Bassett the confidence to keep signing juniors. In 1975, Bassett raided the Marlboros again, signing 17-year-old Mark Napier to a three-year, $200,000 contract.[10] Basset may have enjoyed the attention, but it should be pointed out the underage signings were shrewd hockey moves. Dillon enjoyed a solid NHL career after leaving Toronto. Napier played three seasons for Bassett, scoring an astonishing 60 goals in the 1976-1977 season before he left for the Montreal Canadiens in 1978. Napier became a 40-goal scorer for Montreal and won a Stanley Cup in 1979 with the Canadiens and in 1985 with the Edmonton Oilers.

After moving to Birmingham, Bassett continued to select juniors he felt would help the Bulls. Tony McKegney was a 20-year-old left wing that Bassett signed off the Kingston Canadians in 1978. Sadly, Bassett moved McKegney off the roster under pressure because of dissatisfaction among the Birmingham fan base over the player's skin color. In addition to McKegney, Bassett also signed Kingston center Ken Linesman. The 20-year-old became a pawn in a battle of wills between the WHA, NHL, and Bassett. The WHA, wanting to ease merger negotiations and ameliorate anger from the Canadian juniors, banned Linesman from playing and suspended Bassett for six months.[11] Linesman filed for an injunction that allowed him to play in the 1977-1978 season and Bassett was reinstated after only two months.[12] Linesman finished the season with 38 goals before he was moved to the Philadelphia Flyers. Both McKegney and Linesman also produced solid NHL careers, showing that Bassett had an eye for hockey talent and was not just a man looking to stir up a hornet's nest.

The 1978 offseason saw Bassett's signing of underage players increase dramatically as he saw the handwriting on the wall regarding the Bulls' future. As merger talks continued, the Bulls continued to be left out. With nothing to lose Bassett signed as many of the top junior players as he could for his team. Six under-age players were signed to one-year contracts at $60,000 apiece: goalie Pat Riggin, defensemen Gaston Gingras, Rob Ramage and Craig Hartsburg, and forwards Michel Goulet and Rick Vaive.

Bassett even signed his seventeen-year-old son to a contract to play in a series of exhibition games against the Finnish and Swedish national teams. "In March 1978 I played two games for the Bulls," John C. Bassett said.

> During the regular season two European teams traveled around playing various WHA teams in mid-season exhibition games. In the first game against Finland, there was a fun, five-minute period in which I centered Gilles Bilodeau and Dave Hanson. In the second game of the series against Sweden, I sat on the bench for 55-minutes before the coach put me in. He put me in at center between Frank Mahovlich and Paul Henderson. During that shift Henderson and I did the

give-and-go while crossing the blue line and I came in from the right side and got a shot on goal. The goalie made a block save though.[13]

The "Bullies" were out and the era of the "Baby Bulls" had begun. The agent who represented the "Baby Bulls" remembered Bassett's signings being the impetus forcing a merger agreement through. "The NHL did not want one team to get them all (junior players)," said Bill Waters. "They certainly didn't want Johnny to sell them. That only left the merger."[14] The two leagues agreed to a final merger in which the NHL absorbed Edmonton, Quebec, Winnipeg and New England.

New England Whalers owner Howard Baldwin confirmed that Bassett cemented the merger deal with his spate of underage signings. "When we knew we had struck out in our second round of merger talks, we knew we needed to cause the NHL pain and he really did it when he signed those young players to Birmingham," Baldwin said. "That really hit the NHL below the belt which was a great thing at the time. The NHL owners got mad and upset. They were saying, 'You're going to ruin hockey.' We needed someone who had the balls to stand up to them and Johnny did that."[15] Of course, Bassett's stratagem enriched his luckier peers who merged into the NHL. It did his hockey fortunes less long-term good.

Whether Bassett intended the signings to end the WHA-NHL war is open for conjecture, but his willingness to act in the WHA's best interest is not. By signing so many top-level junior players, Bassett could have commanded an outrageous sum for folding his franchise after the 1978-1979 season. Instead the Bulls owner collected $2.4 million from the four WHA survivors. The multi-million dollar "clean-up" fee was part of the merger agreement and, according to Howard Baldwin, was a typical selfless Bassett deal. "Johnny was instrumental in the merger in that he knew Birmingham wasn't going to get in the league," Baldwin explained. "But Johnny took a position of, 'This (financial settlement) is what I want for Birmingham,' and he never deviated from it. Some people overreached in what they demanded, but Johnny never did. He was straight and told us what it would take, and he offered any help he could."[16] This was no small gesture on Bassett's part. Cincinnati owner Bill DeWitt ended up securing $4.25 million to agree to leave professional hockey, almost two million dollars more than Bassett got for a team full of future NHL All-Stars.[17]

Leaving money on the table may have been Bassett's most selfless act to ensure the future of the surviving WHA teams, but it was not the most impactful. A deal Bassett brokered for a WHA rival resulted in his most memorable gift to the upstart hockey association. The biggest name in Canadian Junior Hockey was convinced by Bassett to join the younger league. The epic deal allowed the WHA to enjoy one last moment in the sun. It also solidified Johnny F. Bassett's reputation in hockey forever.

Bassett's Hockey Legacy—The Great One

Wayne Gretzky was a 17-year-old center from Brantford, Ontario, with a gift for hockey the likes of which had rarely if ever been seen before. Coming off a 70-goal season with the Sault Sainte Marie Greyhounds of the Ontario Major Junior Hockey League in 1977-1978, Gretzky was a phenom whom Bassett had kept his eyes on for over a decade. "My dad found out about Wayne when Gretzky was 6 or 7 years old," John C. Bassett said. "When he was at the *Telegram*, he tried to get a writer to go and do a story about Gretzky."[18]

Bassett followed the progress of Gretzky over the years. As the man who would one day change the face of hockey recalled, it was when he began to play in the same leagues as John C. Bassett that he and Johnny F. Bassett became acquainted. "The first time I crossed paths with him was at the age of ten," said Wayne Gretzky. "John, Jr. was playing hockey and we played against his team and Mr. Bassett was at the game. He was running the *Telegram* and he had a sportswriter named John Iaboni. Iaboni did a story and it was the first national piece done on me. He invited me to Toronto to participate in a shoot-out between periods of a Toros game when I was twelve years old."[19] Gretzky dominated the 1978 World Junior Championship in Montreal by scoring 17 points in just six games. Gretzky received his first professional contract offer from Bassett to play for the Birmingham Bulls during that tournament. Gretzky was all set to sign, but admitted his father put the brakes on any planned signing.

"In 1978, I was playing in the junior tournament in Montreal," Gretzky said, setting the stage for the events of Bassett's offer.

I was only 16-years old, but I was playing with some great wingers and I played really well against 19 and 20-year olds. Two weeks into the tournament, I got a call from Mr. Bassett to meet him in the hotel restaurant for coffee and donuts. I met with him. Now, I'm a 16-year old with no money and a blue-collar father who worked for Bell Telephone. Mr. Bassett explained he had signed Mark Napier, Wayne Dillon, and Ken Linesman, and he really thought I could turn professional and join his Birmingham Bulls. He offered me a two-year contract worth $180,000. When you are 16-years old and can't pay for your own coffee, you decide to sign. I called my dad and said I'm going to sign with the Bulls and Mr. Bassett is offering me $180,000 and I want to be a professional hockey player. My dad said, "That's fine, but you're going to finish 11th grade first." That plan got neutered.[20]

Bassett may have had flashbacks to his father preventing him from signing with the Maple Leafs two decades before, but Bassett never pressured Gretzky to defy his father. Instead, Bassett followed Gretzky's season in Sault Sainte Marie and checked in on Gretzky from time-to-time, keeping his ears open in case the hockey player and his father had a change of heart.

Following his stand out season at Sault Sainte Marie, Gretzky's agent, Gus Badali, was worried his client was so dominant, and the competition so inferior, that his star might risk injury against slower moving players.[21] The NHL was not an option because they still were honoring their commitment not to sign players from the juniors. That left the WHA and the man most noted for signing junior players was forced to demur for two reasons, one financial and the other personal. From a financial standpoint, Bassett was quickly outclassed by WHA teams which knew they would be absorbed in the coming merger. The price for Gretzky's services had grown significantly in just the year since Bassett's $180,000 offer. "Bassett said, 'I cannot pay you what you're asking,'" said Gus Badali. "But I know someone who could."[22] From a personal standpoint, Bassett was concerned that the under-sized Gretzky (6'0", 185 lbs.) might not survive a season in Birmingham, where the other WHA teams were looking forward to payback for the "Bullies'" actions the year before. "My dad had the first option, but he was afraid to be known as the man who killed Wayne Gretzky," recalled John C. Bassett.[23]

Instead, Bassett acted as a broker, cajoling other WHA owners to up the ante before the merger. He found a willing partner in Nelson Skalbania, owner of the Indianapolis Racers, who had also once co-owned the WHA's Edmonton Oilers. The Racers agreed to pay Gretzky the eye-popping sum of $575,000 over four years plus a $250,000 signing bonus. "I really wanted to sign with Mr. Bassett, but out of the blue the New England Whalers offered a contract much greater than what Bassett could do," Gretzky said. "But then the Racers one-upped the Whalers."[24]

Gretzky's stay in Indianapolis was very short. Skalbania's franchise could not dig its way out of debt. After just eight games in a Racers uniform, Gretzky was sold by Skalbania to the Edmonton Oilers, which were owned by Skalbania's former partner Peter Pocklington. Regardless of where Wayne Gretzky ended up in the WHA, the point was that Bassett had safely transferred the greatest talent in hockey out of the risky junior leagues. Gretzky embarked on a legendary career with the Edmonton Oilers and a handful of other NHL clubs during his 20 years in the league. Gretzky retired holding or sharing 61 league records including career goals (894), assists (1,962) and points (2,856). Gretzky also set a record with four separate 60-goal seasons. These career records do not count his statistics from the playoffs, which he participated in many times. Gretzky played in six Stanley Cup Finals, winning four (all with Edmonton). The Hall of Fame career earned Gretzky the nickname "The Great One."

While it is easy to say Wayne Gretzky would have still been "The Great One" had he spent three more seasons in the juniors, it is thought by some that his risk of injury was greater at that level than in the WHA.[25] The temptation to slow down the talented young star by hitting him or tangling him up in a corner would have been impossible for slower but larger players to resist. Also, the Oilers' rise to NHL prominence, including four straight Stanley Cup championships between 1983-1984 and 1987-1988, might not have transpired. Taking one more leap, had Gretzky's debut in the NHL been delayed by three years, he may not have been a member of the Los Angeles Kings in 1988, a transaction that is credited with saving hockey in the City of Angels. "God bless Bassett for that," said Alan Thicke, the late television actor and die-hard Kings fan, on Bassett's rescuing Gretzky from the junior ranks when he did. "We probably wouldn't have a Stanley Cup in Los Angeles if that hadn't taken place."[26]

"Looking back when you are a 17-year old kid that people aren't sure of and your name recognition is confined to southern Ontario, the reality is I probably wasn't ready to sell tickets and carry a franchise in Birmingham or Indianapolis," Gretzky said. "So, I got sold to Edmonton, which ended up being a great deal for me and the WHA teams that merged into the NHL. I could have signed with Mr. Bassett for less money, but as he would say I made the right decision. I always loved hockey uniforms and I thought the Toros/Bulls had the greatest uniforms and I thought maybe one day I could wear that uniform, but it never worked out."[27]

Bassett never took credit for discovering Wayne Gretzky or for his own role in getting "The Great One" to the WHA. Instead, he constantly joked about how he let the greatest talent in the history of hockey play for someone else's team. The move worked for Gretzky, but it also worked for the WHA in that final season. As Bassett's friend Peter Eby recalled, the WHA was a dead league in 1978-1979, and it needed a star attraction. "If Gretzky came to town, it was a success," Eby said.[28] In a real way, Gretzky's WHA stint allowed the league to sail into the merger as a going concern rather than as a failing rebel outfit.

The Baby Bulls

With only six teams in the league that season, Gretzky came to opposing arenas half a dozen times, increasing the average attendance each visit. For that Bassett deserves a lot of credit. He also deserves credit for giving the city of Birmingham, its fans and his players one more season when he did not have to. The fact that his Bulls did not make the cut still irks Bassett's friend John Eaton, who believes the powers that be in the NHL simply did not want Bassett because he had cost them so much money. "I think he did so much to challenge the NHL that they had to listen," Eaton said. "When the WHA folded, it was with the understanding that all teams would be absorbed. One of the cruel things was that the NHL blackballed Johnny. They just couldn't handle him. They would merge, but not with him."[29] If true, these charges do the NHL no credit. Instead of embracing the entrepreneurial zeal of a rival who admittedly hurt them in their pocketbooks, but whose skills could have enriched them all to an even greater extent, NHL owners chose the petty route of keeping Bassett out of their exclusive club. It was many years before the NHL operated on a par with more successful leagues such as the NFL. Had the NHL demonstrated a level of open-mindedness, or even profit-mindedness, it might have accepted Bassett and utilized his skills for its own enrichment.

The Bulls took to the ice in 1978-1979 with huge targets on their backs. The "Bullies'" rough tactics had rubbed many in the league the wrong way and many of Birmingham's opponents were looking for payback. Except for Dave Hanson, all the perpetrators from the previous roster were gone, leaving the underage players to suffer the retribution. After a rough start to the season, the young players started to coalesce under the tutelage of John Brophy, who coached the team that final season. Brophy also recounted that as the season went on, the recriminations against Birmingham stopped because the youngsters were starting to learn how to skate out of danger and take their shots on goal. "They certainly stood up for themselves, but they could also play," said Brophy. "Teams may have wanted to fight but if you put two to three goals on them, you take that out of them."[30] The "Baby Bulls" ended up being good but just not quite ready. They finished the season at 32–42 and out of the playoffs. Despite the losing record, most of the players gave hints of what was to come in their professional hockey careers.

In all, six "Baby Bulls" went on to play for many years in the NHL. Michael Goulet scored 500 goals in his professional career and became a member of the hockey Hall of Fame. Rob Ramage played for 15 seasons in the NHL, winning two Stanley Cups. Rick Vaive played until

1992 and made history as the first 50-goal scorer for the Toronto Maple Leafs in 1981-1982, the first of three straight 50 goal seasons. Craig Hartsburg played for a decade in the NHL and then became a head coach with stints leading the Chicago Blackhawks, Ottawa Senators, and Anaheim Ducks. Gaston Gingras alternated between the minors and the NHL throughout a career that spanned nearly two decades. Pat Riggin played goalie for several NHL teams until 1988. Not a bad legacy at all for the players given their first taste of major league hockey by Johnny Bassett.

"They were all underage guys, but you could tell they were going to go to the NHL," said their coach, Brophy. "They were easy to handle. We didn't worry about them not being developed. They could all skate and play."[31] At season's end the time came to disassemble the Bulls and Bassett's spate of signings paid off in ways that others may not have realized at the beginning of the year.

The only positive aspect of being left out of the merger was that Bassett received a generous monetary settlement which went a long way to alleviating the crushing fiscal pressure he was under from the folded Northmen and Toros/Bulls. Another asset in Bassett's favor was the demand for players under control to him on personal services contracts. "When people knew the WHA was going to fold, his players became available," Brophy explained.[32] Signing Bulls players to NHL contracts required compensation to their current employer. Bassett's partner Peter Eby explained the payment was a requirement of the merger. "They would have to purchase the contracts," Eby said of the NHL teams that wanted the "Baby Bulls." "There was a lot of sharing of resources in the league to get the merger deal. The teams that were going to move needed to share with the teams that weren't."[33] The money for the contracts combined with the $2.4 million clean-up fee Bassett was due for not being invited to merge meant that he could leave the WHA without debt and his reputation for integrity intact. The money allowed him to satisfy all Bulls debts and even debts related to the WFL, which endeared him to employees and creditors alike.[34]

"It never crossed our mind that we wouldn't get paid. Word got out that it was a good place to play," said coach John Brophy. "It is easy to talk about Mr. Bassett. He was a good guy, first of all. He was a busy man. He wasn't always around, but he would show up a lot and never interfered, never criticized."[35]

In addition to his own team, Bassett took a "league-first" mindset, constantly helping other teams even if it was to the detriment of his own franchise, such as getting Wayne Gretzky to Indianapolis. Part of Bassett's revenue went not just to his own team, but often to others as well.

"People with other teams would come and ask him to take them over because they needed the cash," Brophy said.[36]

The true legacy of Johnny F. Bassett's time in the WHA, what made him beloved, was the impact he had on the player selection system. Hockey players gained a level of control over their own careers that they have never relinquished and that their predecessors only dreamt of. Bassett's signing of multiple junior players to professional contracts gave the WHA star appeal and a reason for fans to watch. Just as the American Football League took away just enough business from the NFL to force a merger, so had the WHA made the NHL agree to a merger. This led to more jobs for hockey players, more NHL franchises in Canada and the United States, and proof that a team in the Deep South could work. Even though the Atlanta Flames fled to Canada, a precedent for hockey in the South had been set by Bassett. The Tampa Bay Lightning, Florida Panthers, Nashville Predators, and Carolina Hurricanes would not exist without Bassett's foray into Birmingham. "He was such an innovator," Gilles Leger said. "He was one of the last, great original individual owners in hockey. He helped to grow the game by giving so many guys the opportunity to make money. It helped that he could relate to them because of his own hockey and athletic background."[37]

Bassett got an idea of how much his contributions to hockey were appreciated one night when he and Steve Ehrhart were on a business trip in Oklahoma in the early 1980s. According to his friend, they took in a minor-league hockey game and an impromptu tribute broke out. "We were at a minor-league hockey game in Tulsa and nobody knew who we were in the arena," Ehrhart recalled.

> We went down by the bench and some of the players and coaches started banging their sticks against the boards in tribute to Johnny. They knew how iconic he was in hockey, having created so many jobs for so many people in the WHA, in Toronto, and in Birmingham. Johnny kind of shrugged it off, but the respect for him in the hockey world was enormous. He just joked it off, reminding everyone that he was the only man dumb enough not to sign Wayne Gretzky.[38]

In the opinion of Wayne Gretzky, the work of Bassett in the WHA paved the way for juniors to become professionals, hockey teams to find home in warm-weather locales, and the sport itself to become a national presence in the United States. "He was very much an innovator," Wayne Gretzky said about Bassett's position on junior players and expanding hockey to new markets.

> He didn't believe that because a league made a rule that it should become a law. He thought the laws that governed society were bigger than what a sports owner dictated. The rule was no 20-year old players and he just didn't believe that. The only Southwest team when I played was the Los Angeles Kings. No one had the

foresight that, Dallas, Phoenix and San Jose could do it (be viable NHL locations). The Bulls really opened a lot of doors, not just for those cities' success, but from a television marketing point of view. That team in Birmingham helped pave the way for hockey to become more of a national sport in the United States. Kids in the South and Southwest now grow up wanting to play hockey and that is part of his foresight.[39]

Bassett's Ottawa Nationals/Toronto Toros/Birmingham Bulls was just one of five franchises to survive all seven years of the WHA.[40] During that time Bassett further burnished his reputation as a sports idealist, a talented business operator, and a marketer extraordinaire. Honest, creative and shrewd, Bassett had navigated very turbulent waters and came out as crisp and clean as any man could. There were naïve missteps which gave credence to a dark chapter in history, but also a successful quixotic quest to change hockey for the better. Constantly adapting to change, every team Bassett put on the ice was at the least interesting and at the most competitive. Bassett was left out of professional sports as the 1980s dawned. He was rescued from financial ruin but was far removed from the income bracket he inhabited when he entered professional sports seven years before. A construction project with a tangential connection to a game he loved provided the funds necessary to jump back into football ownership yet again when another upstart league offered the opportunity in late 1982.

ELEVEN

Tennis, the USFL
and the Bandits

Johnny F. Bassett followed the trend of many North Americans in the early 1980s by moving to the Sun Belt, in his case, to Florida. During the 1970s, the so-called Sun Belt came into national consciousness as the destination for citizens relocating from former industrial communities in the North and Midwest. Florida was a leading recipient of new citizens searching for work and a sunny lifestyle. The sandy beaches, temperate climate, and lack of a state income tax all helped increase Florida's population. Florida was home to nine of the twelve fastest growing cities in the nation in the early 1980s.[1]

Bassett settled into Longboat Key, a small village just southwest of Tampa on Florida's Gulf Coast. Longboat Key and other locales had been the site of past Bassett family vacations in which the patriarch attempted to cram as much quality time as possible in with his children. Many of these vacations included his infectious laugh and attempts at what are now called "Dad Jokes." "At a vacation on Lake Placid, dad came down to the dock after having played golf," recalls youngest daughter Heidi Bassett-Blair.

> He was still wearing his golf pants and golf shirt. He said, 'I'm going water skiing and I'm not going to get wet and I'm going to land on the dock and be perfectly dry still in my clothes.' He tried a flying start from the dock and sank immediately and got sopping wet! Then he wiped out a few times and missed the dock landing. He comes out of the water with everyone laughing at him and he's laughing at himself. He never took himself too seriously and always had a way to laugh things off.[2]

Bassett also tried his best to take part in the hobbies and interest of his children. He allowed his son to skate in two exhibition games with the Bulls. He shared stories with Vicky and allowed his free-spirited daughter to accompany him on the road. "I had nothing but a good time with him," Vicky said. "I got to go on business trips with him. My dad

Johnny F. Bassett engaging in one of his favorite activities in Longboat Key, Florida. Bassett was a top-ranked tennis and squash player in Canada and played for Canada's Davis Cup team. Bassett was also a supporter of Nick Bollettieri's tennis academy and an admirer of Murray "Murf" Klauber, who established the area's tennis bona fides with The Colony Beach and Tennis Resort (courtesy the Bassett family).

would send me out to buy cigarettes. I wasn't old enough to drive or smoke, but he told me 'If you get pulled over, just cry a lot and I'll pretend to yell at you when the cops bring you home.'"[3] He also encouraged Carling's love of films and Heidi's passion for photography. "We both loved the movies," Carling said. "I remember going to double-features with him and afterwards going to the deli to get corned beef on rye. Growing up the way I did, we were always active and entertained."[4] Heidi had the rare treat of going on a cruise with her parents without the other children and an impromptu purchase by her dad made a vast difference in her life. "It was a nice trip and the only one that was just the three of us," Heidi recalled. "We walked into a store in St. Thomas and he bought me a Minolta 35mm camera. It was very spontaneous. That was the camera I started shooting with and I ended up being a photographer. He was very spontaneous but very meaningful in his giving."[5]

Johnny F. Bassett's love of life and desire to maximize the time he had with his children made him the fifth teenager in the house in many ways and led to some spontaneous purchases that Vicky Bassett remembered presenting Sue Bassett with household challenges. "He was so impulsive," Vicky Bassett said of her father. "One day he came home with snowmobiles and my mother did not like that at all. She told him to get rid of the snowmobiles, so of course he came home with motorcycles. He had traded the snowmobiles in for them!"[6]

The entrepreneur no longer owned a sports team, so he threw his all into researching a news business strategy and watching the burgeoning professional tennis career of his daughter Carling. Carling Bassett joined the women's professional tour in 1983 and enjoyed moderate success, once taking the legendary women's champion Chris Evert to the limit in the Amelia Island Championships. A competitor at the highest level, she was one of the best players in the world by any fair measure. Bassett followed his daughter from tournament to tournament and was her biggest fan. Carling still looks back in appreciation, knowing how difficult it was for her father to make the time and afford the travel while simultaneously attempting to start a new business and follow his cancer recovery procedures. "My dad loved being at the tournaments," Carling said. "I don't think it was too good for his health, though. He would smoke about 40 cigarettes during a match and constantly pace around. I know he was really, really proud."[7] His daughter's success no doubt spurred his current interest in tennis. The former Canadian champion and Davis Cup participant reentered the game in an impactful manner.

The Player's Club and Bassett's Tennis Legacy

The business that Bassett slowly built in the early 1980s was condominium development. Family vacations to Longboat Key in the 1960s made an indelible impression on Bassett. In addition to Longboat Key, Bassett became aware of all the natural and man-made attractions popping up throughout Florida in the 1970s and 1980s. "He fell in love with the place," explained his son, John C. Bassett. "He called the area between the Gulf, Tampa, and Orlando 'The Golden Horseshoe.' A person had access to beaches, sun, water, attractions, and a major airport."[8] Bassett studied the surrounding condominium developments and learned they had two main characteristics in common. First, most of them were built around golf courses. Second, most of the clientele were

Bassett with his daughter Carling in the 1970s on the tennis courts of The Colony. Carling Bassett-Seguso played tennis professionally from 1981 to 1988, winning two titles, and became the eighth-ranked player in the world at age 17. Carling was 11 when she became a student at Nick Bollettieri's tennis academy in Longboat Key, Florida (courtesy the Bassett family).

retirees. In fact, the Suncoast, as the Gulf coast cities in the Tampa Bay area are known, had a large population over the age of 65. This mirrored the state's overall aging demographic in which 17.4 percent of Florida's population exceeded that age.[9]

Bassett felt that a condominium complex built around tennis, a sport he was passionate about, would differentiate his project from most Florida condos and attract a younger, more dynamic crowd. Drawing on his connections in the sport, Bassett envisioned a community that would feature top of the line condo units built around a world class collection of tennis courts. The development would cater to professional athletes and wealthy amateurs. Bassett had an excellent template to follow in Longboat Key. The Colony Beach and Tennis Resort, established in 1952 as a beach resort but transformed in the late 1960s by Murray "Murf" Klauber into a tennis-themed luxury resort, was an international destination.[10] Bassett felt his development would add to the sterling tennis reputation Longboat Key had earned thanks to The Colony. The name Bassett chose for his vision underscored the clientele he hoped to attract: The Player's Club. To accomplish this goal required capital, so Bassett prepared himself mentally and physically to put together a proposal for lenders and investors. "I only wear a suit and tie when I go to the bank," Bassett once joked. "My hair is short when I'm raising money and long when I'm spending it."[11]

The vision slowly came to life as Bassett found lenders and raised money from friends such as Peter Eby and Donald Dell. The Player's Club was built between 1981 and 1983 and became an important part of the Longboat Key community. Donald Dell was a partner in The Player's Club and Carling Bassett's agent at ProServ. Dell explained that Bassett worked hard to market The Player's Club to professional tennis players, banking on their celebrity appeal to attract high-end tenants. "It wasn't just for tennis players, but Johnny wanted a celebrity type investor," said Dell. "We had clients of Pro Serv who bought. Yannick Noah bought a unit. There were four hundred units in four buildings. It certainly helped us at the start, and it was a very successful real estate deal for Johnny. It was a lot of fun and we made a lot of money."[12]

Bassett's wife remembers a litany of tennis greats choosing The Player's Club as their home and the positive impact it had on her husband. "It was such a wonderful condominium complex right on the Gulf of Mexico," Sue Bassett-Klauber said. "Johnny just loved that area. Having tennis on Longboat was the best of both worlds. There were days when it was literally 'The Player's Club,' as Donald Dell, Tom Okker, and a great deal of sports people became investors. That was the reputation. It was a place with real tennis players. It became a place with a lot of tennis energy."[13] The Player's Club secured a profitable occupancy rate before it opened in 1983. Another advantage to developing The Player's Club was it kept Bassett close to his daughter Carling as she began taking classes at an interesting Longboat Key school.

Nick Bollettieri was a career tennis coach with an innovative idea. He opened a tennis academy at The Colony in 1978, what later became known as IMG Academy, which provided a school curriculum in the morning and tennis training in the afternoon. The Bassetts enrolled eleven-year-old Carling and Bollettieri's tutoring helped her become a professional at fifteen and she climbed as high as eighth in world rankings. Bassett also donated vehicles and other material support for Bollettieri's school.[14] The Bollettieri Academy blossomed and became the starting point for the careers of players such as Andre Agassi, Monica Seles, Jim Courier, and Maria Sharapova thanks in part to Bassett's belief and support.

The Player's Club became one of Johnny F. Bassett's greatest legacies and exemplified his idealistic approach to professional sports. Making a great deal of money on a beachfront development was not enough for him. What made The Player's Club memorable as opposed to just another beach condo is the lasting impact it had on the game of tennis and Longboat Key. Bassett's commitment to following the work of Klauber and Bollettieri made Longboat Key the place to be in tennis. Players from around the world flocked to Longboat Key either to be trained or to live in a community geared to meeting their every need. That Bassett made a small fortune out of the deal was gravy compared to what The Player's Club came to symbolize. Peter Eby could tell just how important The Player's Club was to his lifelong friend. "Johnny would get just as excited about The Player's Club as he did one of his sports teams," Eby said. "It was wonderful. It was a very good development for the times. I bought a place there and had a great time with the kids growing up there. A number of us from Toronto bought places at The Player's Club."[15]

Bassett made quite a bit of money from the development of The Player's Club, more than enough to help him regain his financial footing following his time propping up the WFL and WHA. In his mid–40s, Bassett had reached a point in his life where someone might have been inclined to slow down and enjoy the fruits of their labor. With money in the bank, successful children, a loving wife, and a dream house on the Gulf of Mexico, a man who had been through many financial and health battles could be forgiven for wanting to spend his days overseeing his Canadian and American business holdings from the comfort of a chaise lounge, or while travelling the world to follow Carling. Bassett was always looking for something new, however, and his son picked up hints of the restlessness. "When dad developed The Player's Club, he'd get his friends to buy in, but then he would put the money into something else," John C. Bassett said.[16] One of those business opportunities came in 1982 when Bassett was approached by a man starting another rival professional football league. After initial hesitation, Bassett jumped into this new endeavor with both feet. This second Tampa Bay–based start-up provided Bassett with his greatest sporting achievement.

The United States Football League

The new professional football league Bassett threw himself into had been nearly two decades in the making. New Orleans businessman David Dixon surveyed the landscape of professional football in 1965 and saw opportunity. The NFL and AFL were beating each other bloody in their battle for supremacy in the fall, but Dixon saw the spring and early summer as a vast expanse of territory just waiting to be filled with footballs. "I've never believed Americans buy chewing gum only in the spring, make love only in the fall, and go to movies only in the summer," Dixon told potential investors.[17] Some of those potential investors were big names in sports, entertainment, and industry. "Paul Brown said, 'Dave, never let anyone talk you out of this,'" Dixon told *Sports Illustrated*. "The Ice Follies people were ready to go all the way, Gussie Busch of Anheuser-Busch, Kemmons Wilson of Holiday Inn, Gerry O'Neil of General Tire & Rubber, Nelson Bunker Hunt. Believe it or not, Walter O'Malley (owner of the Los Angeles Dodgers) wanted a piece."[18]

While Dixon crafted a spring/summer football plan that he successfully sold, the idea sat dormant while he worked to place an AFL or NFL team in New Orleans. Dixon promoted AFL exhibition games in New Orleans in the early 1960s, writing in advertisements that "attending now will put you in the front row of those fans who will put New Orleans in the major-league column."[19] Dixon organized the 1964 AFL All-Star Game to be played at Tulane Stadium to showcase New Orleans as a major-league city. Unfortunately, New Orleans embarrassed itself by refusing to shelve its Jim Crow legacy, even at such a late date. Black players were refused cab service, were turned away from restaurants, and generally made to feel unwelcome.[20] This led to a player boycott of the game, which was hastily rescheduled for Houston, Texas. The AFL soured on New Orleans because of the All-Star Game fiasco, but Dixon's promotions of football events gave him political leverage in dealing with NFL commissioner Pete Rozelle. Dixon had support from powerful United States Senator Russell Long and Congressman Hale Boggs, who assisted the NFL in avoiding anti-trust complications related to the AFL merger. Rozelle and the NFL awarded an expansion franchise to New Orleans to begin play in 1967 as repayment for their efforts. Christened the "Saints," New Orleans' new NFL team took up a great deal of Dixon's time over the next decade. Dixon was not an owner, but he still played a major role in the franchise, including the construction of the Saints' modern stadium, the Louisiana Superdome, in the mid–1970s.

Dixon came across numerous articles on the advent of cable television, including the founding of an all sports network, ESPN, in 1979. Realizing that cable channels needed thousands of hours of programming, Dixon dusted off his spring/summer football concept and hit the road seeking out new investors. Dixon also commissioned a study by Frank Magrid Associates to determine the viability of such an undertaking.[21] Dixon was greatly buoyed by the findings. Magrid's poll found that 76 percent of those who considered themselves football fans would want to watch football in spring/summer; 63 percent said they would buy tickets to attend spring/summer games; 53 percent said they would prefer football to baseball in spring/summer.[22]

Dixon studied the success of the American Football League and the folly of the World Football League and crafted a business plan for his new league, which he named the United States Football League. In what came to be known as the "Dixon Plan," Dixon laid out how his league would work. First, he would put teams in major markets so a national television contract would be easier to negotiate. All teams would play in NFL quality stadiums so fans would perceive the experience as major league. All players on a team's roster would come primarily from colleges and universities in the team's geographic area so fans would be familiar with them and want to see them. Finally, and most importantly, fiscal integrity would reign supreme. Teams would have player budgets dictated to them from the league office with each team putting up a $1.5 million line of credit and a pledge to budget for $6 million of operating costs over three years.[23] Dixon had a plan. Now he needed owners. One of the first presentations he made was to the man he considered the cream of the WFL.

Bassett Finds His Sweet Spot

Bassett was 42 years old and enjoying every minute of being Carling Bassett's father when David Dixon met with him in the spring of 1981. Bassett was the best owner in the WFL and arguably in the WHA too, but he was not keen on being the standard bearer for yet another under-financed, poorly run sports league. "I bought him (Dixon) lunch and told him he was crazy," Bassett said of the initial meeting.[24] He felt better after meeting with Dixon again and reading carefully over the new league's prospectus. Bassett allowed himself to dream again of establishing a model sports franchise, this time incorporating all the lessons learned from his past failures. Bassett felt a sense of confidence in the USFL that the WFL and WHA never provided. A key component was Dixon's stressing of fiscal responsibility in salaries and having a league-wide program to assist struggling owners. Bassett had reached deep into his own pockets to assist his WFL and WHA peers and knew he could not do so again. "My dad used to joke that in the WFL days he was the richest owner, but in the USFL days he was the poorest," said John C. Bassett. "My understanding is that he was asked to come in as the sane voice of someone who had been through all this before, who would show some guidance. He could also provide expertise on not overspending money."[25]

Bassett agreed to a USFL franchise but surprised many when it was not located in Memphis, Birmingham, or Toronto. In keeping with the league's edict of putting teams in metropolitan areas that already had NFL franchises or NFL quality stadiums, Bassett elected to start his franchise in Tampa. Bassett met with Tampa area sportswriters shortly after the USFL was announced in May 1982. The taint of the WFL's failure hung over him even though Bassett's Memphis Southmen franchise was a successful endeavor to its fans. Why, Bassett was asked, would his Tampa franchise in the USFL be any different? Bassett was candid in stating the WFL suffered self-inflicted wounds, but that the USFL approach was different and that he would personally build the Tampa Bay area a first-class football organization. "Well, fans were not the problem," Bassett said of the WFL. "The ownership was the problem. We will have $6 million up by the time we kick the ball off. We will be well-financed. We start now to begin a new business. We will look for space, for staff, for a public relations firm, for a nickname, a logo, players, jockstraps, the works."[26]

One of Bassett's first tasks was to generate excitement in the community. To start, he invited season ticket holders of the Tampa Bay Buccaneers of the NFL and Tampa Bay Rowdies of the North American Soccer League (NASL) to a meet and greet event at the Tampa Marriott in June 1982. The new USFL owner asked the fans for their input in creating an ideal stadium experience. What did the Bucs and Rowdies do right and wrong, in the fans' opinion? The meeting lasted well over 90 minutes as Bassett and the fans informally "exchanged ideas about the new USFL team and what he could do to make the enterprise more endearing and entertaining for fans."[27] Bassett explained that the meeting was illustrative of his philosophy that you must give the fans what they want to succeed in sports.

The ideal professional sports team, Bassett said, is the one which treats the man in the bleacher seats with the same respect as the man in the luxury box. "It was very interesting and quite refreshing to talk to one of the people who pays the freight," Bassett said after the meeting.

You don't often hear from that kind of guy, and he's the most important person. The guy who is last in line is the guy who counts. It's not the guy who builds the house. It's the guy who buys the house. It's not the guy who writes the news story. It's the guy who puts out the quarter to read the story. The fan is most paramount and he's the one who gets jacked around too much. The fan and what he is thinking is too often overlooked.[28]

This simple gesture made Bassett a beguiling figure in the region. It also taught him that a successful team in Tampa needed to counter-program the Buccaneers, emulate the Rowdies, *and* celebrate native Floridians, a demographic that for decades had their needs and heritage shunted aside in the name of tourism.

Bassett did not see competition in the Rowdies and Buccaneers. Instead he saw prime examples of what to do and what not to do. The Rowdies played a sport that had yet to be fully embraced in America in a league which expanded too rapidly and folded in 1985. Such perilous circumstances required the Rowdies to engage in creative marketing. Wearing colorful green and gold jerseys and playing quality soccer, the Rowdies also had a catchy jingle that appealed to its fans. People could be heard singing the team's slogan, "The Rowdies are a Kick in the Grass," all over Tampa Bay. The marketing combined with the fact the Rowdies had won one NASL championship and played for others led to sell-out crowds, a novelty in the NASL. When Bassett went to a Rowdies game in the summer of 1982, he was impressed that the large crowd included 13,103 children.

The NFL Buccaneers, on the other hand, played a popular sport before large crowds, but the miserly ways of their owner, Hugh Culverhouse, and the sarcastic humor of their coach, John McKay, kept fans at arm's length despite recent playoff appearances. Culverhouse was, to put it bluntly, a skinflint. He was averse to spending more than necessary, which was frustrating to fans since the team was on the verge of greatness. McKay's acerbic jokes resounded with appreciative reporters, but fans found his humor too barbed. For example, when asked after a loss about his team's execution, he cracked, "I'm all for it."[29] The Buccaneers also did not engage in very creative marketing, believing in the outmoded philosophy that an NFL game was an experience in and of itself.

John C. Bassett explained that his father's research on the major professional sports teams in the area revealed that the Rowdies were the better and more beloved organization:

> He loved how the Rowdies had marketed themselves. When he first arrived there, he saw Rowdies posters all over the place and he wanted to learn what made them successful. He wanted to learn because he thought they were the most successful franchise in the NASL. He knew the market was there. He knew the passion for sports was there. In the Rowdies, he saw that fans wanted to be passionate about something and there wasn't a lot of passion for the Buccaneers then.[30]

Bassett also recognized the latent anger and resentment many native or long-time Floridians held toward tourists. Bassett was a Canadian "snow-bird," a part-time resident of Florida who still maintained his residency in Toronto. Despite his willingness to build businesses in Florida, Bassett's dual residency embodied the mindset that Florida governor Bob Graham (1979–1987) called the "Cincinnati Factor." Graham's term described residents who had moved to the state physically, but their emotional connections were still to their hometowns such as Cincinnati, Ohio.[31] A more damning description of such residents is that they were merely treating Florida as a warm and temperate way station before their death.[32]

This resentment was not only generated by the perceived emotional neglect of Florida, but also by a perception that native Floridians were merely props in a fantastical version of the state. Florida beaches were refuges from the cares of the world and Orlando's theme parks, particularly Disney World, created a fantasy world which successfully transported guests from the real world into a relative virtual world of make believe. Native Floridians, derisively referred to as "Crackers" by tourists, grew disenchanted by their treatment. "Do native Floridians even exist, or are they merely faceless robots, standing by to change beds, take tickets, and serve fast food to people on the go?" an observer asked.[33]

By 1978 one of every eight jobs in Florida was generated by tourism, with the bulk of those jobs being low-paid and low-skilled.[34] In addition to the degrading jobs, Floridians viewed the increased traffic congestion, increased cost of living, and corresponding property tax spikes with a jaundiced eye. More egregious was the white washing of Florida heritage. A state with settlements dating back to the sixteenth century and a diversity of ecological wonders saw little of this bounty celebrated. Instead trick-performing orcas, water-skiing bathing beauties, and a very popular cartoon mouse were sought after.[35] The Tampa Bay Buccaneers were even named after a fictional pirate, Jose Gaspar, whose legendary pillaging of the Gulf of Mexico and Tampa Bay led to the annual Gasparilla Festival. There is no proof that Gaspar ever existed, but his legend boosted tourism in the Tampa Bay Area and spurred many "pirate cruises."[36] Local residents holding the integrity of their heritage as a priority blanched at the state of their state. Orlando was a fantasy world and the Gulf beaches were the nation's sandbox.[37]

Bassett had a clear understanding of the needs of the Tampa sports fan in 1982. There was a clamor in the native populace for a professional football team more embraceable than the Bucs and more aligned with the family-friendly Rowdies. There was also a uniquely Floridian cry for any kind of institution to recognize the personality and talent of the state's natives and long-time residents. Bassett promised to build it, step-by-step.

Overwhelming the Bucs

Bassett was true to his word and over the summer his team quickly took shape. Some of the leading names joining Bassett's franchise as investors were: Stephen Arky, a prominent Miami lawyer and civic leader; Ralph Campbell, an insurance executive who Bassett had gotten to know through both men's association with Nick Bollettieri; and, in a move that increased Tampa Bay's national USFL profile immensely, Burt Reynolds, Hollywood superstar. "Bringing Burt Reynolds on board was a tremendous marketing move," said Jim McVay, the Director of

Bassett (left) with Bandits general partners Burt Reynolds (center) and Stephen Arky (right) at Tampa Stadium before "Burt's Bash," a January 1984 fan festival in which the Hollywood legend mingled with fans in a pre-training camp party. The event attracted 25,000 fans and featured food, music, giveaways, and player autographs, exemplifying Bassett's belief in treating fans to more than just a football game (courtesy Steve Ehrhart).

Marketing for the still unnamed team, and one of Bassett's first hires. "Burt was bigger than Tom Hanks, George Clooney, and Brad Pitt combined. He was a king. In addition to being a movie star, he had been a football player at Florida State University."[38] Jim McVay came to the USFL with a good idea of how Bassett operated. McVay's father John was the head coach of the Memphis Southmen in the WFL and young Jim remembered hearing about the energetic, idealistic man his father reported to. "I'm sure I met him in Memphis, but it would have just been a quick meeting," McVay said. "But I knew he was a brilliant guy. He had a lot of thoughts on a lot more than sports. He was just a lot of fun to be around."[39] Within a matter of months this genial Canadian could be easily confused with a native of Clearwater, Bradenton, or Ocala. First, he needed to counter the Buccaneers.

Professional football fans in Tampa Bay were looking for a football team to fall in love with in 1982. The NFL suspended operations after the second week of the 1982 season as the battle over salaries between the owners and players boiled over. The NFLPA demanded over 50 percent of gross revenues while the owners were far from willing to make that concession. The NFL went dark following the second Monday Night Game of the season. The strike left fans of professional football with nothing to watch on Sunday afternoons but Canadian games and Division III collegiate contests. Instead of being able to satisfy their hunger for professional football, fans found themselves on an unwanted crash diet, and they were not happy about it. One man many players and fans blamed for the stalemate was Tampa Bay Buccaneers owner Hugh F. Culverhouse. A self-made millionaire, Culverhouse was one of the keenest legal and financial minds of the time. A former boxer and IRS executive, Culverhouse advocated taking a hard line against the players even if it meant sacrificing an entire football season. To be fair, Culverhouse was not the only owner to take this view, but in Tampa it was easy to view him as the face of the strike.

In addition to his scorched earth strategy in labor issues, Culverhouse also earned a reputation as someone who raked in a windfall profit at the expense of his players and fans. The NFLPA released figures on team revenue in relation to salary shortly before going out on strike. The information was particularly damaging to Culverhouse. The Tampa Bay Buccaneers took in $17.04 million in gross revenue, good for fifth highest in the league in 1981. Culverhouse did not spend much of that revenue on keeping his team competitive, however. The Bucs were in the bottom quarter of the league in salaries, paying an average of $76,761 per player.[40] Fans could be forgiven for thinking that their favorite team's owner was more concerned with milking the franchise to enrich himself rather than getting over the top and into a Super Bowl. Hugh Culverhouse was a Southern-style Harold Ballard: stubborn and not willing to change. A sports owner grown complacent with making millions off a franchise that was the only game in town. Culverhouse knew the fans had to come because there was no viable alternative. He saw no reason to extend himself when it came to marketing, amenities, or much of anything else.

Bassett could not have dreamt of such a stroke of luck as finding Harold Ballard's double in Tampa. Pleasing fans was in Bassett's DNA. Bassett had intuitively known how to get under Ballard's skin. He intended to do the same to Culverhouse. Over the next several months Bassett marketed his USFL team as the anti–Bucs just as he had marketed the Toros as the anti–Leafs. Bassett was going to win the attendance war this time, and he was going to do it with an emphasis on making his newly named Tampa Bay Bandit's "Florida's Team" the way the Dallas Cowboys embraced their unofficial title of "America's Team." First, he needed players.

A Team of Floridians for Floridians

Bassett and his organization invited over 550 players to try out for the team one October weekend. The try-outs were held at Tampa's Jesuit High School and led to the signing of only two players: center Ray "Chubby" Davies and kicker Alvaro Arenas.[41] The weekend did not produce many legitimate players, but that was beside the point. Bassett's motive in inviting hundreds of Floridian gridiron Walter Mitty's was to encourage their dreams and to make the Bandits relatable to the common fan. "Everybody has something inside him that says he can play professional football," Bassett said. "You can't take that dream away. Everybody wants to be Burt Reynolds or Bert Jones. And there's nothing wrong with that. If I weren't 43 and owned the team and had bad knees, I'd be out there too.... To be good-looking, rich and famous, that's what America's all about. That's why all these people are out here."[42] At the very least, Bassett knew that 553 fans would go home and brag about the time they had a tryout with the Bandits, and all of them had family and friends.

Florida became particularly renowned for college football in the early 1980s. The programs at Florida, Florida State, and the University of Miami were all national title contenders. Each school had fielded top teams at various points, but this was the first time they were all excellent together. Bassett's staking of the Tampa Bay claim for the USFL did not just gain him a large fan base, it gave him access to the cream of college football. Because of the USFL's mission to build teams with local talent, the Bandits had first dibs on arguably the finest college players in the country. Florida State quarterback Jimmy Jordan was one of Bassett's earliest signees. A Tallahassee native and Tangerine Bowl MVP, Jordan led the Seminoles to an 11–0 record in 1979. A draft choice of the New England Patriots, Jordan was cut shortly after the end of training camp in 1982. Jordan felt betrayed and was ready to walk away from football when his family received a call from Bugsy Engelberg, Bassett's director of football operations. "There is a new league and we have a team in Tampa owned by Johnny Bassett and Burt Reynolds," Jordan recalled Engelberg telling him. "We've got a national television contract with ABC and we're going to be a big deal. We want you as a quarterback."[43] Talk about an offer he could not refuse. Many similar conversations took place throughout the Sunshine State. Within weeks, the Bandits were loaded with dozens of players who played at either Florida, Florida State, Florida A&M, Bethune-Cookman, or the University of Miami. These included wide receiver Eric Truvillion and quarterback Nathaniel Koonce (Florida A&M), linebacker Paul Piurowski and guard Ron Simmons (Florida State), and quarterback John Reaves (Florida).

The signing of Reaves was one of Bassett's more controversial personnel decisions. Reaves was well into the second half of his career at 33 years of age. A star at Tampa's Robinson High School, Reaves became a record-setting quarterback at the University of Florida and then a first-round draft choice of the Philadelphia Eagles in 1972. Reaves' NFL career was solid if unspectacular. Unfortunately, Reaves became addicted to narcotics and he admittedly hit rock-bottom in the late 1970s and early 1980s. "I went on a binge for around six to eight months," Reaves stated in an early 1980s interview. "I got to using cocaine and Quaaludes every day. Not long after, my liver was swollen. I was strung out. I couldn't quit."[44] His career took him to Cincinnati and Minnesota, as well. Reaves was arrested multiple times for driving while intoxicated and getting into a fight with a bar manager, but he turned his life around and dedicated himself to Christ.[45] At the same time, he rededicated himself to football. Bassett did not view Reaves as a risk. He viewed him as a local hero well on his way to redemption. That was a story that the owner thought would have gate appeal. If the ticket buying public still wanted to see the former Gator star throw the ball around, that is what Bassett would give them. It also helped that the head coach Bassett hired knew a little something about throwing the ball around.

Stephen Orr Spurrier did not have much national name recognition, but in Florida he was football royalty. A quarterback, Spurrier won the Heisman Trophy at the University of Florida in 1966, the first player in school history to achieve that feat. Spurrier also led the Gators to their most successful era at that point, winning games in dramatic fashion. Spurrier led his team from behind to defeat Auburn 30–27 during his Heisman-winning season, a game in which Spurrier kicked the game-winning 45-yard field goal. It was a performance that is still discussed in awed tones around Gainesville, Florida, half a century later. Spurrier's collegiate success did not translate to the NFL. He was used primarily as a back-up in San Francisco, during a career that lasted for a decade. Spurrier returned to the Sunshine State in 1976, as the starting quarterback for the expansion Tampa Bay Buccaneers and played on a team which lost all fourteen games. Due to Spurrier's popularity and solid performance, the Tampa media named him the team's Most Valuable Player. His lengthy time as an NFL backup gave him plenty of opportunity to observe and analyze the professional game, which bore dividends when he became a coach.

Spurrier stayed in the game as a quarterback coach at Florida and Georgia Tech before taking the offensive coordinator position at Duke. Duke was a basketball school with low football expectations, but Spurrier saw no reason why the Blue Devils could not field an imaginative and winning team. He and Bassett were on the same wavelength when it came to football style. Bassett wanted a coach who could run a high-powered, imaginative offense. It was his belief that an ideal team gave the fans an exciting, wide-open offense that put up points by the bushel, not the ground and pound game the NFL was putting on the field. "I want my team to be interesting, exciting and fun," Bassett said. "We're not looking for any 7–6 ballgames."[46] *Tampa Tribune* sports columnist Tom McEwen was a big Spurrier fan and put a bug in Bassett's ear about the coach. Bassett, who was seriously considering former NFL coaches Jack Pardee and Howard Schnellenberger, along with former University of Tampa coach Fran Curci, agreed to interview Spurrier, but as an offensive coordinator.[47] Spurrier recalled being contacted by Bassett's emissary Bugsy Engelberg.

"Engelberg called me up to offer me the job of offensive coordinator," Spurrier said. "Now, Bugsy called everybody 'Bubba.' And when someone calls you Bubba, you call them Bubba right back. He said, 'Bubba, we want you as offensive coordinator.' I said, 'Well, Bubba, I'm already an offensive coordinator and the next time I move, I'm going to be a head coach.' He said, 'Really?' and I said, 'Yep, really.' He said, 'Well, I'll tell Bassett you want to be head coach.'"[48] Bassett was impressed with Spurrier's chutzpah and flew to Durham, North Carolina, to interview the bold young man. "At Duke in 1982, we were fourth in the nation in total offense, so we were doing pretty good," Spurrier said of the hand he played against Bassett in the interview. "We had a good time. Bassett had a steak he liked, and we had some vodka martinis he really liked. On the way back he said, 'Steve, I want you to come down and be my head coach.' I said, 'Mr. Bassett, I will take that job.'"[49]

The naming of the 37-year-old Steve Spurrier as head coach thrilled his home state. There was excitement in Tampa Bay at the prospect of the local football hero getting his first head coaching job. Bassett beamed at the introductory press conference. In Steve Spurrier he had found a creative offensive mind, but more importantly, a Florida football hero with great name recognition. To top it off, Spurrier's brief affiliation with the Buccaneers meant he had a marketing coup over his inner-city rival, and he tweaked Culverhouse by bringing up one of the Bucs' darkest hours. "Some people said it was an unwise decision to go with a player who quarterbacked a team that didn't win a game," Bassett said. "But I notice he was named their most valuable player that year. I think he'll make a hell of a coach."[50]

Meanwhile, over at One Buccaneer Place, Hugh Culverhouse fumed at being one-upped. If USFL owners did not realize what Bassett had in Spurrier and a bevy of Florida and Florida State players, the Bucs owner did. "Tampa is one of the most rabid 'Gator Nation' cities in the state of Florida," Culverhouse's son, Hugh, Jr., said. "Their head coach and quarterback are former Gators. You couldn't throw dirt in the face of my dad more and it was the smartest marketing thing."[51] Clearly, Bassett knew that.

For his part Spurrier promised Bandit fans that he intended to employ a wide-open offense that would counter the run-oriented offense preferred by the Buccaneers. He also hinted that Bandit players would be a part of the community, a philosophy perfectly in line with Bassett's. "We're going to throw the ball around," Spurrier announced. "I believe you can have a wide-open attack and still play safely. We're going to make it exciting for the fans. We want a team they can be proud of. We're going to have the kind of players who will get out in the community and we'll be accessible and available at all times."[52] Bassett had not just hired a head football coach. He hired a man whose views on football and promotion aligned perfectly with his own. The impact on tickets sales was immediate.

The Tampa Bay Bandits sold 10,000 season tickets before Spurrier was named head coach.[53] After Spurrier was hired, they sold thousands more. While season tickets are nice, what Jim McVay remembered is that the Bandits became the "in" thing in Tampa. People who bought single-game tickets would buy the best seats because they wanted to be close to the action that they were certain Spurrier would provide. "We sold all the best seats," McVay said.[54] This was particularly important considering where the Bandits were going to play their games. Bassett inked a deal with the Tampa Sports Authority for the right to play at Tampa Stadium beginning in 1983. Tampa Stadium, with a seating capacity of 72,000, was the largest venue for a Bassett team. The size could prove to be a problem if Bassett could not fill the seats. The sight of WFL stadiums at less than quarter capacity helped kill that league and Bassett did not want to be the overseer of a repeat. The idea that a USFL team was becoming the biggest news story in town made the Bandits unique in the league. Elsewhere, teams settled for being a new attraction for the spring, but Bassett wanted his Bandits to be a year-round attraction.

There was also the added benefit of Bassett's lease breaking the stranglehold Hugh Culverhouse held on Tampa Bay football. The owner had worked for years to make his Buccaneers a Tampa football monopoly, going so far as to battle Miami Dolphins owner Joe Robbie over televised games. The NFL mandated for years that if a home game did not sell out within 72-hours of kickoff, the game could not be televised in its home market. This was done to protect ticket sales. Culverhouse went one step further, however, and instituted a secondary blackout. This meant that if the Bucs did not sell out a home game, then neither the Bucs game nor any Dolphins game could be shown on Tampa television.[55] In short, if Culverhouse could not convince enough Floridians in his area to buy Bucs tickets, he would make sure they could not watch any games involving Florida teams. This decision initiated a feud between Culverhouse and Robbie that culminated in the Bucs and Dolphins cancelling their very popular annual pre-season games known as "The Battle of Florida."[56]

Culverhouse became unhinged when Bassett signed his Tampa Stadium lease, viewing it as an act of treason by the Tampa Sports Authority. He took it very personally. The Bucs' owner retaliated through petty and self-defeating means. Culverhouse fired the Buccaneers' statistician, a contract employee, when he learned the man was also going to keep statistics for the Bandits. Culverhouse later cancelled a contract with the local department store that provided uniforms for the Swash-Buc-lers, the team's cheerleaders, when he learned it was also making uniforms for the Bandits' cheerleaders.[57] Bassett received the news of his chief's competitors' mania warmly as he worked to establish a gridiron bulwark in the hearts and minds of Floridians everywhere. Bassett emerged as a positive, cheerful, energetic owner while Culverhouse appeared cranky and small-minded.

Bassett opened a merchandise shop in the Tampa Bay Center Mall, located directly across the street from Tampa Stadium. Opened just in time for the Christmas season, the store could not keep up with demand. The most popular item was a glow in the dark t-shirt depicting the Bandits logo, a lone horseman. The logo became tremendously popular. Sales figures showed Bandits merchandise outselling Tampa Bay Buccaneer merchandise before the inaugural season kicked off.[58] This demand for tickets and merchandise led many in the USFL to realize that Johnny F. Bassett was crazy like a fox and that his choice of Spurrier was inspired. The amount of people who came out to watch practices was staggering.

The regular season opener against the Boston Breakers was just over a month away when the Bandits began training camp in early February. In a testament to the effectiveness of Bassett's marketing campaign, the opening of training camp was a leading news story in Tampa and throughout the state of Florida. Over 300 fans turned out to watch the Bandits perform simple calisthenics and workout. The Bandits held an unpublicized intra-squad scrimmage later in the week. Simple word-of-mouth attracted more than 1,200 fans to come out for the scrimmage.[59] Attendance at a scrimmage was free, but the fans also proved to be willing ticket-buyers. Twenty-eight thousand single-game tickets for the opener were sold as well as 20,000 season tickets. Season tickets were sold on an installment plan and the Bandits were pleased to learn that 82 percent of the passes had been completely paid for.[60] Bassett was proving his point that Tampa Bay was the perfect laboratory for his experiment in sports idealism. "Fans here are just very supportive," said team publicity director D.J. Mackovets. "It's an excellent sports town. We've sold 20,000 tickets on fluff, hype and promises before anyone even saw a football. It's amazing that we are doing so well. Fans are just now starting to see the real product."[61] Bassett proved how far he was willing to go to create "Florida's Team." Midway through training camp, he defied USFL executives so that fans from Key West to Pensacola could see the Bandits' real product on television.

The Bandits Take the Field—Very Early

Pre-season exhibition games have been around for decades. The games are a chance for coaches to evaluate players in a live setting during a game that does not count in the official standings. They have become a rite of football training camp. The USFL decided to forego this rite during their inaugural season. Steve Ehrhart explained the USFL did not schedule pre-season games in deference to their broadcast partner ABC. "ABC wanted the very first week of the season to be a premiere week," the former USFL executive said. "They didn't want to dilute the product by having exposure in advance."[62] Bassett felt that stance was ridiculous and said so. "In the NFL, they play four pre-season games and they're looking to replace maybe six players," Bassett said, understating the number of players typically released. "We're starting from scratch. The NFL teams don't need pre-season games. We do."[63]

Standing by both his football principles and his desire to create buzz for his team across the peninsula, Bassett arranged a series of pre-season games against the Boston Breakers, Washington Federals, and Philadelphia Stars. The games were scheduled in Orlando and Jacksonville to broaden the Bandits appeal throughout Florida. Going one step further, Bassett sold the television rights for the games to Tampa independent station WTOG. In a coup for Bassett, WTOG was a cable station which meant the games could be broadcast in every major city in Florida. When pressure was applied on the USFL by ABC, Bassett compromised—a bit. He agreed to not stage "games." Instead he converted the games into "controlled scrimmages," which meant no kick-offs, no 30-second clock, no two-minute warning, no penalties, no advancing of fumbles or interceptions, and coaches in the huddle and on the field during play.[64] The compromise was accepted, but many in the USFL and at ABC were not thrilled. "There was an awful lot of anguish over that, but Johnny went ahead and did it," Steve Ehrhart said. "He covered it by saying, 'These are just scrimmages. I'm inviting a team over because they are in Florida for training camp.' Other teams scrimmaged, but Johnny sold the broadcast rights. He always pushed the envelope."[65]

"Johnny would find a way to do whatever he wanted to do," said Jim McVay. "It was not an actual game. He knew the other team wanted to get some practice in. When you have a new league, you want any revenue stream you can get."[66] Bassett's son is quite familiar with his father's methods, particularly his ability to parse terms. "Read between the lines, I'm not breaking any rules," John C. Bassett said of his father's mindset.[67] The Bandits defeated the Boston Breakers 10–3 in Orlando. The scrimmage was a financial success for WTOG, which sold the game to multiple sponsors. The scrimmage was also a marketing victory for Bassett. While only 247 fans attended due to torrential rain, the mere fact the scrimmage was televised was historic. No NFL scrimmage had ever been shown on live television before, much less on a syndicated network.[68]

"The league didn't want us to play on TV. They didn't even want us to play," a defiant Bassett said. "Of course, they've never been involved in putting together a franchise and I have. If we weren't playing any pre-season games our opening day product would be significantly reduced. Any team in this league that doesn't play two or three head-knockers will be in serious trouble."[69] Bassett was buoyed by the spirit of the few fans who showed up. In a shrewd move, he promised them free tickets to the next Orlando scrimmage, making positive inroads to Tampa's neighbor to the northeast.[70] The other two scrimmage also produced victories, 20–7 over the Washington Federals in Jacksonville and 31–3 over the Philadelphia Stars in Orlando. While not box office draws, the Bandits got notoriety throughout Florida and the team got quality practice which is precisely what Bassett wanted. His defiant tone against the USFL also struck a chord with Floridian football fans. There was the obvious joy over watching a new team play a sport they loved, but more than that, fans were excited when the Bandits' owner stood up to the powers-that-be in New York and forced them to accept a compromise. It seemed their new owner was standing up for their new team, and the bond between Bassett and the fans grew even stronger. This was a grand scene to witness for generations of Floridians forced to kowtow to New Yorkers and Chicagoans through their jobs in the tourism industry. That, more than any other cultural pattern, resonated along Florida's Suncoast.

Twelve

‖‖‖‖‖‖‖‖‖‖‖‖‖‖‖‖‖‖‖‖‖‖‖‖‖‖‖‖‖‖‖‖

Bandit-Ball

The Tampa Bay area, also known as the Florida Suncoast, is composed of the counties which surround its eponymous body of water. Included in these counties are the well-known cities of Tampa, St. Petersburg, and Clearwater along with the famous Gulf of Mexico beaches Clearwater Beach, Indian Rocks Beach, Treasure Island, and more. Early travelers to the region were financially well-off Northerners who spent weeks at Henry Plant's Tampa Bay Hotel, now the administration building of the University of Tampa. Travel to the area became possible for more and more Americans in the early twentieth century and Tampa Bay became a popular destination with the first mass wave of New Yorkers vacationing in the area in 1909 and travelers from the Midwest arriving en masse in 1913.[1] The region became a national destination for more of these travelers in the 1920s when numerous hotels were built primarily in Pinellas and Hillsborough Counties.[2] Many of these travelers returned to Florida during their "golden years." Senior communities dedicated to retirees from primarily New York and the Midwest sprouted up throughout the Tampa Bay region. The most famous of these is Sun City Center, a 12,000-acre senior community 25 miles south of Tampa whose demographics in the 1970s and 1980s included retirees primarily from New York, Michigan, and Illinois.[3] Culturally, retirees remained loyal to their home cities, eschewing local customs and traditions for their own, which they viewed as superior. The birth of the Tampa Bay Buccaneers is a vivid illustration of the phenomenon.

The NFL expanded into the Tampa Bay area in 1974, but even this civic accomplishment was muted somewhat by the strategic placement of the franchise divisionally for the benefit of Northern transplants to Florida. The Buccaneers were placed in the NFC Central Division, a division which featured the Chicago Bears, Detroit Lions, Green Bay Packers, and Minnesota Vikings. This put the Bucs at a distinct disadvantage. The team was required to make numerous long-distance flights during the season. Worse for neophyte Bucs fans, the NFL advertised the placement as a wonderful opportunity for retired and relocated fans of the Midwestern teams to see their favorite clubs at Tampa Stadium and for fans still in the North to take a Florida vacation to see a game.[4] The NFL eventually realigned in 2002, placing the Bucs in a division with teams in Atlanta, Charlotte, and New Orleans, but this did little to assuage Floridians in the 1970s and 1980s who felt everything in their lives was liable to be altered for the benefit of New York and Chicago.

Bassett shrewdly exploited the "us" vs. "them" mentality Floridians held towards New Yorkers and Midwesterners by painting the Bandits as a scrappy band of Floridians who would fight against the inherent tyranny of outsiders from New York, Chicago and the rest of the Midwest. Fortunately, USFL teams from Chicago and New York played right into Bassett's hands.

We Don't Care How You Do It Up North!

Bassett was a firm believer in the Dixon Plan and its rule that USFL franchises should adhere to strict budgets when acquiring players. Chicago Blitz coach George Allen violated this rule immediately. Allen believed in spending on veteran players and did not want a budget dictated to him as he was procuring talent for the Chicago franchise. Allen created a stir by signing "big-name" former NFL stars such as quarterback Greg Landry and stealing Chicago Bears third-round draft choice Tim Wrightman. As an advocate for the Dixon Plan, Bassett held firm and went toe-to-toe with Allen. Bassett and other Dixon Plan supporters carried the day. The 1983 budget for USFL players was $1.8 million per team. As a caveat to Allen and those who wanted unfettered spending, the committee agreed that $1.2 of the $1.8 million could be spent on 38 of the 40 roster players, leaving $600,000 to spend on "marquee players."[5] George Allen continued the "future is now" philosophy he had employed as the boss of the NFL Washington Redskins. In addition to Greg Landry, the Blitz signed NFL players Luther Bradley, Joe Ehrmann, Karl Lorch, Ed Smith, and Stan White.[6] The signings took the Blitz well over the agreed upon budget. Bassett worried that Allen's signings were a shot across the bow of the NFL, an act of aggression that would cause a bidding war the USFL could not possibly win in the long term. Ironically, Bassett had fired such a shot when he signed Larry Csonka, Jim Kiick, and Paul Warfield. Those signings had a ripple effect which raised player salaries. The higher cost of doing business killed the WFL because it did not have the financial wherewithal to sustain itself. Bassett worried a repeat of that mistake was happening in the USFL. "We have never factored the NFL into our program at any point," Bassett said in explaining how the USFL wanted to avoid the mistakes of the WFL. "The first couple of years we will be non-competitive with the NFL."[7]

"George Allen was once charged with exceeding an unlimited budget," quipped Steve Ehrhart, who witnessed Bassett and Allen engage in lively conversations at owner's meetings during the roster-stocking phase of the USFL. "Johnny was telling George, 'You're going to blow up this league if you keep spending.'"[8] Bassett made a public enemy out of Allen and castigated the coach and his Chicago team for months as exemplars of big city spenders out of touch with the goal of the USFL. Wrapping himself up in the garb of the Floridian everyman, Bassett once chided Allen without naming him, broadly equating Allen to the stereotypical Northern industrialist who selfishly promoted his own goals at the expense of everyday Floridians. "I think the biggest problem in the league is spending too much money," Bassett said bluntly.

> That's because ego gets in the way. And because of guys who don't know how to run their teams and can't sell tickets by doing their jobs properly. So, they have so much money they go to their wallets and figure if they sign Joe Ace here and Harry Ace there and So-and-So Ace there, their teams will win, and people will come. Then the next guy has to do it. History shows you're in the last throes of a dying civilization when you're paying athletes, gladiators and entertainers more than you pay your presidents. That's a joke. When your third-string linebacker makes more than a captain in a police force, something's wrong. Or more than a high school principal. Or more than a college professor.[9]

Allen grew tired of Bassett's haranguing and growled that both Bassett and the Bandits were a group of softies, relying on finesse and a roster full of beach boys.[10] The public back-and-forth worked for Bassett at the ticket window. A great number—46,585 fans—turned out to Tampa Stadium the first time the Blitz came to town. Unfortunately for Bassett, a marketing victory was all he got as Chicago rolled over Tampa Bay 42–3. Bassett eventually got the last laugh over Allen. Dr. Ted Dietrich, owner of the Chicago franchise, lost a great deal of money during the inaugural season. The Blitz averaged only 18,000 fans per game, drawing fewer than 14,000 on five separate occasions despite Allen's team of "stars."[11] Dietrich lost so much money he traded the entire franchise to Arizona so he could at least stay closer to his Phoenix home. In an unusual deal, all Blitz players, coaches, and personnel were traded for the entire roster of the Arizona Wranglers.[12] Witnessing a team lose money and abandon a major media market was a black eye for the USFL but in Bassett's opinion, the Blitz problems were the result of one man's vanity. "Chicago is a great sports town," Bassett said. "I remember watching WFL games in Chicago with 53,000 people. The problem with Chicago is all the damage George Allen did last year. He refused to go out and shake hands and sell tickets. Instead he was over in Europe with Ronald Reagan selling people on jogging around the block."[13] Allen's ambassadorial trip in his role as President Reagan's chairman of the President's Council on Physical Fitness and Sports was not without importance. In Bassett's mind, however, if Allen was going to overspend on talent, the coach had an obligation to the USFL to sell the league with vigor.

Instead, Allen had created an untenable financial situation which required other USFL owners to provide emergency funds to prop up the Blitz. This was a system Bassett had demanded when he joined the USFL after his experience watching team after team in the WFL simply fold and leave him holding the bag. Bassett had no compunction in explaining how Tampa Bay's plan saved the USFL. "In Chicago, the system proved itself," Bassett said.

> The Chicago situation was perfect. The mechanism was tested, and it worked. First of all, we funded it out of the letters of credit, a million and half bucks apiece. Then the teams sent an assessment. The financial structure of the league that was set up—and I have no bones about telling you it was set up by our franchise, all the motions to do it that way—was a direct result of the WFL.[14]

Bassett also took time out to tweak Hugh Culverhouse again when critics argued the Blitz failure was indicative of the entire USFL. "The NFL shored up Leonard Tose," Bassett said, comparing the USFL's bailout of Chicago with the NFL's actions to keep the Philadelphia Eagles solvent due to the gambling losses of Tose. "Did people go around and say the NFL is in financial trouble? The league paid his payroll for half the year and Mr. Culverhouse lent him money or signed a note for him or what have you, which is a damn fine thing for one partner to do for another, but you didn't see all kinds of stories about the NFL did you? What's the difference?"[15]

Bassett's public relations-fueled enmity against Chicago paled in comparison to his public denunciations of the USFL's New York area franchise. The irony behind Bassett's pronouncements is that he was privately in favor of the New Jersey Generals violating the salary cap to sign the most famous collegiate player of the early 1980s. The USFL unanimously approved the Generals making football history by signing an underclassman, the University of Georgia's Herschel Walker. The signing was sensational news because Walker had not yet completed his junior year of college. Walker, the 1982 Heisman Trophy winner, was not eligible to play in the NFL because that league did not sign underclassmen, but that was not true in the USFL.[16] The new league, mirroring Bassett's argument against the NHL ban on junior hockey players, believed the NFL's policy violated anti-trust law and agreed to allow Walker in the league. Commissioner Chet Simmons hand-picked Generals owner Walter Duncan to sign Walker, and the owner quickly accomplished the goal, inking Walker to a three-year, $3-million contract.[17]

Bassett sensed a great opportunity to continue his strategy of marketing the Bandits as a team of scrappy everymen. Bassett picked a fight with the league through the media and passed himself off as incensed, even though he had approved the signing. Bassett claimed facetious outrage at both the contract's size and the fact that the USFL hand-delivered the best college player in the country to a franchise without allowing open-bidding. Bassett also argued that under the auspices of the Dixon Plan, the University of Georgia was a territorial school of Southern USFL teams such as Birmingham and Tampa Bay, so Walker should have been their player to bid on. If nothing else, Bassett wanted monetary compensation to make up for what he felt was a competitive disadvantage bestowed on his club. "We would have signed him and wanted the opportunity," Bassett said.

> The Generals didn't have rights to Walker and yet they got him without compensation to any of the other clubs. That's why there must be compensation. The league should have put the contract on the table and let every franchise have a shot. It is the policy of this football team to expect meaningful compensation from New Jersey, because the Tampa Bay Bandits would have been in the running for Walker.[18]

Those who knew Bassett admitted the Tampa Bay owner was not genuine in his umbrage. From the start, Bassett knew having the country's best player in the league's biggest media market was best for the USFL. He was also practical enough to know making a public stink about it would be the best thing for Tampa Bay. "We had caucused and had the full support of everybody in the league, including ABC, to get Herschel into New York," said Steve Ehrhart, who orchestrated the signing for Chet Simmons.

> Johnny was one of the few guys who knew what was going on behind the scenes and was absolutely supportive. Johnny was aware and said, "That's the greatest thing to get Herschel in New York, but I'm going to come after him in the press and my fans are going to love me. I'm going to raise so much hell about how Herschel got to New York. We'll create a huge rivalry and when the Generals come to town, we'll get a great crowd!"[19]

Bassett's marketing ploy was nothing short of genius, but the benefits were lost on Walter Duncan. The Generals owner did not understand what Bassett was doing and grew confused as to why the Tampa Bay fans were being whipped into such a frenzy over the goings-on in

New Jersey. "Johnny did it all based on marketing," Ehrhart said. "Johnny was league-first in this instance, but he said, 'Wait and see. My fans expect me to stand up for Tampa Bay. I'll never say it was wise for Herschel to go to New York publicly.' Now Walter Duncan was such a fine gentleman, he just didn't understand it. 'I thought Bassett was for it,' Duncan told me. I said, 'He is Walter. This is his way to sell tickets.'"[20] Bassett won the public relations battle with Duncan, attracting over 40,000 to the Tampa Stadium contests with the Generals. Bassett's team also split the four games the Bandits and Generals played during the USFL's lifespan. When the Bandits held Walker to just 39 yards on 19 carries in Tampa Bay's first victory over New Jersey, Bassett enjoyed a golden moment on the sidelines of Giants Stadium in East Rutherford. Bassett experienced many such moments in the USFL, buoyed by a marketing strategy and playing style that made the Tampa Bay Bandits the talk of the nation.

Bassett and Burt Reynolds drawing a winning raffle ticket during a Bandits fan festival at Tampa Stadium. The imaginative Bassett believed the ticket-buying public deserved more than a game for the admission price. Bassett spearheaded numerous promotions including a mortgage burn-off and a million-dollar giveaway. Photograph from 1984 Bandits Bulletin courtesy of Steve Ehrhart.

The Redneck Chic Team

Bassett's team needed a name to capture the imagination of the Florida Suncoast and capture its culture of defiantly demanding something Floridian in the face of tourists, snowbirds, and retirees. Bassett gave thought to names as diverse as Commodores, Captains, Thunderbirds, Sunbelt, and Sun Bandits.[21] Bassett eventually arrived at a name that was closely associated to one of his co-owner's film franchises. Burt Reynolds had been the star of two *Smokey and the Bandit* films by the time Bassett was ready to officially christen his team in August 1982. The Tampa Bay Bandits were named for Reynolds, but the elder Bassett and his son tried their best to tweak the public by claiming the name came from something less sensational. "We had a German Shepherd named 'Bandit,'" said John C. Bassett.[22] Johnny F. Bassett stated at the team's launch party that the name of the team was in honor of the family dog, but was willing to let the legend of *Smokey and the Bandit* grow to take advantage of the appeal of both films. "It's named after the family dog," Bassett told the media. "But don't tell Burt that."[23]

Bassett may have played fast and loose with the truth about the etymology of the team's name, but there was no doubt who the star of the team's launch party was. "This is the first time I've ever owned a sports franchise and not been the focus of attention," a delighted Bassett beamed as Burt Reynolds schmoozed with reporters while being escorted by two extremely attractive cowgirls. One writer wrote the press conference was the first he attended that possessed "an open bar, a three-piece country-western band and very, very attractive cowgirls."[24] Reynolds held forth at the party, working the room like a politician. "I'm going to play linebacker," Reynolds said. "We're going to play Greenville Prison (the fictional setting of his film, *The Longest Yard*) and Dom DeLuise is the coach."[25] Bassett let the press lap it all up. The next day's papers were filled with positive stories about the Bandits in direct comparison to stories about the Bucs and the player's strike. It could not have worked out any better and Bassett knew it. "I just wanted to be different," he said. "I wanted it to be fun. I just wanted to have people mixing, rather than preaching."[26] Mission accomplished.

Bassett's invitation of Reynolds into the franchise's ownership group was part of his multi-pronged strategy to associate his team with American popular culture's recent fascination with the Deep South, a trend which had strong ties to Florida. Bassett surmised he could attract national followers to the Bandits by incorporating the themes of Southern pop culture into the marketing operations of the team. This was a time when Southern culture was nationally attractive.

Reynolds starred in numerous Southern-themed movies in the 1970s and 1980s. His inclusion in the Bandits ownership group provided Bassett with unfettered access to the biggest names in entertainment, and the Canadian quickly went about using their talents to craft the team's image.

Southern-themed music, television, and film so dominated the American landscape in the late 1970s and early 1980s it was referred to as "Redneck Chic."[27] During this time the term redneck, a former vituperative description of a backward thinking white Southerner, became a badge of honor for a subset population of Americans with scores of Americans considering themselves "half a redneck ... driving pickup trucks, listening to country music, watching stock car races, and flying Confederate flags."[28]

Country music, long thought of as "too rough-hewn for Yankee eyes and ears," became immensely popular in the early to mid–1970s as its imagery of cowboys, mountaineers, working-class heroes, and other rugged individualists infatuated the nation.[29] Country songs with cross-over appeal such as Loretta Lynn's "Coal Miner's Daughter" (1970), Lynyrd Skynryd's "Sweet Home Alabama" (1973), and John Denver's "Thank God I'm a Country Boy" (1975) were among several country songs to climb to the top or near the top of the pop charts.[30]

Televised sports also began to have a distinctively Southern flavor in the 1970s and 1980s. The weekly races of the National Association for Stock Car Auto Racing (NASCAR) were traditionally shown on a tape-delayed edited basis until 1979. In 1979 CBS broadcast the Daytona 500 live from Florida for the first time and received solid ratings.[31] Two years later, neophyte cable sports broadcaster ESPN began weekly telecasts of several NASCAR races, slowly growing the appeal of the Southern-based sport throughout the nation.

The final example of Redneck Chic is the rise in popularity of Southern-based films during this time. Dozens of films during this era featured Southern protagonists exploring the romantic themes of the South: rugged individualism, defiance of authority, grace, and loyalty to a cause. Perhaps no other actor became more associated with this era of Redneck Chic than Burt Reynolds. Reynolds starred in more than a dozen Redneck Chic movies between 1972 and 1984, with several of the films featuring Florida. Reynolds is best known for his role in *Smokey and the Bandit*, a film about two truck drivers attempting to win a farcical bet by racing across the Deep South with bootlegged beer. The film features a country music soundtrack, Southern backdrops, several scenes of lawlessness and defiance of authority, and loyalty to friends. Released while the nation was engaged in an energy crisis, the protagonists racing muscle cars and semi-trucks heedless of fuel conservation was a great method of escapism for citizens of a country who could only fuel their tanks on certain days of the week. While not exactly *Citizen Kane*, the film was the second-highest grossing film of 1977, finishing behind *Star Wars*. *Bandit* catapulted Reynolds and his on-screen persona to the status of folk hero. Bassett appreciated the fascination with the persona of the Bandit and its appeal. "There is something subliminally appealing about being a Bandit," he said when asked about the team name.[32]

Five years later Reynolds was still playing a variation of "The Bandit" when he mingled with reporters and guests at Bassett's launch party. The team's color scheme and logo quickly obscured Bassett's claim that the Bandits were named after the family dog. The Tampa Bay Bandits uniform consisted of a red jersey, similar in color to the shirt Reynolds wore in the film, striping of the same black as the Pontiac Trans-Am the Bandit drove, and a logo depicting a lone rider atop a black stallion (named "Smokey") similar to the painting on the side of Bandit's semi-truck. The importance of Reynolds' persona to the team's image was further cemented when the team's inaugural media guide featured a photo of the smiling actor in team regalia on the cover.

Further muddying the distinctions between the on-screen Bandit and the on-field Bandits was the team's issuance of a 45 rpm record featuring the team's new fight song "Bandit-Ball." Replete with region-specific lyrics set to banjos and electric guitars, the song was an homage to Florida and Southern pop culture. The line "We come from down in Gator Country" made reference to the 1978 hit "Gator Country" by the Florida-based band Molly Hatchet and the popular University of Florida football team. In fact, the Bandits' lone rider logo also evoked the rider on the cover art of Hatchet's eponymous 1978 album which included "Gator Country." The song was performed by country western star Jerry Reed, who played Reynolds' best friend and partner Cledus "Snowman" Snow in *Smokey and the Bandit*. Reed's vocals, best known for his two top hits "When You're Hot, You're Hot" (1971) and "East Bound and Down" (1977), were instantly recognizable. The singing of Reed and the references to Southern-themed rock, lifestyle, and football further entrenched the Tampa Bay Bandits as a gridiron exemplar of Redneck Chic. The song even hinted at a new style of Southern football created by University of Florida alum Steve Spurrier: "We're gonna be runnin', gonna be throwin', gonna be showin' everyone that Bandit-Ball is a brand of ball that's an awful lot of fun."

Spurrier made sure that Reed's lyrics were prophetic.

The Strategy of Bandit-Ball

Steve Spurrier had been given complete control over the X's and O's by Bassett and he ran with the freedom the same way a sixteen-year-old given keys to the family car does. Spurrier spent the three months between leaving Duke and the start of Bandits training camp adapting and refining an offensive system which employed a base formation few teams in professional football used unless they were in a desperate late-game situation. "We had a formation of three wide receivers, one tight end, and one running back," Spurrier explained. "It was developed mainly up at Duke. It got started back in 1982. It got developed a little more in Tampa and we named it 'Bandit-Ball.' The formations would be called 'Bandit Left,' 'Bandit Right.' I still called it 'Bandit' (thirty years later) at South Carolina."[33]

Most football teams of that era ran offenses with two receivers and one tight end while employing three men in the backfield: quarterback, fullback, and tailback. With the "Bandit-Ball" formation, Spurrier deployed three outside receivers and a tight end while lining up a solo tailback behind the quarterback. The formation required the defenses to put an extra cornerback into play, eliminating a linebacker or safety. This opened more space downfield to run routes. It also created the opportunity to run a wider variety of pass patterns which put pressure on the opposing defense to cover more ground. The Bandits also ran the offense without a huddle, putting extra pressure on defensive substitutions.

A precursor to the "Fun and Gun" offense Spurrier ran during his national championship years at the University of Florida, Bandit-Ball was unveiled to his first team when Tampa Bay reported to training camp in February 1982. One of Spurrier's quarterbacks felt as though he was seeing football for the very first time. "The smartest quarterback coach or offensive mind I have ever been around," said Jimmy Jordan, who had been coached by another legend at Florida State. "Nothing against Coach (Bobby) Bowden. Bowden was hands-on with everything, but Steve would get out there and throw the ball with you. He'd get up there with you on the blackboard and challenge you to draw plays. He'd challenge you from the sideline and in the film room."[34]

Bandit-Ball was a big hit with minority owner Burt Reynolds. Reynolds enjoyed bragging about the Bandits and was completely enamored with the team's playing style. "Bandit-Ball was unpredictable," Reynolds said. "It was totally spontaneous and wonderful. It was colorful."[35]

The 1983 season opener against the Boston Breakers at Tampa Stadium was the first official USFL game, kicking off two hours before the other Sunday slate of games on March 6. The 42,437 in attendance were treated to a great deal of star power and Bandit-Ball from the start. Jim Nabors, former star of *The Andy Griffith Show* and *Gomer Pyle, USMC*, and a friend of Burt Reynolds, sang the national anthem. Burt Reynolds was a no-show, but the former Florida State tailback's absence was mitigated when another ex-Seminole scored the first touchdown in franchise history. Ricky Williams had the honor of scoring the inaugural touchdown. John Reaves threw for 358 yards and three touchdowns, the last a 33-yard strike to Willie Gillespie with ten minutes to play. That toss proved the difference in a nail-biting 21–17 victory not decided until Bandit defender Ken Taylor made a goal-line interception late in the game. "That's Bandit-Ball, wide-open, with a lot of passing," Spurrier explained about his game plan. "That's the way we like to play."[36]

The game plan was pure Bandit-Ball. The first seven offensive plays for the Bandits were run without a huddle, catching the Breakers off guard. With two minutes to play and the Bandits nursing a four-point lead, Spurrier elected to go for it on fourth-and-one from deep in his own territory, eking out the needed conversion with the assistance of a Boston penalty. The game winning-throw by Reaves came on an improvised play. When Reaves came to the line of scrimmage, he saw that Gillespie, normally a kick-return specialist, was drawing single coverage. Finding the missing puzzle piece that Spurrier always spoke of, Reaves uncorked a long pass to the player Boston least suspected to run to the end zone. "I just said, 'Let's go for it,'" a joyous Reaves recounted in the locker room.[37]

The win gave the Bandits a 1–0 record, the same as half the teams in the USFL after one week. The difference was how well the Bandits executed. A complaint from the first weekend of play had been the stupefying boredom generated during many USFL games.[38] The majority of USFL teams looked sloppy and sluggish, just as Bassett had predicted would happen without pre-season games. Bassett for one was pleased with the debut. In a wonderful example of wordsmithing, Bassett explained that fans should not expect a title while at the same time promising more fun than the Buccaneers provided when they started operations. "Give it three stars, recommend it for future viewing and call it a fine day," Bassett told the press. "This wasn't the stuff a Super Bowl is made of—there is no point in making such illogical comparisons—but neither was it a day at the office in 1976 and 1977 when the Tampa Bay Buccaneers had a tough time finding their own dressing room."[39] Somewhere Hugh Culverhouse had to be seething.

The Tampa Bay Bandits remained competitive as the season progressed despite being relegated to their third and fourth string quarterbacks, Nathaniel Koonce and Mike Kelley, when John Reaves broke his right wrist and Jimmy Jordan suffered a severe shoulder sprain. Things got so bad that a shirtless Spurrier began heaving passes at practice and Bassett floated the idea of making the 38-year-old a player-coach in an emergency situation. "We were going to dress Steve, he was going to play," Bassett said, somewhat jokingly, before admitting another plan was to sign two famous NFL quarterbacks engaged in acrimonious contract negotiations to one-game contracts. "We discussed signing Dan Fouts and Doug Williams. They could be a reliever for a couple of games, like (New York Yankee pitcher) Goose Gossage."[40]

As unrealistic as procuring the services of Fouts and Williams, starters for NFL teams in San Diego and Tampa Bay respectively, might have been, it was equally unrealistic to expect a team down to its fourth string quarterback to remain in playoff contention. But there the Bandits were with a record of 9–3. That they were doing it against teams with bigger names and salaries made it all the sweeter to Bassett and his marketing staff, who delighted in putting forward the image of the Bandits as a scrappy, well-run organization intent on showing the big money boys how to play the game. "We were winning games we really shouldn't've," Jim McVay admitted. "Bassett followed the salary cap and other owners didn't. It really was a combination of almost every favorable element you could ever dream of as a marketing person."[41]

Jimmy Jordan saw his profile change rapidly in 1983 when he was thrust into the starter's role. He also discovered that working for Johnny F. Bassett meant a rapid rise in pay as well. "Mr. Bassett was really good to me," said Jordan.

> When John got hurt, Mr. Bassett called me into his office and said, "My starting quarterback is not going to make this kind of money, so we need to get you some more money." He asked me what I thought, and I said I need to call my agent. He said, "There's not going to be any agents. You tell me what you think is good." I didn't have a clue! I mean, I was making real good money for somebody coming out of college. There is no way with a criminology degree I was going to make that kind of money anywhere. Mr. Bassett said, "All right, I'll write something down." I looked down and said, "I'll do that!" He said, "Okay, I'll include some incentives such as completions, touchdowns, and playoffs." And that's what I got paid for the rest of the year. We just shook hands on the deal, and it was done. He said the deal was done and it was. I don't have a bad thing to say about Mr. Bassett. He was a good guy, he really was. I doubt you'll find anybody who has a bad thing to say about him.[42]

The injury-plagued Bandits finally came undone in the final quarter of the 1983 season. Even with the development of Jordan, the Bandits found themselves overmatched during the playoff push. Eventual USFL champion Michigan beat the Bandits 43–7 at the Pontiac Silverdome. The score reached 40–0 before the Bandits scored a face-saving touchdown. The Bandits also lost to eventual USFL runner-up Phila-delphia 24–17 and 31–8 to the Chicago Blitz. The second loss to Chi-cago was particularly galling to Bassett. Getting outscored 73–11 in two games against his nemesis George Allen did not sit well with Bas-sett. Interestingly, despite Chicago's NFL roster, the Blitz only finished one game ahead of Tampa Bay in the standings. For all that spending, the Blitz won only one more regular season game than the team that embodied the Dixon Plan. The Bandits, forced to play multiple games with reserve players and outspent by almost all USFL teams, had much to be proud of. The season had a feel-good element that the end did not erase.

Bassett also had much to look back on with pride. He had created a truly Floridian team which resonated with residents throughout the region. They adopted the Bandits and fell in love with them. His ros-ter was filled with Sunshine State stars led by a local hero. He contin-ued to exploit regional animosity between the North and South, but his championing of Floridian-ness against big-money tourists was tamer and more genteel than his cooption of Lost Cause mythology, and argu-ably more effective with his new audience. Further, Bassett's exploita-tion of the icon of Redneck Chic, Burt Reynolds and his *Smokey and the Bandit* persona, had a broader national appeal than anything he had done before. Bassett finally achieved his dream of establishing a sporting nirvana on the Gulf Coast and looked forward to growth of his team's potential and expansion of the USFL in 1984. The 1984 sea-son was Bassett's apotheosis, the happy realization of all his sporting dreams come true. The Bandits became the face of the USFL, and Bas-sett's string of promotions garnered him headlines around the country. The year of 1984 also saw the introduction of Bassett's veritable doppel-ganger into the USFL, an adversary intent on becoming the face of the USFL himself.

THIRTEEN

The Model USFL Franchise

The Bandits fell short of the playoffs in 1983, finishing with a record of 11 wins and 7 losses, but they were winners on the balance sheet. USFL teams lost an average of $2.5 million per franchise in 1983.[1] The only team to make a profit was the Denver Gold. The Gold finished $150,000 in the black but earned a reputation around the league for being cheap.[2] Bassett's Bandits lost just $150,000 for the season and finished second only to Denver in attendance. Denver averaged 41,735 per home game to Tampa Bay's 39,000.[3] Bassett felt the team's attendance could have been better had the Bandits played more night games. Bassett and the USFL had not anticipated just how brutally hot Tampa Stadium could get in May and June. The stadium's concrete bowl lacked shaded sections and was lined with tens of thousands of aluminum benches. A sunny, 90° day could generate in-stadium temperatures of close to 110°, making fans feel like baked potatoes in a convection oven. Bassett also discovered that the Bandits needed to compete with the siren call of the tropical beach breezes during day games.

"If I have my way, when they put the schedule together for next year, we will not play any Sunday afternoon games after April 15," Bassett said following a home game played in 92° weather in front of 35,000 sunburned spectators. "You've got to admire the fans. It was really too hot for them to be here, but they showed up anyway. This time of the year, Sundays are for beaches and boaters, not football. Playing on Sunday may have cost us 10,000 fans. If playing Saturday night means we have to rent out the stadium for the entire weekend, we'll do it, even if we have to have bingo or backgammon on Sunday."[4]

Bassett's success in 1983 attracted a lot of attention from both inside and outside the USFL. The NFL's Tampa Bay Buccaneers headed into the 1983 season without quarterback Doug Williams, who refused Hugh Culverhouse's low-ball contract offer and chose to sit out the season. Ticket holders for the Buccaneers quickly changed their allegiance to the Bandits, who announced that 27,000 season tickets for 1984 had been sold. This got the attention of Hugh Culverhouse. Bassett might have started the season hoping his team and league could compete indirectly with the Buccaneers in terms of quality product, but the Bandits had showed staying power and were now viewed as a threat by Tampa's NFL franchise. Once again, Bassett set the standard for owner excellence in a league with a widely varied ownership. "The things he was doing down in Tampa Bay, drawing season-ticket holders from the Buccaneers, the NFL was very concerned about that," said Paul Warfield, who moved from playing for Bassett in Memphis to a front-office job with the Cleveland Browns. "I went to owners' meetings and we discussed what we had to do to be more competitive in Tampa Bay. The NFL also wanted to study what Mr. Bassett was doing down there to enhance its own product. The NFL had a lot of respect for his concepts."[5] So did many USFL owners. Orlando Renegades owner Donald Dizney freely admitted that he was cribbing Bassett's note. "We're copying everything that John Bassett has done," Dizney told reporters.[6]

Bassett and the Bandits topped themselves in 1984, both on the field and at the box office. A string of promotions which strained credulity at the time captured the imagination of Bandit fans around the region and kept the turnstiles going. Spurrier's imaginative offense kicked into a higher gear and brought the Bandits to the precipice of a title. Bassett should have enjoyed the success, but just as his organization hit its stride, he was confronted by the vanguard of a new type of sports owner which came into the USFL amid much glitz and glamor. The newcomer personified Tom Wolfe's "Masters of the Universe" as laid out in his contemporaneous novel *The Bonfire of the Vanities*. A high-roller from New York, used to operating with a piratical spirit that drew positive attention in the tabloids, this new owner forced Bassett to fight a rear-guard action to keep the USFL true to its mission. That new owner was a New York commercial real estate heir named Donald J. Trump.

The Greatest Showman in Sports

Tampa Bay area commuters were treated to a billboard in January 1983 the likes of which had not been seen before. The photo on the billboard was so sensational and pleasing to the eye that red-blooded drivers hardly minded the traffic jams at "Malfunction Junction," Tampa's notorious interchange where interstates 275 and 4 meet. In fact, commuters might have wished for a delay so they could take the time to observe the advertisement in fuller detail. The billboard featured Loni

Anderson, buxom star of the American sitcom *WKRP in Cincinnati* and romantic companion of Burt Reynolds. Anderson wore a mega-watt smile and little else except for a pair of too-tight football pants and a midriff baring football jersey. Not content with titillation, Bassett and his marketing team also emblazoned the billboards with the phrases "Special Thrills Coming This Year" and "All the Fun the Law Will Allow."[7] The latter phrase became the Tampa Bay Bandits' team slogan. The billboards garnered Bassett's football team national attention.

Newspapers across America reproduced the billboard in stories. The *New York Post* went so far as to put the billboard on their front page.[8] Loni Anderson's football photo became so popular that the Bandits' marketing staff made posters and distributed them for free around the region. In just over a month of distribution, 275,000 of the posters were given out.[9] "That poster has been the best thing since popcorn," publicity director Jim McVay told the media at the time. "The interest has been overwhelming. She is a very attractive woman. Maybe that poster is symbolic of the type of fun we're going to have this year. Football is at the heart and soul of our operation. Giving fans exciting professional football is the most important thing, but we want to offer fans a total entertainment package."[10] Sexism might offend, but sex always sells.

"We led the league in promotions," McVay claimed recently, providing a litany of events Bassett hosted during Bandit games at Tampa Stadium from 1983 to 1985.

> Johnny was a very creative guy with a brilliant marketing mind. Every game we had something spectacular happen to complement and supplement what was happening on the field to distinguish ourselves from the Bucs and the rest of the USFL. Johnny liked a lot of commotion. We had bikini contests, diamond giveaways, car giveaways. He wanted to make it spectacular for the fans. He wanted a lot of fun. He needed a lot of fun. That was our philosophy with the Bandits. You've got to do that with a new league. Johnny wasn't right every time, but he was right most of the time. He had a good feel for what the fans wanted. He was even going to bring a fire truck to hose the fans down when it got hot down there.[11]

Bassett may have also needed to hose down the male spectators for other reasons. In addition to the Anderson poster, Bassett proved he was not above appealing to the lowest common denominator by crafting promotions based on titillation. A Dolly Parton lookalike contest was scheduled, with spectators voting on the largest bust size, and a bikini contest led one local writer to comment: "It was a skin and sex spectacular. Ninety-eight curvaceous beauties wearing nothing more than Pepsodent smiles, teeny-weeny bikinis and plunging bathing suits parading around in high heels."[12] The skin show promotions make for uncomfortable retelling today and were plainly sexist, but they worked in 1983: almost 47,000 spectators made the trip to Tampa Stadium and witnessed this unusual halftime show.

Bassett's promotions in the inaugural 1983 season reached their peak during the week of a home game against the Oakland Invaders. Pam Yonge, Bassett's personal assistant, explained that her boss was flying during the week on business when a chance conversation with a fellow passenger in business class (Bassett did not travel in first class as a standard practice) provided him with an epiphany. "He was on a plane and he asked a passenger, 'If a genie could pop out of a bottle and grant you a wish, what would it be?'" said Yonge. "The passenger answered he wanted someone to pay off his mortgage. Well, Johnny came back into the office and said, 'Okay, next game we're going to have a drawing and pay someone's mortgage off.' All the lawyers were going no, no, no. But Johnny said, 'This is what the people want.'"[13]

That week Bassett announced that at halftime of the Bandits-Invaders game he would draw a ticket stub from a container and the lucky winner would get their mortgage paid off.[14] Bassett called the contest "The Bandit Burnout." It generated headlines across the country. Customers wanted to see if their wish would come true—43,389 came out to the game. The drawing went off without a hitch but for one small detail. The winner of the contest was one of the wealthiest men in Tampa Bay. Mike Pappas, part-owner of the famous Pappas restaurant in Tarpon Springs, held the winning ticket. Pappas did not have a mortgage to pay off, so Bassett agreed to grant him a $10,000 certificate of deposit instead.[15] The string of promotions paid off for Bassett and his team. The Bandits drew an average of 39,895 fans per game during the 1983 season. Bassett's innovative and imaginative strategies were noticed by the rest of the USFL. "Johnny was always upbeat and coming up with something new," recalled Carl Peterson, general manager of the Philadelphia Stars and an avowed Bassett fan.

As the 1984 season approached, Bassett came up with an idea inspired by a common complaint of NFL season ticket holders. NFL season ticket holders are expected to pay for two pre-season games as part of their plan. These games do not count in the standings, and primarily serve the coaching staff as an evaluative tool for setting the regular season roster. They are glorified practice sessions, yet season ticket holders must buy them at regular season prices. To encourage purchases of Bandits' season tickets, Bassett did the unthinkable. The Bandits advertised that season ticket holders would be admitted to the team's pre-season games free of charge. This was not a small concession considering the Bandits had sold 27,000 season tickets.[16] Tampa Bay's season ticket base was the largest in the USFL.[17] A crowd of 42,247 came out to see the Bandits defeat Oklahoma 15–6.

The number of fans in the stands was impressive, but what they were wearing also proved the efficacy of Bassett's methods. Tens of thousands of Bandits hats, t-shirts, sweatshirts, jerseys, and other assorted collectibles were visible in the stands. Bassett had not just created a successful football team; he had created a merchandising giant. "We would drive out to the malls and see people clamoring for Tampa Bay Bandits gear," recalled Steve Ehrhart. "Johnny was always a step ahead. He spent so much time marketing. At that time, Tampa Bay merchandise was number two in the country only to the Dallas Cowboys."[18]

Bassett ingratiated himself to two of the most rabid college football fan bases in the state with his next promotion. Bassett purchased 27,500 tickets to the September 1, 1984, game between the University of Florida Gators and the defending national champion University of Miami

Bassett (right) and USFL executive Steve Ehrhart (left). The two men travelled the country (not in this car) looking for prospective owners of USFL expansion teams in 1983 and 1984. This photograph was taken by future Charlotte Hornets owner George Shinn with the caption "Would you buy a football franchise from these guys?" Shinn never became an owner but Ehrhart eventually became President/GM of the Memphis Showboats (courtesy Steve Ehrhart).

Hurricanes. The game was scheduled for Tampa Stadium and was eagerly anticipated. Bassett's purchase guaranteed a sell-out, which meant the game would be shown on television in Tampa. The game would have most likely sold out without Bassett's intervention, but his motivation for buying the block of tickets was inspired. Bassett proposed to sell the tickets for $15 apiece to Tampa Bay's 27,000 season ticket holders. By guaranteeing his patrons access to the biggest game in the history of Florida college football, Bassett became a saint in the eyes of Bandit fans. "The Bandits hold all the tickets and they're going to our season ticket holders," Bassett proudly said, explaining that he wanted his fans to have the chance to see one of the three biggest games in the history of Tampa Stadium, Super Bowl XVIII, the USFL Championship Game, and UF-UM. "There are a lot of people down here who can't get to see Super Bowls."[19] The gambit was not without risk. By tying up all the ducats, Bassett kept non–Bandit ticket holders from attending the big game. The bold Bandit boss did not seem broken-hearted by that. "I'm not interested in the people that are mad at me," Bassett said. "I'm interested in our season ticket holders. You go with those that go with you."[20]

The ticket plan was just the latest Bassett promotional/marketing stroke to pay dividends. For many who worked around the owner it seemed that Bassett had as much fun coming up with promotions as he did in winning football games. Bassett did not deny it. "It's great fun, great fun," Bassett told the local papers. "I try to think of something every week so nobody will go out and buy concessions. I get them so mad at me at the stadium because nobody goes out to buy a beer or hot dog at halftime. They want to have approval of my promotions because we're hurting them."[21] In another interview, Bassett gave an overview of how Bandit-Ball and his marketing vision complemented each other. "The whole program, from the name, to the logo, to the ad campaigns, to the attitude of the office staff, the open practices, all that stuff, the crazy promotions, all of that is consistent with the way the team plays football," Bassett said. "We've been fortunate that we've won. We've done a good job there. But you can't guarantee winning. If you don't win, you hope that with all the other things you do, the fan, when he leaves the stadium, can say that he had a good time."[22]

Former Bandit Director of Marketing Jim McVay is still in awe of his former boss's bold moves, including tying up all the UF-UM tickets. What appeared a crazy notion had its roots in a calculated business strategy. "Everybody wanted tickets, but he bought them all," McVay marveled. "The plan is, if you control the inventory, you make them buy your tickets. It was a high demand game. He knew what was going on. He could get a feel for a market real fast."[23]

The local and national media began noticing the Bandits. The Bandits were a calm ship chugging ahead in the USFL's sea of red ink. Averaging 46,000 fans per game, the Bandits were viewed as the best organization in the USFL. "It is known around the league that if you want to know how to run a franchise, then you come to Tampa to watch the Bandits," USFL commissioner Chet Simmons told the *Sarasota Herald-Tribune*.[24] "The Bandits were the model franchise of the USFL, and I don't think you'll get much of an argument on that," said filmmaker Michael Tollin, whose production company produced the weekly USFL highlight show. "They were winners, they packed the stadium, they were colorful, they had their own theme song, they had a horse as a mascot, they had Burt Reynolds as an owner, Steve Spurrier as a coach, John Reaves as a quarterback. As the group back in Manhattan making highlights, we always looked forward to Bandits games. They always gave us great material. Spurrier had that wide-open, zany offense with trick plays and a take no prisoners approach. As their slogan said, it was all the fun the law allows."[25] In short, the Bandits provided the element that Bassett never overlooked: fun.

The perception of Bassett and his Bandits changed significantly in the eyes of the Tampa Bay media as well. The team was held at arm's length at first as Bassett's past relations to the WHA and WFL gave off warning signs of leagues gone belly-up. The successful 1983 season and the repeat in 1984 made it apparent Bassett's franchise was now viewed as the best run team in town, despite the continuing struggles of the USFL to turn a profit outside of Tampa Bay. "In Tampa sits the Tampa Bay Bandits, an entertaining and imaginative team with an energetic young coach, Steve Spurrier, and shrewd, practical owner John Bassett, who has the interest of fans at heart," wrote Patrick Zier in a positive review of the team in the *Lakeland Ledger*. "To us, the Bandits are the USFL, and we tend to extrapolate from them that they are representative of the struggling new league, when in fact they are not. The Bandits are, as it were, a mighty oak in a sea of Dutch Elm disease."[26]

All previous promotions paled in comparison to Bassett's 1985 *pièce de résistance*. Bassett announced on April 1 that if that weekend's game drew a sell-out crowd, he would give one million dollars to a single fan. Bassett assured everyone this was no April Fool's Day joke. "I said to myself, 'What will it take to get somebody to one of our games who has never been to one, and what will it take to get him back?'" Bassett told the press. "I figured this would be a good way. The odds are one in 73,000, that's better than you'd get in a lottery. We just hope it sells out. We think football is entertainment, and we think this is fun. And having a sell-out would be a great way to show the league that spring football is here to stay."[27] The Bandits defeated the Jacksonville Bulls 31–17 that weekend, but the game did not sell out. A very good crowd of 51,286 attended so Bassett resorted to a late-announced Plan B to generate publicity. The owner announced before the game that if there was not a sell-out, he would give one fan one dollar for every seat sold over 40,000. A seat number was called out at halftime and Thomas Landi of St. Petersburg won $11,286.[28]

Bassett renewed the one-million-dollar promotion for the following home contest against the Denver Gold. This time 54,267 attended, still short of Bassett's goal of a sellout, but the promotional maverick decided to go ahead with the giveaway. WFLA radio announcer Jack Harris called out the seat number of one George Townsend at halftime. The lucky engineering technician and football fan came to the field to accept a contract directly from Bassett stipulating that, starting in 2005, Mr. Townsend would receive a payment of $50,000 a year for twenty years from an annuity. Attempts were made in researching this book to track down Mr. Townsend to verify if he did start to receive payments in 2005. Those attempts were unsuccessful, and no information has come to light through news searches or other interviews. "The annuity was sold, and we lost track of those people a long time ago," Jim McVay said.[29] Recent books on the USFL also failed to determine if Townsend was paid. Whether or not Mr. Townsend received payment in 2005, the one-million-dollar promotion in 1985 worked so well that even the Bandit players could not help but be distracted during their halftime preparations. "There was interest when he gave away a million dollars," defensive tackle Fred Nordgren said. "We had to stay focused at halftime, but we were curious to learn what happened."[30] Fortunately for Nordgren and his teammates, the Bandits maintained enough focus to complete a 33–17 defeat of the Denver Gold.

"I've sat in owners' meetings in many leagues, and there is no question Johnny Bassett is the single most creative sports owner I have ever known," Steve Ehrhart said.

> He was a guerrilla owner. He was always fighting against the odds and he had to be the most creative. He pioneered so many sports marketing promotions that are de rigeur today. Johnny knew how to create commotion. When Johnny Bassett came into the room there was commotion. He would flail his arms and say, "Let's do this! Let's do that! We can make this happen!" And he had such a great, cackling laugh. "We'll stir 'em up! Burn a mortgage, ride a horse into the stadium!" Nowadays, you go to many sporting events and they have the same music and themes he did.[31]

Bassett's promotions, trinkets, and baubles would be meaningless if Steve Spurrier and the players did not win games. People who shop for a steak dinner may be attracted by the sizzle, but the meat better taste good or they will not come back. The Bandits were a very good team. They finished the 1984 season with 14 wins against only 4 losses and secured a spot in the playoffs. A healthy John Reaves led the second most productive offense in the USFL and executed Spurrier's bevy of trick plays to near perfection. The combination of winning football and imaginative promotion kept the Bandits' ticket office busy. The team averaged more than 46,000 fans per game, including a season-high 59,000 for a game against Oakland.[32] The Bandits also made history by becoming the only USFL team to outdraw its NFL counterpart. The 1984 Buccaneers drew 45,000 to their games, 1,000 less than the Bandits. The Bandits fell short of a title in 1984. They lost a playoff game to the Birmingham Stallions, 36–17. The Bandits enjoyed another playoff year in 1985, churning up the yards on offense and setting scoreboards ablaze with Bandit-Ball. They also outdrew the Buccaneers for the second consecutive year. The Bandits drew 45,000 per game in 1985 while the Bucs only drew 38,000. The Bandits fell short of a title again, however, losing a playoff to the Oakland Invaders 30–27.

Bassett and his son John C. (center) and Bandits head coach Steve Spurrier (right) before an exhibition game with the Philadelphia Stars at London's Wembley Stadium in 1984. John C. covered kickoffs as part of the Bandits special teams during the exhibition. This was the younger Bassett's second time playing for his father's team. He also took the ice as a member of the Birmingham Bulls in exhibition games against Finland and Sweden in 1978 (courtesy the Bassett family).

The end-of-season losses may have dampened the players' spirits, but Bandit personnel never had to worry about paychecks or being treated poorly. Just as he had done in Toronto, Memphis, and Birmingham, Bassett gained a reputation for probity and integrity, qualities which too many of his USFL counterparts sorely lacked. More than one opposing player commented on how they wished Bassett were their boss. "If you talked to other players in the league, we were by far the better team in the league," said Fred Nordgren. "I know people would have loved to play for him in Tampa. There were guys on teams in big cities where the owners didn't care. Johnny just understood the way to market and get people interested. He would encourage us but didn't mess around. He came to practices. This is a guy who got it and was pretty down to earth"[33]

The reason for Bassett's popularity among his players was not just because paychecks were steady and bounce-proof; it was because he had carefully crafted an environment where players were treated like family. This was far different than what so many had experienced in other USFL cities, where confusion and chaos often surrounded teams. It was also a far cry from the cold business of the NFL, where sentiment came second to profit in every case. "There is a lot of arrogance in the NFL, but I think people were a lot more helpful and friendly in Tampa," Nordgren said.[34] One of Bassett's most recalled ploys was taking different groups of players out to dinner. A night on the town with the Bandits' nine offensive lineman set Bassett back $1,400.[35] In 1985, Bassett and Burt Reynolds organized a team dinner during a road trip to Los Angeles, replete with a guest list including Dom DeLuise, Ricardo Montalban, and, of course, Loni Anderson. "Loni Anderson was serving us appetizers!" an astonished Nordgren recalled.[36]

The highpoint of both the Bandits' and Bassett's time in the USFL was 1984. Bassett built a model franchise for the new league and seemed to be the living embodiment of the USFL's mission to provide a fan-friendly version of the sport at lower prices than the NFL. The off-season approach was a success, proving that fans enjoyed the sport whenever it was played. Through shrewd, and sometimes over-the-top, promotions, Bassett crafted his version of a sporting nirvana. While unorthodox, Bassett represented an old-school approach to sports: study a market, provide a quality product at a low price geared toward that market, innovate operations to differentiate from competitors, and follow through on promises to compete for titles. Furthermore, Bassett employed a "league-first" mindset in which he realized his team was only as strong as the league it belonged to. Unfortunately for the USFL and sports in general, a new type of owner came into the new league that year. This ownership model mirrored the anything goes approach to enterprise often associated with the 1980s, which, to its detractors, was called "The Decade of Greed."[37] Instead of operating the sports team to satisfy a competitive itch, generate profit and goodwill, and maintain the competitive balance of the league for the betterment of all, this new type of owner viewed a franchise as an opportunity to promote their personal brand and catapult themselves to a higher economic strata.

A New Type of Sports Owner

Capitalists were the American heroes in the early 1980s, politically and culturally. President Ronald Reagan became the champion of a conservative movement within the Republican Party that viewed the federal government as too restrictive on private business and equated businessmen with the heroic cowboys of old. Reagan won the 1980 Presidential election on a campaign envisioning a country where the free market reigned, and government's role was vastly reduced. "What I want above all," Reagan said, "is that this country remains a country where someone can always get rich."[38]

The 1980s saw not the business-building titan of old, but a new form of capitalist hero, the corporate raider. High-flying hedge fund managers or bond traders epitomized the new ethos, and their lavish lifestyles helped fuel their image. The decade became an era in which manhood needed to be tested, not in battles of strength against strength, but in the manner of "the schoolyard bully, defeating weaker foes."[39] Glamorization of the pursuit of vast sums of wealth regardless of its impact on others permeated 1980s popular culture.

In the early 1980s the super wealthy became heroes rather than villains. This was the time when *Lifestyles of the Rich and Famous* seemed like aspirational television. Authors, producers, scriptwriters, and directors portrayed the wealthy as personifications of the American Dream, particularly on television which romanticized the accumulation of wealth without regard for the consequences such pursuit had on innocent bystanders. This was seen in the popularity of shows such as *Dynasty, Knots Landing,* and *Dallas.*[40] The epitome of unrestrained 1980s capitalism was stockbroker Ivan Boesky, famously convicted of insider trading, who told the graduating class of the University of California that the pursuit of wealth was admirable. "Greed is all right, by the way," Boesky said. "I want you to know that. I think greed is healthy. You can be greedy and still feel good about yourself."[41] Boesky's speech would be paraphrased by Gordon

Gekko, Michael Douglas's character in the 1987 film *Wall Street,* who famously said, "Greed is good."[42]

This giddy madness began to permeate sports as well. The history of sports ownership shows that franchises were generally family-run businesses prior to the 1980s. The revenues produced by professional teams were too paltry to be of interest to titans of industry.[43] There were exceptions from time to time, such as a period in the 1910s when wealthy men like gum manufacturer William Wrigley and brewer Jacob Ruppert purchased the Chicago Cubs and New York Yankees, respectively. These purchases discomfited other owners, who feared executives like Wrigley and Ruppert would be interested "solely in the bottom lines" and would spend as little as possible to put a quality team on the field.[44] Starting with the CBS purchase of the New York Yankees in 1964, numerous corporations became sports owners in the last four decades of the twentieth century: the Tribune Company purchased the Chicago Cubs, the DeBartolo Corporation purchased the San Francisco 49ers, and Turner Broadcasting the Atlanta Braves, Atlanta Hawks, and Atlanta Flames.[45] A key individual equated with both 1980s avarice and 1980s sports is Donald J. Trump, who eventually became the 45th President of the United States.[46]

Donald Trump purchased the New Jersey Generals from Walter Duncan following the 1983 season. The league's franchise in the nation's media capital was an underperforming disappointment, and Trump figured to garner plenty of headlines and, presumably, field a winner. A real estate magnate in his mid-thirties, Trump was not all that different from Johnny F. Bassett in many ways. The scion of a wealthy real estate entrepreneur, Donald Trump was energetic, visionary, and eminently quotable. His real estate transactions and social pursuits made him a household name in New York, but he wanted national headlines and believed purchasing a professional football team would grant him such a platform. Trump quickly became the face of the USFL as he made one bold player transaction after another after buying the Generals. Trump persuaded numerous NFL players to jump to his USFL franchise starting with quarterback Brian Sipe, the 1980 NFL Most Valuable Player with the Cleveland Browns. After Sipe, Kansas City Chief All-Pro safety Gary Barbaro joined the Generals, followed by Seattle Seahawks cornerback Kerry Justin, Cincinnati Bengal offensive lineman Dave Lapham, and San Francisco 49er linebackers Willie Harper and Bobby Leopold.[47] The signings quickly escalated the Generals' status in the USFL. Already the home of Herschel Walker, New Jersey was a *bona fide* title contender.

Bassett saw the logic in the signings even though they clearly violated the salary structure agreed upon during the founding of the USFL.

He realized the value of having a strong team in America's leading media market. It was a delicate balance. Making a New York team strong would keep the USFL in the national eye but it would make it more difficult for the other USFL teams to compete. Bassett appeared both wary and complimentary of the new owner as the 1984 season approached. "Trump is doing a great job for the team in New York, but he's making it tougher on everyone else," Bassett said following the signings. "But don't get me wrong. I think he's doing a great job. If I lived in New York, maybe I'd be doing the same thing."[48]

In a perfect world Donald Trump and Johnny F. Bassett could have been friendly rivals. Bassett could continue his public Tampa versus New York marketing strategies while privately engaging in witty banter with his Generals' counterpart. Just as he had with Walter Duncan, Bassett would have equated the Generals with all that was unfair and unjust in sports to the press and his fans while at the same time working with Trump for the betterment of the league. It could have been an attractive and lucrative personality clash to which fans might relate, provided it stayed within bounds. In the beginning of Trump's ownership, it seemed the two were aiming for a rivalry that might prove mutually profitable. "They weren't arch-combatants," Steve Ehrhart said.

> Johnny had been very outspoken as an owner and when Trump came in, he took over the mantle of brash owner. There was so much emphasis on coming into New York and Trump challenging the New York Yankees and George Steinbrenner. The first few months everybody thought it was great because New York needed to be a strong franchise and Trump got the Generals on the back page of the *Daily News*. Johnny certainly welcomed Donald to the league, and they were convivial for a time. They were both young and full of drive, articulate guys, and dynamic. If there was a "Dynamic Duo," those were the two guys. 1984 was probably the high point of the league.[49]

Trouble was brewing within the USFL, however. Bassett knew that the necessary evil of allowing Trump to build a powerful New York area team meant he and his Bandits would need to be even more creative in crafting rosters and marketing plans. Bassett accepted the challenge and succeeded, overseeing a team which won fourteen of eighteen games and attracted more fans than any other league team. Unfortunately for the league's fortunes, many owners—perhaps feeling competitively inadequate next to the brash New Yorker—felt the need to out-Trump Trump, matching his player spending dollar-for-dollar regardless of their means. This is a common plight in professional sports ownership. Wealthy men are used to being perceived as leaders and do not generally accept that someone else can possess something they cannot. Their egos dictated illogical moves. This rush to be seen as equal to Trump by owners who simply were not as rich, and whose markets were not New York, devastated the USFL and Bassett. The wannabe owners never caught on to the fact that Donald Trump viewed them not as peers, but as pawns. His larger quest was to leverage their franchises in an attempt to gain an NFL team for himself. He viewed the USFL simply as a vehicle with which to gain control of the New York City market which the NFL had technically abandoned by moving the Giants and Jets to New Jersey's Meadowlands sports complex. Trump was also willing to entertain owning an NFL team elsewhere if it came to that. The USFL was merely a temporary expedient toward these plans.

Johnny F. Bassett quickly caught on to Trump's motives and the tone of the Bassett-Trump feud quickly transitioned from good-natured banter to personalized invective. At the center of the feud was the future of the USFL itself with Bassett fighting for a commitment to spring and Trump advocating for a move to fall. The no-holds barred battle which ensued has been seen by some as a preview of Trump's political style and a reflection on Bassett's fierce commitment to his fanbase. When Bassett's health quickly deteriorated over the course of 1985, the battle also became one in which Bassett knew he was fighting for his legacy and the outcome made Bassett's efforts all the more poignant.

FOURTEEN

The Death of the
USFL and Bassett

Donald Trump never intended to stay in the USFL for the long haul. In his 1987 autobiography *Trump: The Art of the Deal*, Trump explains that his purchase of the New Jersey Generals was intended as a low stress way to make a short term killing in the market, what he referred to as a "lark." His goal was to either force his way into the NFL with the Generals or sell out of the USFL to make enough money to purchase an NFL team on his own.[1] Doing so would adhere to his self-described business philosophy of using leverage to get what he wants regardless of the needs of others.[2] It was not always safe to be his business partner.

USFL owners were either blind or oblivious to Trump's intentions and began to spend uncontrollably. Million-dollar contracts were handed out like candy as the USFL raided NFL rosters and snatched college players right off campus. Mike Rozier secured a $3 million contract from the Pittsburgh Maulers, making the former Nebraska Cornhusker the second consecutive Heisman Trophy winner to land in the USFL.[3] Pittsburgh Steelers quarterback Cliff Stoudt and Buffalo Bills running back Joe Cribbs signed lucrative contracts with the Birmingham Stallions. Average-skilled collegians and professionals such as Alabama quarterback Walter Lewis and Dallas Cowboys backup quarterback Glenn Carano signed mega-deals, including one million dollars for Lewis, who had middling stats in a run-oriented Crimson Tide offense.[4] The most mind-boggling contract was a 40-year, $40 million contract given to Brigham Young quarterback Steve Young by the Los Angeles Express.

Bassett watched the signings from afar with a dreadful sense of *déjà vu*. Bassett had addressed the league owners just weeks before the spate of signings. He advised the owners that it was clear that all USFL teams needed to embrace the low-cost tenets of the Dixon Plan after all but one team lost money in 1983. "Our goal must be to deepen our market penetration as strongly as possible, with as positive an image as possible, at the lowest possible expense," Bassett said at the meeting in Houston, Texas. "In plain business terms, reduce costs and maximize sales."[5] That meeting was also Donald Trump's introduction to the USFL and his early public comments about seeking to hire Miami Dolphins head coach Don Shula and going after New York Giants linebacker Lawrence Taylor took precedence over Bassett's in the sports sections of the nation.[6]

Whereas Bassett preached patience, adherence to the original plan, and a long-term build-up to financial stability, Trump made a splash. When Trump spoke, many of his fellow owners had stars in their eyes. In contrast, Bassett's speech fell largely on deaf ears as the owners tried to emulate Trump. Bassett could only ruefully chuckle about the event. "Sports history is full of the likes of this," Bassett said of the big-money pronouncements and grandiose visions of Trump. "All of this reminds me of the old commentary that goes: When a man with money meets up with a man with experience, the man with experience usually ends up with the money and the man with the money ends up with the experience. I have no intention of going bankrupt signing wealthy players. I have lost my $10 million."[7]

Fight for the Future of the USFL

Bassett became angrier as the large-money signings continued. Bassett argued that many of his contemporaries were lazy, unimaginative, and prone to delusions of grandeur in which they thought they could be just like Donald Trump. "Those agreements weren't worth the price of the paper they were written on," Bassett told the press, emphasizing the asset difference between Trump and the rest of the owners.

> I call it a rule of saneness. The problem is there are people who don't know how to market and manage teams. We still have a bunch of neophytes running teams. It's too easy to spend money. Too many people feel they can buy the market. Politicians think they can do that, then the people find out what they're really like and vote them out. For Trump to go out and get a player is like you buying a box of chocolates for your wife.[8]

Bassett targeted Donald Trump and the Generals as a natural rival for his Tampa Bay Bandits. Bassett spent a great deal of time railing to the press and his team about how the Generals were a franchise that needed to be defeated in order to prove the validity of the Bandits blueprint, but now the intensity of the message changed and his players noticed the shift. "Yes, we did get the feeling he wanted us to beat New Jersey," recalled defensive lineman Fred Nordgren. "He never came out and said it, but we knew he was pretty irritated with Donald Trump so there was a lot of animosity between the two teams."[9] Nordgren's teammate, quarterback Jimmy Jordan, agreed. "We didn't know how much was going on between Bassett and Trump, but we knew it was like Florida vs. Florida State and that we needed to put in even more effort against the Generals," Jordan said. "Mr. Bassett sure did like to beat those guys."[10] Off the field Bassett tried his best to get along with Trump despite the latter's anti–Dixon Plan actions. "My dad did his best to get along with Donald because he knew that was where everybody was going to put their marbles," said John C. Bassett. "I don't think Donald was afraid of anybody and I think my dad was the only owner in the USFL Donald respected."[11] The younger Bassett's recollection is of a pre–April 1984 relationship prior to Trump's decision to disregard the USFL's original mission to stake out a modest but ultimately profitable spring football niche.

Shortly before the Bandits' 30–14 defeat of the Generals, Donald Trump stunned Bassett and many other USFL officials when he told the *New York Times* that the league was going to move to a fall season in 1987 and compete head-to-head with the NFL.[12] Trump first started advocating for a move to fall shortly after taking ownership of the Generals in October 1983. Trump told his fellow owners he did not sign on to be in a "minor league" and that a move to the fall was where the big money could be made. Trump believed the NFL had lost popularity because of the 1982 players' strike and was vulnerable.[13]

At an ownership meeting in January Trump attempted to organize a vote on moving to the fall but was foiled by USFL Commissioner Chet Simmons and Bassett.[14] Blocked by the league, Trump sought to conjure a move to the fall into fact by releasing a bogus decision to the press. "If I thought this league would not have gone for a fall schedule, I would not have come into this league," Trump was quoted as saying in the *Times*. "It is the only logical way for the league to continue. There's virtually no chance that it's not going to happen."[15] Here, the break with the USFL's origins was total. Instead of avoiding the oppressively popular NFL and claiming an empty part of the calendar, Trump said he wanted to directly compete with the senior league. Bassett countered quickly, with anger in his tone.

"The story was totally and completely wrong," Bassett said. "I'm livid about it. I'm trying to negotiate a television contract and to have this come out at this time is like shooting me in the stomach with a machine gun. To release a falsehood that the league has voted to do this is totally irresponsible. It has been Mr. Trump's dream and desire, his number one objective and for him to release this story to the *New York Times* was irresponsible and a detriment to everything we are trying to do."[16] Bassett further explained that a move to fall would be particularly difficult on teams which shared stadiums with NFL teams and that is the reason Trump's desire for fall was a non-starter. Bassett and the owners of such teams were concerned such a shift would require them to possibly abandon their markets, markets like Tampa which Bassett had spent a great deal of time and money cultivating successfully.

Trump was unimpressed with Bassett's arguments so their professional relationship rapidly soured. A method of Trump's that became apparent in his Presidency is the pattern of publicly insulting opponents. Trump explained in his autobiography that in order to succeed in business you must fight back against those you perceive have crossed you. "I'm very good to people who are good to me," Trump writes. "But when people treat me badly or unfairly or try to take advantage of me, my general attitude, all my life, has been to fight back very hard."[17] Bassett's success in Tampa adhering to the Dixon Plan, his belief in the validity of the spring schedule, and his genial, but to Trump insulting, anti–Generals marketing made him a target. Trump was overheard short-selling Bassett's previous professional sports experience by dismissively lumping him in with the failed owners of the WFL. Trump would refer to Bassett as "John Bassett of the World Football League" when he wanted to make that point.[18] Trump also passively aggressively spoke of an imaginary owner who "shuddered at the notion of any direct confrontation with the NFL, they were quite content to play in the obscurity of the spring, and they spent much more time thinking about how to keep their costs down than about how to build the league up."[19] It did not take much imagination to determine who Trump was speaking of. Not all insults were shrouded in mystery. Trump often referred to Bassett as "erratic," "vicious," "terribly frustrated," and "angry."[20]

Bassett overlooked Trump's personal slights but drew the line at attacks against members of the USFL who he felt were simply acting in the best interests of the league in advocating for continuing to play in the spring. Shortly after Trump referred to USFL commissioner Chet Simmons' report on the viability of spring football as "bullshit," Bassett sent a letter to the New Jersey owner warning the New Yorker he would be punched in the mouth the next time he insulted Bassett or other USFL personnel.[21]

In addition to writing private missives, Bassett continued as the enthusiastic public face of spring football. He stressed patience and argued that within four to five years he envisioned the NFL and USFL forced to either merge or alter the professional football calendar. But always, his message was that future plans depended upon keeping to the original design of a slow build-up to profitability and the USFL was not there yet. "I keep saying this and my fellow owners get mad at me, but the history of pro sports in every league shows that new leagues are either taken in, accommodated, merged or go out of business," Bassett said.

> I think one of those things has to happen. There is no way five years from now, that the Bucs can be playing here in the fall and we can be playing in the spring, and both of us can be making money. I went into the spring and summer football business. We've got a winning team, and we're second in attendance. Our fans like it. We're 10,000 people a game ahead of what we'd figured we'd be after the first two years. We've been doing very well, thank you. It's not necessary to change. If something's working, why bother to fix it.[22]

Bassett had facts and history on his side, but in the world of professional sports, those are frequently not enough.

Bassett's arguments held sway in early 1984 but momentum began to work against him as his former Chicago nemesis George Allen, now in charge of the Arizona Wranglers, unreservedly endorsed Donald Trump's aim to move the USFL to the fall. "I think Donald Trump has done a tremendous job for the Generals and the USFL as well," Allen said shortly after Trump's inaccurate story to the *New York Times*. "He represents the type of ownership this league needs. I didn't get into this league to be in the minor leagues. I don't think we have to wait until 1987 (to move to the fall). I think that is too far down the line. Some teams in this league right now could compete with some teams in the NFL."[23]

Trump's brashness did generate headlines and attention in the nation's largest media market. The financial failures of teams in Los Angeles and Chicago, the second and third largest American markets, respectively, provided Trump with leverage over owners who felt the need to placate him. By doing so, they hoped that they could keep him in the league. They connected their league's future to the owner who saw it as merely a temporary convenience. Unfortunately, unlike Bassett, who put the league first in giving up his territorial rights to Florida by approving expansion franchises in Jacksonville and Miami, Trump was in it for himself. This was evidenced by his meeting with NFL Commissioner Pete Rozelle in which he stated the USFL was small potatoes and that he was willing to walk away if the established league would absorb his Generals.[24]

A trial vote of owners was taken to gauge the willingness to play one more spring season in 1985 and move to fall permanently in 1986. This happened at a hastily arranged league meeting in August 1984. Twelve franchises voted to move, four voted against and two franchises were not present.[25] Joining Bassett in voting against a move were Michigan, Philadelphia, and Pittsburgh. Not coincidentally, all shared homes with popular NFL teams. Most of those voting for the fall move aligned with Donald Trump's belief that by moving to the fall, the USFL could land more lucrative television contracts. The USFL had an exclusive contract with ESPN and the NFL desperately wanted cable dollars. By moving to the fall on ESPN and staging weeknight and weekend evening games that did not go head-to-head with the NFL, the USFL could theoretically force the NFL to seriously consider making financial accommodations to the USFL or absorb franchises in a merger. A merger—which could not include every USFL team since there were shared markets—would have the instantaneous effect of making any franchise that did make it into the NFL far more valuable. That was the siren call: gaining access to the NFL's brand. Steve Ehrhart and Memphis, who played in a non–NFL market, were in favor of a move to the fall. He explained his reasoning for breaking ranks with his friend. "We had ESPN and the NFL could not get on ESPN because they would have violated anti-trust law," Ehrhart said, explaining that having their games televised on the rapidly growing network gave the USFL clout. "We would have kept ESPN as our distributor. Just showing up and being in games is half the battle."[26] Of course, the USFL had spring television to itself when it came to football. That was its reason for being, but that seemed less appealing than the chance to cash in during the fall.

While the vote did not officially signal a move to fall was imminent, it increased the likelihood and it prompted teams to take strategic action. Many teams left their home markets or merged with other USFL franchises. In a move that benefited Bassett, the moribund Washington Federals decided not to go head-to-head with the extremely popular Redskins. The Federals moved to Orlando, Florida, and took on the nickname Renegades. With his territorial rights to Florida, Bassett collected a hefty payment from Orlando owner Donald Dizney.[27]

The mergers, relocations, and dissolutions brought the total number of USFL franchises down from 18–14. As other USFL owners prepared themselves for ball in the fall, Bassett remained steadfast in his belief that his Bandits would play spring football. The Tampa Bay owner made no attempt to merge his team or gave any hint that he would abandon his fans by folding the franchise. "I am not in the least bit worried that we will be up against the Tampa Bay Buccaneers of the NFL and college football teams," Bassett answered when asked about 1986.[28] The August vote was meaningless as far as Bassett was concerned. Until he received proof that the USFL would receive a king's ransom in television revenue for switching to the fall, he doubted the owners would actually move. He felt their hopes for a rich fall television contract were far-fetched.

In addition to beating the drum for a move to the fall, Donald Trump continued to spend money on player salaries which exceeded the original USFL charter. His acquisition of Heisman Trophy-winning quarterback Doug Flutie garnered most of the attention when the Generals travelled to Tampa for both team's pre-season opener. The five-year, $7 million contract Flutie signed was worth almost the entire payroll of many USFL teams.[29] The only consolation for Bassett was that his Bandits once again defeated New Jersey, 21–7.

Weeks before Bassett set the promotional world ablaze with his million-dollar giveaway, he sat down for an interview with local reporters and revealed that his chief Tampa competitor once warned him the fate of the USFL was pre-ordained. "Culverhouse told me what was going to happen," Bassett recounted of their 1982 conversation when the two men sat down for what Bassett termed a "Let's get along" meeting. "He told me that even though USFL owners were talking about not going after big-name players, they would. And once that started, it would drive up the salaries in both leagues."[30] Culverhouse's prediction was coming true and Bassett knew it. Bassett hinted that if the upcoming vote on officially moving to fall football went against him, he would have to consider other options for his Bandits. "I'm tired of the hassle," Bassett said. "We will not play in the fall. There's no point in rowing a boat that is full of holes. I think the fall people have had their chance for '86 and as far as I'm concerned, they have failed. We're sure sanity will prevail. If it doesn't, we don't intend to go to the fall. For four years I've tried to do what is best for the league. Now I'm doing what's best for Tampa Bay."[31]

A Desperate Bid for the Bandits

Just days before the vote Bassett announced that he would pull the Bandits out of the USFL if the league moved to the fall. Bassett reassured Bandit fans that pulling the team out of the league did not mean the end of their beloved franchise. Bassett intended to make the Bandits the keystone of a new spring/summer sporting league he planned to develop that would include football, golf, tennis, indoor soccer and Olympic events.[32] Bassett's son recalled some of the details. "He called the league the First All-Nation Sports (FANS) league," John C. Bassett said. "He wanted a variety of sports teams in the league with various celebrities in the ownership groups. He envisioned people like Martina Navratilova, Burt Reynolds, Clint Eastwood, and Bruce Springsteen. There were to be musical concerts with the games."[33]

A prospectus Bassett crafted for his proposed league predicted teams in various sports to be based in Miami, Tampa, Jacksonville, Atlanta, London, Philadelphia, Berlin, Charlotte, Montreal, Boston, Honolulu, Tokyo, Los Angeles, Oakland, Vancouver, Denver, Minneapolis, Chicago, Detroit, Houston, San Antonio, Dallas, and Washington, D.C. While the idea of so many teams and sports across the globe is almost unfathomable, Bassett got a veritable who's who of sporting and Hollywood celebrities to lend their names and capital to the project including golfers Jack Nicklaus and Tom Watson, tennis stars Martina Navratilova, Chris Evert, John McEnroe, and Jimmy Connors, entertainers Burt Reynolds, Sylvester Stallone, Barbara Mandrell, and the Gatlin Brothers among others. Even burgeoning basketball star Michael Jordan was listed as an owner of the Charlotte entry along with future NBA owner George Shinn, race car legend Richard Petty, and the Billy Graham Foundation. Bassett had kept this prospectus close to his vest, keeping everyone's involvement secret until he was ready to launch. "Everyone who read and agreed to the prospectus had to sign a non-disclosure agreement," John C. Bassett said. "Even though it was viewed as grandeur, it was applauded by the participants. Most of them agreed with my dad that it was the sports league of the future."[34] This was typical Johnny F. Bassett. Instead of folding his hand, he planned a newer, grander spring venture.

Bassett had earned a reputation for giving fans what they wanted. As far as he was concerned, his team's fans wanted spring football and showbiz. "This decision is being made because our fans have told us what they want," Bassett said of his threat to leave the USFL. "They want the Tampa Bay Bandits to play in Tampa Stadium in the spring and that's what they'll get. This is our team, our fans and our time of the year and that's when we are playing."[35] Bassett was fined $10,000 for the comments by new USFL Commissioner Harry Usher. Usher felt Bassett's threat to leave the USFL was hurting the league's television negotiations. Bassett countered that there had been no movement in fall television contracts for six months and the lack of movement was proof a move to the fall was foolish. "I said the Bandits are not going to the fall unless Harry Usher can come up with a gigantic television contract," Bassett argued after the fine. "It would have to be big enough to cover all of my operating expenses with nobody in the stands."[36]

Bassett's son recalled his father being quite consumed during this time. Johnny F. Bassett had always had a hard time relaxing, but now he was in full battle mode and it started to wear on his patience and out-look. The youthful, energetic-looking executive now gave off the appearance of someone 15–20 years older than his true age of 46. He was haggard, exhausted, and irritable. "I don't think he was ever content," John C. Bassett said.

> He just couldn't wind down. Maybe at the opening kickoff he'd relax, but then he would start counting seats. He just couldn't turn it off. I'm sure he was miffed about the audacity of a certain person coming in and taking over a team and trying to recreate the rules. The rules were there for a reason and that's why my dad was in the league. Perhaps he was seeing something that he had seen before and had a bad sense of, "Here we go again."[37]

Bassett expressed his discontent during an interview conducted three weeks before the final, deciding vote on whether the USFL would move to the fall. In it the Bandits owner, head of the only team to have the same owner, coach, and hometown for all three USFL seasons, comes across as a man who is very tired of the unnecessary ordeal. "This is just no fun at all anymore," Bassett said.

> It was supposed to be fun. But the business side has overtaken sports and I never got into sports because of business. All I've ever wanted to do is our thing in spring. I mean could you imagine the Bucs going to the Super Bowl and the Bandits going to the championship game within an eight-month period in the same stadium? That was the golden dream. Look, we sell more tickets when the Bucs win than after they lose. How else do you get half-a-million people to celebrate? Either you win a Super Bowl or a war. That's what makes this fun. I want our fans to know we are here and we're not changing, and they can count on us. I think a lot of people are afraid to get too attached to us. They're afraid they'll lose their baby. They figure if we go to the fall, they won't be able to support two teams, so they're holding back on coming to our games. I want them to know we're here to stay.[38]

Subsequent events made the return unlikely, however.

The USFL voted almost unanimously to move to the fall during their April 1985 ownership meetings. The final vote was 12–2 with Denver Gold owner Doug Spedding the only person to join Bassett. It was no surprise considering Spedding and Bassett were two owners who would face head-to-head competition with an NFL team in their home markets during the fall. "There was a split between teams in NFL markets and those who weren't," said Steve Ehrhart, whose Memphis Showboats did not have to fear direct competition with a local NFL team. "That's why you saw teams combine before the 1985 season; everyone was trying to find a market free of the NFL."[39]

The vote went against him, but Bassett's performance was a *tour de force* during arguments. Bassett conducted a presentation that consisted of 60 pages of prepared notes and a 12-minute film highlighting the positive aspects of spring football.[40] Bassett also offered a rough outline of his new spring league featuring a variety of sports. According to Bassett and Denver owner Doug Spedding, the new league had interested groups in Chicago, Philadelphia, Miami, Detroit, Milwaukee, Minneapolis–St. Paul, Denver, Los Angeles, Charlotte, Honolulu, Mexico City, and Rome.[41] The vast majority of USFL owners were unmoved. The league Bassett was proposing was too unorthodox, especially for owners now uncomfortable with playing their sport in a different season. No league comprising so many disparate sports on multiple continents had been tried before. The USFL owners on the fence were simply more comfortable risking it all in the fall then entering a completely different sports dynamic. Despite their reservations, one voter was extremely impressed with the amount of passion and ingenuity Bassett showed. "Johnny is a conceptual guy," said Don Klosterman, general manager of the Los Angeles Express. "He put a lot of work into it, no doubt about it. It was so vast. But obviously he gave it an awful lot of thought."[42]

Sadly, most of the voters shared the opinion of Baltimore Stars owner Myles Tanenbaum, who now hoped to slide his team into its new NFL-caliber home. Long a supportive ally of Bassett's in upholding the tenets of the Dixon Plan, even Tanenbaum viewed going to the fall as a safer bet than Bassett's proposed league. "There will not be a new league to even tempt success," Tanenbaum said. "That is my judgment. None of it made any sense to me. At a certain point, it's easier not to listen. And that's where I was."[43] Bassett left the owners' meeting angry and disappointed. Commissioner Usher was answering questions from the media as Bassett walked down the hallway. Coincidentally, Usher was asked if Tampa Bay would be granted a new team in the USFL to replace the Bandits just as Bassett walked by. Bassett heard this and shouted out at the commissioner, "The Bucs really need the competition, don't they?" An embarrassed Usher said, "I would think not." When Bassett was later asked if he was surprised at the outcome, he put on a brave, defiant face. "Nope, not a bit," he said, blaming Trump without naming him. "There is nothing like peer pressure. You've got a couple of guys in that room, and they can convince some other people to vote the wrong way in my opinion." Bassett further argued that his franchise was the best run organization in the USFL, and he was not willing to simply watch it wither away. When he was told the commissioner had said Bandit players could not just leave the USFL for his proposed new league, Bassett thundered his rebuttal. "I'm not going to just sit back and be told what to do by a bunch of people who don't know how to run a business," he said. "Last time I looked my name was on their paychecks. I think that the chances of the United States Football League being successful in the fall are very slim."[44]

In the opinion of both Bassett's son and a close friend, the public bluster hid the fact that Johnny F. Bassett knew he had no chance to win and that for the most part his Tampa Bay Bandits were going to disappear from his life. "I think he knew he was going to lose, that's why he started work on the new league," John C. Bassett said.[45] "It was a last gasp," said Bassett's friend Steve Ehrhart. "His love for his team was evident. Johnny was looking out for everyone, his employees and players. He was striving to leave a legacy and take care of the people he wanted to be loyal to."[46]

The word legacy was an interesting choice by Ehrhart. For better and for worse the legacy of the USFL was transferred from Johnny F.

Bassett watching his Bandits during pre-game warm-ups at Wembley Stadium in 1984. The happy-go-lucky bravado masked an intense competitor. As Donald Trump's attempts to move the USFL into the fall gained momentum, an intractable Bassett intensified his campaign against the man who became the 45th President of the United States. Bassett's illness and Trump's ill-advised strategy conspired to end the USFL prematurely (courtesy Jill Massicotte-Barreto).

Bassett to Donald J. Trump following that vote in April 1985. Bassett's vision mirrored the reason the league came into being. A spring league offering the most popular sport away from direct competition with the most powerful league in sports. Trump's scheme was to face-off against the NFL, resulting in either unfriendly coexistence or forced entry into the senior league. Fairly or not, the USFL is now remembered as the league Trump helped to kill rather than the league Bassett helped build. Trump's plan to raise the value of his Generals by signing high-priced players worked for a little while but when ABC, CBS, and NBC refused to agree to televise the USFL in the fall, the value of his franchise and all remaining USFL franchises plummeted.[47]

Trump's response revealed what was most likely his main option all along. He organized an anti-trust lawsuit against the NFL, claiming that their exclusive contracts with the three television networks constituted restraint of trade. His hope was that the NFL would either be found guilty or settle out of court. Either way, he reasoned, the NFL might decide to make the problem vanish by accepting his team and perhaps a few others, which would make his initial investment savvy indeed. He nearly got his wish. The NFL was found guilty, but the USFL's demise was held to be largely its own doing—meaning, Trump's. The jury sided with Trump, but only awarded the USFL one dollar, trebled to three dollars under anti-trust rules. The jurors felt Trump's actions, particularly advocating for a move to fall over the learned objections of peers like Bassett, was a self-inflicted wound.[48] Trump walked away from his football "lark" relatively unscathed, beneficiary of a burgeoning career of self-promotion and access to lucrative real estate deals. His investment in the USFL was merely what Trump repeatedly called "small potatoes."[49] The USFL owners who followed him were forced to shutter the league. They had no television contract, no teams, and no future in football. These men with money had met a man with experience in Trump, and in the end, they were all left with much less money and one hell of a painful experience just as Bassett had predicted. The players, coaches, and, most importantly, fans, who had devoted years of blood, sweat, and tears to the USFL were left without recourse and some would never be involved with professional football again.

The legacy of Bassett and the USFL is secure in Tampa, however. The fun that the team epitomized made for long-cherished memories. "I still see Tampa Bay Bandits license plates around town, and this is thirty years later," said Bandits public relations director Jim McVay. "Johnny just had that rare ability to connect with everybody: coaches, players, fans, writers."[50]

Unfortunately for Bassett and the Tampa Bay area, the entrepreneur never had the opportunity to reconstitute his Bandits and place them in his proposed FANS league. His cancer was back.

The End of It All

The final battle started with a series of headaches that Bassett just could not shake. Bassett had excruciating headaches in late 1984. Bassett and his wife chalked the episodes up to the stress and fatigue of consistently engaging in USFL battles. Things became more serious when the couple escaped for a week to watch one of Carling's tennis tournaments. Bassett was laid low by pain so severe it prompted him to return to Canada on the verge of Bandits training camp. "At the very beginning of 1985, we were at a tennis tournament in Delray Beach, Florida and he got these headaches that he couldn't understand," said Bassett's wife, Sue Bassett-Klauber. "He'd be up all night, restless, he just couldn't sleep. He'd sit up and smoke."[51] When Johnny and Sue returned home to Toronto, he took in a hockey game with his brother Douglas. Bassett told his younger brother during the game he was planning to visit a doctor. "We were at Maple Leaf Gardens," Douglas Bassett recalled. "Johnny said he had a headache and was going to get an x-ray."[52]

Soon after attending the game with his brother, Bassett visited a doctor and submitted to numerous tests, including x-rays and CAT scans. While the doctors waited for the results of the tests, Bassett flew back to Tampa Bay for the beginning of the 1985 USFL season. Shortly after Bassett's appointment, the doctors received dreadful results. In this era before cell phones and 24-hour accessibility, none of the doctors had Bassett's Tampa phone number. As Bassett busied himself with thoughts of million-dollar giveaways, negating Trump's power play, and multi-sports leagues, Sue Bassett received a horrible phone call from one of Johnny's doctors. "He was diagnosed with two malignant, non-operable brain tumors," Sue Bassett-Klauber said.[53] Sue was caught completely off guard. Her husband had shown no signs of illness, nothing to indicate a return of the melanomas that had plagued him in the late 1970s. As active and outgoing as ever, Bassett never had a hint of public ill-health since his brush with skin cancer. With stealthy impunity, the cancer that had once been visible on Bassett's shoulder secretly spread to his brain over the intervening years. If the news of inoperable brain cancer was not bad enough, the doctors had to break the worst news of all to Sue Bassett. Her husband had just six months to live.

Sue Bassett steeled herself for a extremely difficult phone call. When she reached her husband, she found him in a celebratory mood.

The Bandits had just defeated the Orlando Renegades in the season opener, 35–7, before a good crowd of more than 30,000. The traumatic nature of the phone call and the intervening 30 years have robbed Sue Bassett-Klauber of the specific details of her conversation with her husband, but not its impact. "I forget bad things," Sue Bassett-Klauber admitted. "But I do remember having to make that phone call to Johnny."[54] Even though the specifics of Bassett's verbal reaction to his diagnosis have been lost, there is no doubt that given the course of his actions over the next 16 months he eventually chose to go on the attack.

In the first half of 1985, Bassett made routine trips to Toronto for a series of treatment sessions in the oncology department at Toronto General Hospital. The first attempts at treatment were three separate four-and-a-half-hour radiation doses in late winter/early spring.[55] The treatment caused Bassett to slowly lose his blonde hair but did little to arrest the development of the two tumors. The slow loss of hair meant Bassett could keep his condition low profile. Unless you were an intimate acquaintance of Bassett, you may not have noticed any difference in his appearance at all.[56] "I didn't know he was ill until the day he told me," friend Peter Eby said. "We were going out to dinner one night and he just said he had brain cancer. That hit us like a bolt. He didn't go into a funk. He just picked himself up and kept going."

The slight change in appearance also allowed Bassett to inform the Bandits that he was sick without having to go into a lot of detail. Bassett did not miss much time at the office during his early treatment, putting in the same twelve to fourteen-hour days he had always put in. When coaches and players saw Bassett feeling under the weather, they chalked it up to the fatigue of the many draining days Bassett spent dealing with USFL politics or believing he had a bad case of the flu.[57] The radiation did not have the desired effect after a couple of months so Bassett entered a second phase of treatment.

When radiation failed, Bassett underwent an intensive regimen of chemotherapy drugs designed to kill the cancer cells in his brain. The chemotherapy Bassett endured caused him to suffer the treatment's ominous side-effects, including debilitating nausea, wildly fluctuating weight gains and losses, and continued loss of his hair. "He would go up and down thirty pounds during the treatments," said John C. Bassett. "It was such a vicious illness."[58] Unfortunately for Bassett, the only impact the treatment had was its detrimental effect on his physical appearance. The treatments made it clear to all who followed the USFL and the Tampa Bay Bandits that something more than fatigue and frustration was affecting Bassett. Bassett's presence for games against Arizona and New Jersey in the season's fourth and fifth weeks caught the attention of many. The loss of hair and weight gain were noticeable to all.[59] When Bassett received a game ball following the Bandits' 23–13 victory over Arizona, his first ever such honor, Steve Spurrier commented only that he knew Bassett was ill, but not the extent to which the owner was suffering.[60] Wild rumors began to swirl throughout the Bandits' offices, so Bassett shared the news with his team. Shortly after the New Jersey game, kicker Zenon Andrusyshyn announced to his teammates that Bassett had cancer. The news hit the Bandits hard. The team did not have the adversarial owner-player relationship so prevalent in professional sports. Bassett drove as hard a bargain as any man, but he had spent more than a decade redefining the labor-management relationship in professional sports. He viewed players as equals and genuinely enjoyed their company. This attitude engendered deep devotion among his employees, so the thought of their boss suffering severely affected them.

"We all felt he cared about the players," said defensive lineman Fred Nordgren. "One of our defensive backs in the first year was talking to Bassett and said he needed to get home to visit his family. Bassett made it happen for him. That showed his care and compassion for the players. It did affect the way we thought about things. We knew he had beaten cancer before. He was courageous and positive. We had a great deal of respect for Mr. Bassett, but it was apparent he wasn't feeling real well."[61] Quarterback Jimmy Jordan was shocked and saddened by the news. Jordan also recalled the impact the announcement had on head coach Steve Spurrier. "It affected Coach Spurrier, no doubt," Jordan said.

> He'd get emotional a few times. Bassett had given Spurrier an opportunity nobody else had. That is how you get close to somebody. I think Johnny and Steve were very close. We didn't see a lot of it because we weren't in their meetings, but Mr. Bassett was such a hands-on guy. He was on the sideline and at all practices. He just really enjoyed that team. I'm telling you, he did so much for so many people. That was a big distraction. He's our owner, but he's a good man too. We'd have barbecues out on the practice field. Mr. Bassett would hire a truck to come out and the families and the kids would enjoy the day. You just don't see that in professional football very often.[62]

The media in Tampa Bay was still in the dark. The press did not receive official word until shortly after the players were informed in early April. During the Bandits' 31–17 victory over the Jacksonville Bulls at Tampa Stadium, Bassett met with *Tampa Tribune* sports editor Tom McEwen. Bassett told the well-respected writer that he was diagnosed with two brain tumors and explained his reason for not announcing the news earlier was simple. "My health is none of anybody's damn business," Bassett said.[63] Using a less defensive tone, Bassett admitted that he was touched by the outpouring of concern and good wishes, but that he did not want to be treated differently and that he was in complete control and would beat the disease. "I don't want people coming up to me with ashen looks saying, 'I'm sorry John,' or looking like they want to do that," Bassett said.

> The doctor said I was 150% healthy except for those two little things. I've read six books on the subject. Diet and attitude. Well, I'm eating right, and my attitude is great. I am going to manage my Bandits, be with my family, and smell the roses. I am convinced attitude is number one and you are going to see the greatest attitude anyone ever had with these things. No sad songs, please. They're out of place.[64]

Even a cynic would have been moved by his spirit. Bassett may have kept a positive attitude about his health, but when it came to his beloved Bandits, he was forced to watch things slowly fall apart.

Bassett tried desperately to keep his football team together in May 1985 but was forced to work from a distance while receiving treatments in Toronto. A 38–14 loss to the Memphis Showboats in his former Tennessee home was the final game Bassett attended.[65] The radiation and chemotherapy treatments took such a toll on the owner that he was forced to cede control of day-to-day operations to Bandits Director of Business Operations Ralph Campbell. When Bassett did make appearances, he came across as erratic, especially regarding his promotion of his multi-sports league, FANS. Always quixotic, Bassett now fell victim to both disease and desperation to hold onto his Bandits. The cumulative effects damaged his amazing ability to balance his fanciful pursuits with sound business principles, such as when he signed NFL draft choice Randall Cunningham to a FANS contract despite not being in a league.

Family and friends agreed that the effects of aggressive treatments were not just altering Bassett's physical appearance. The fatigue caused by radiation and chemo wore him down emotionally and mentally, causing him to become irrational, or at least to act very differently than he ever had before. The visionary thinker was suddenly scattered, lacking the focus that had made him so successful. Despite his diminished physical state, Bassett still attempted to have a say in the Bandits from afar, get FANS off the ground, and fight the USFL. "He was impetuous, competitive, a fiery personality," Sue Bassett-Klauber said of her husband, adding that she was worried that at this point he had finally bitten off more than he could chew. "Certainly, when he was ill, he did not have control because of all the drugs."[66]

"When he got sick, I think there were some behaviors that became erratic, probably the result of chemotherapy," said Steve Ehrhart. "Even during the period of time when his brain was affected, he was still so kind in every way. His idea was to recreate the league and reform the league. It was an off the wall kind of thing. But he was just trying to take care of the people that were important in his life even though he was misguided. But we all understood that Johnny was trying in these late stages to reach out to his friends."[67] Bassett may have suspected that his idea for FANS was never going to come to fruition. The sheer scope of the endeavor is almost incomprehensible: One league encompassing football, soccer, golf, tennis, track, and other Olympic-style events on multiple continents with multi-national corporations such as Xerox, Labatt's, Mitsubishi, Nabisco, and many others in the Fortune 500 as sponsors for teams owned by powerful celebrities with carefully crafted public images. This enterprise would have been audacious and challenging for Bassett in perfect health. In a slowly diminishing state, it was becoming apparent that his final attempt at crafting sports to his ideal would never come to fruition.

Bassett's condition deteriorated rapidly. He checked himself into Toronto General Hospital in mid–March 1986. In early May, he was moved out of his room and into intensive care. The nursing coordinator of Toronto General informed the press that Johnny F. Bassett was failing fast. "There's been a very rapid change for the worse," Bryan Crocker said. "I think they (doctors) feel he needs the services of our intensive care unit."[68]

Bassett was still aware of his surroundings but growing a little less lucid each day. "He was aware, and he fought until the end," Sue Bassett-Klauber said. "He would tell me about funny dreams. He would say, 'Listen to that music, it is so beautiful.' But there wasn't any music we could hear."[69] It was at this time that Sue Bassett told her children they needed to come to Toronto. "I lived in Calgary at the time and had booked a flight to Toronto," John C. Bassett said. "Two nights before I was to leave my mom called and said I needed to get there. A huge snowstorm moved in right after I left so if I had left on my original date, I wouldn't have made it. I made it to his room within the last 30 seconds."[70] John C. Bassett made it to the hospital on the morning of May 14, 1986.

"He died just before noon," Sue Bassett-Klauber said.

> I had been at home because I had spent so many overnights at the hospital. It was a beautiful, sunny morning and I was picking some flowers from our garden to take to John's room. Then when I walked back into the hospital a doctor called me and said overnight John had slipped. He said you must let it happen. I walked into his room and saw Johnny slowly letting go. He fought until his last breath with all his children surrounding him. A peaceful and new journey had begun.[71]

Bassett's death was announced during the national media coverage of the USFL's civil suit against the NFL. It is cosmically, morbidly appropriate that the end of the league coincided with the death of its most ardent champion. The personal loss to Sue Bassett and her children was immeasurable. They lost a husband and father in the prime of his life. The loss to professional sports has yet to be properly accounted, but many argue that the industry has been much less interesting and personable in the thirty years since Bassett's demise and ponder aloud what a difference he could have made.

Fifteen

Conclusion

Johnny F. Bassett was laid to rest on Saturday, May 17, 1986, in the cemetery of St. John's Anglican Church in Willowdale on Toronto's west side. Bassett's funeral and burial were held three days after his passing. The friends and family who attended were amazed at the number of people who travelled across North America on short notice to say good-bye. "You couldn't get in the church," said friend Sigmund Levy. "There wasn't a dry eye in the place. There were sports figures from all over the world. I didn't know Johnny very long, but when I was at the funeral I cried like a baby and so did everyone else including the hockey and football players."[1] It is worth noting that sportsmen, executives, and athletes are not customarily known for public displays of emotion, so the depth and sincerity of the grief was clear to all present. The funeral service, conducted by St. John's pastor James O'Neil, played to an overflow crowd which spilled out the door and into the churchyard cemetery. The mourners included luminaries of stage, sport, business, and politics. The eulogy and assorted speeches included remembrances of mortgage burnings, daredevil goalies, and enjoyable days and evenings. It was the kind of ceremony Bassett would have orchestrated had he been in charge. "Johnny would have loved to see this production," said his brother Douglas.[2]

Bassett would have also appreciated the news coverage. The Toronto daily newspapers recounted the service on their front pages, devoting numerous articles and columns to celebrating the life of the departed. The articles recalled with fondness Bassett's litany of sporting successes and his daring, imaginative promotions of hockey, football, and tennis. Nostalgic recollections of diamond giveaways, battles with the Canadian Parliament, daring player signings, and verbal sparring matches with Donald Trump filled the column inches. Bassett had even been the subject of a massive five-part biographical series by Paul Rimstead of the *Toronto Sun* in the months immediately preceding his death.

In death, he received adulatory press coverage that made it clear that his role as a Canadian maverick was finally understood and embraced in his hometown. As Toronto grew more diverse and sophisticated, it also came to appreciate Bassett's singular personality.

Among those who came to say good-bye were former Toros/Bulls Frank Mahovlich, Paul Henderson, and Vaclav Nedomansky. Bassett's former Davis Cup teammates were in the pews as were members of the Tampa Bay Bandits, including head coach Steve Spurrier. Also attending were Pam Shriver, one of Carling's close tennis mates, and local and national politicians. Even former Bassett hockey rival Harold Ballard came to say good-bye to the man he called "a classy guy."[3] Ballard was not one for conciliatory gestures, so his presence signaled a respect that underlay his previously contentious attitude. Donald Trump did not attend the funeral, but did crassly mention Bassett in his 1987 autobiography, *The Art of the Deal*. In that book, he argued that Bassett's illness affected his judgment and was the reason the Tampa Bay owner refused to go along with a move to Fall.[4] This was palpably false, yet of course Bassett was unable to counter the claim.

"The funeral in Toronto was unbelievable," said Douglas Bassett. "They all came up from the United States. It was the only time I met Steve Spurrier and I was so impressed by him."[5] Spurrier had not seen Bassett in months. Following the dissolution of Bassett's ownership of the Bandits, Spurrier had taken the head coaching job at Duke, where he soon had the Blue Devils playing bowl-caliber football far above their customary level of performance. During those final hectic months with the Bandits, Spurrier and Bassett did not have a lot of time to talk. In fact, Spurrier said their last chance to spend time together was when he and the owner defeated Bassett's daughter Vicky and her former husband in tennis before the 1985 season. "Sadly, the next time I went to Toronto was for his funeral," Spurrier said.[6]

Those who worked with Johnny F. Bassett would miss his energy, honesty, and passion. In the words of friend and former partner Herb Solway, "When I think of Johnny, I think of life. He created for the people he knew well the same zest for life as he had. Johnny was as creative a person as I've ever met. He made knowing him a very exciting experience. I'll miss him very much."[7]

Memories of Johnny F. Bassett

The unfortunate coincidence of Johnny F. Bassett and the USFL both passing away around the same time has done much to intertwine their memories, especially as his former nemesis unexpectedly ascended to the White House in 2016. Athletes and sportsmen struck down in their prime provide mythmakers the opportunity to "lament the loss of (their) untapped potential while celebrating their accomplishments and constructing their legacies."[8] Bassett's death at the age of 47, occurring shortly after his greatest entrepreneurial triumph, helps to explain the mythmaking which occurred shortly after his demise evidenced by the media coverage. The few who remember him now, however, have placed him as an ancillary character in larger histories of upstart leagues. That character is based on the iconic trope of the man who dies at the same time as his visionary work of art and it is called up again and again in our collective sports memory.

Johnny F. Bassett's current and long-term role as the conscience and face of the USFL was secured by the work of Michael Tollin, a film director once responsible for the USFL's weekly highlights show. Tollin's daily video diary of the Tampa Bay Bandits during the 1985 season became the basis for a well-received documentary, *The Final Season*. Tollin released the film in 1988, two years after Bassett's death. The delay was caused by the tragic fact that Johnny F. Bassett was the film's benefactor and funding dried up when he passed away. Determined to get his film made, Tollin managed to find alternate financing. The result was an intimate portrait of a man and team navigating uneven terrain, all while fielding an excellent on-field product and having fun while doing it. *The Final Season* showed Johnny F. Bassett in something approaching true-to-life style. The owner is shown as affable and no-nonsense, caring and vulgar, and, most jarringly, healthy and ill. The film is well-regarded in sports circles but did not become a financial success. "*The Final Season* was not distributed widely at all," Tollin said. "The funding had disappeared. I spent a lot of my own money. It took three years and it wasn't a successful commercial venture, but I'm glad I did it."[9]

Twenty years later, Tollin released another USFL-related film. *Small Potatoes: Who Killed the USFL?* was produced for ESPN's *30 for 30* series of sports documentaries. *Small Potatoes* introduced Johnny F. Bassett to a new generation of football fans, showing him as the antithesis to Donald Trump. Throughout *Small Potatoes*, Tollin attempts to determine who was responsible for the downfall of the USFL. Many of the people interviewed in the film agree that Johnny F. Bassett and Donald Trump were on different ends of the spectrum and for the most part the informants intimate that it was Trump who killed the league. Trump comes across negatively. The film concludes with his derisive remark that the entire league was "Small potatoes."[10] Trump makes but a brief reference to Tampa Bay and never mentions Johnny F. Bassett by name.

As someone who lost his job when the USFL folded and was a fan of Bassett's methods, Tollin admits *Small Potatoes* was an important film to him, personally. "To be able to make *Small Potatoes* and get closure while paying homage to Johnny Bassett, I can't tell you how good that felt," Tollin said. "It meant a lot to me. It's pretty clear where my allegiance was. That was more exposure for that part of Johnny's story."[11]

Donald Trump's presidency is another milepost which has helped to shape the collective memory of the league and Bassett. The controversies of the Trump administration and the detailed and frequently investigative reporting of his business practices offer a new dimension with which to view his tactics in moving the USFL to a fall schedule. Simply put, reporters and pundits with strongly negative opinions about President Trump looked for and found antecedents to the practices they deplore in his earlier USFL career. Stories along these lines place Bassett in a foreshadowing role, and he is interpreted in similar position to those combating the presidential agenda. This fact explains why the perception of Bassett has become one of sympathetic underdog.

Many figures interviewed for this book opine that rather than think of Bassett as the sympathetic underdog, it is fairer to compare him to one of the most visible owners in the NFL today, Dallas Cowboys boss Jerry Jones. Jones made a name for himself by disregarding conventional league wisdom inherited from deceased commissioner Pete Rozelle, and instead cultivated a maverick approach. That maverick approach is the binding tie to Bassett, the Canadian's former colleagues believe. They feel such comparisons are the best way to memorialize Bassett. Many also wonder what an NFL with Johnny F. Bassett would be like. To a large extent, they think the league would be better and more fun.

"Jerry Jones of the Dallas Cowboys is a Johnny Bassett–type guy," said former Memphis Southmen wide receiver Paul Warfield. "They are both about making their team and league more vibrant. Johnny proved that he had ideas that were creative and produced revenue. The NFL was changing from the old guard to the new guard and he would have been one of the younger owners who wanted to change the league into what it is today."[12]

"I would not argue with the Jerry Jones analogy one bit," said Larry Csonka, Warfield's teammate in Miami and Memphis. "Jerry goes a bit with his heart, and I don't know how much he thinks things through, but Bassett would think things all the way through, considering every angle. That is why he was able to orchestrate our signing. I can't argue with that."[13]

"I think the comparison to Jerry Jones is very good," said Philadelphia Stars executive Carl Peterson, who worked closely with both men.

"I have great regard for Jerry and without a doubt he is the finest marketing man in the NFL. Jerry shares a lot of similarities with Johnny. Johnny was a great loss. He made all of us smile that's for sure."[14]

"Johnny would have been a spectacular NFL owner," said Jim McVay, Bassett's director of marketing in Tampa Bay. "Johnny just had that rare ability to connect with everybody: coaches, players, fans, writers. There are a lot of different owners in the NFL, but I think those guys would have enjoyed him especially when the NFL moved forward progressively in providing in-game experiences."[15]

Interestingly, Johnny F. Bassett's son thinks his father would have not stayed in the NFL for long. He thinks this for no other reason than that the senior Bassett was not happy unless he was taking on something new. "I think he would have loved being in the NFL, but then after a couple of years he would have said, 'What's next?'" said John C. Bassett. "He would always look for something else."[16]

What Is the Proper Legacy of Johnny F. Bassett?

Johnny F. Bassett was so much more than the USFL. That league's rediscovery in the wake of President Trump, along with two recent high-profile attempts to restart spring football, revived memories of the Canadian owner, but in a limited context. Bassett's contributions to professional sports over a twelve-year span (1973–1985) were consequential and numerous, going far beyond the USFL. His commitment to competition and spectacle follows the pattern created by P.T. Barnum in the nineteenth century which was subsequently transferred to professional sports in the 1920s by original athletic promoters Tex Rickard, the first boxing promoter, and Rube Foster, founder of the Negro Leagues. These were figures who understood that, at the most fundamental level, they were in the entertainment business. Entertainment means amusing the fans and not taking the attractiveness of one's job for granted. True entertainment geniuses know that they must promote their offerings to create a "must-see" atmosphere. In the second half of the twentieth century, Lamar Hunt, founder of the American Football League, and baseball's Bill Veeck pushed the boundaries of sports promotions even further and provide further appropriate comparisons to Bassett. None of these figures made their mark by following the rules of established leagues like the NFL, where marketing mainly means continuing to maintain a successful brand. All of them began by creating something new and figuring out ways to secure press and public attention. These were also Bassett's talents.

Bassett's passion for organizing and promoting competitive sports had ripple effects throughout the industry. His efforts expanded the number of major league markets and increased job opportunities and salaries for players. His advocation of a league-first operating ethos is evidenced by his financial and emotional commitment to the WHA, WFL, and USFL. The WHA added hundreds of jobs to players deemed unworthy of the NHL and helped to increase the average salary in the sport from $18,000 in 1970 to $90,000 in 1977-1978.[17] Similarly, football salaries increased from $23,000 in 1970 to over $90,000 in 1982 as a result of the introduction of competition for players by the WFL and USFL.[18] In this regard, Bassett is a peer of Lamar Hunt. Hunt brought professional sports to the virgin territories of Buffalo, Dallas, Denver, Houston, Kansas City, and San Diego where it grew and thrived and forced the NFL to raise its salaries to attract top talent. He experienced successes and failures, made his mark in football, but also kept promoting soccer as a growth sport for the future. While Bassett never conceived of a sporting event to equal the majesty of the Super Bowl, itself a Hunt creation, the on-field and box office success of his teams in overlooked sporting communities did redefine the parameters of what constituted a major league city.

This was particularly true in the sport of hockey. Prior to Bassett's improbable Birmingham foray, hockey's approach to the Sun Belt was diffident at best. But today, the NHL has teams in Southern California, Arizona, Texas, and Florida. This broadening of the sports map was arguably greater than the impact of Hunt's AFL. Hockey in Florida? Texas? Arizona? Fans of the Panthers, Lightning, Stars, and Coyotes can thank Johnny F. Bassett. Also thanking him should be NHL Commissioner Gary Bettman, who made Sun Belt expansion a keystone of his tenure.

To market these franchises, Bassett surpassed even the great Bill Veeck in originality. Veeck created the concept of Ladies' Day in MLB ballparks, installed outdoor showers for hot days, allowed fans to call plays, and once sent the 3'7" Eddie Gaedel to pinch hit, but only Bassett gave away one million dollars to a single fan, offered to pay off the mortgage of a paying customer, organized turkey shoots, and placed a nationally renowned daredevil in goal. Like the fans of Veeck's Cleveland Indians, St. Louis Browns, and Chicago White Sox, the fans of Bassett's Toronto Toros, Birmingham Bulls, Memphis Southmen, and Tampa Bay Bandits embraced his antics and considered them part of the gate appeal. Fans went to the games not just to root for their favorite team, but to see what their favorite owner might try next.

It is fruitless to speculate about what else Johnny F. Bassett could have undertaken had he the gift of more time, but while he was alive, Bassett had an impact on sports that is still felt today. For years, professional tennis was filled with players trained at Nick Bollettieri's academy in which Bassett played a pivotal role. The NHL enjoyed a boom in the 1980s and 1990s, moving to markets such as Nashville, Charlotte, and Dallas, following the trail set by Bassett in Birmingham, Alabama. The NFL followed Bassett to Tennessee in 1997 and has profited from the success of the Titans. It was Bassett who saw that a state known for college football fanaticism could and would embrace the professional variant. Most compelling of all, the Tampa Bay Buccaneers, once one of the least imaginative franchises in the NFL in terms of marketing and cultivating their fan base, changed the entire face of their franchise in the post–Hugh Culverhouse era. The Bucs undertook a massive rebranding, which included new uniforms, and they play in a stadium designed to look like a pirate cove, complete with a galleon that fires cannon shots throughout the game. In other words, the staid old team now plays in a football theme park. This is to some extent a result of the regional shadow still cast by the Bandits, who reminded fans and their NFL neighbor that football is supposed to be fun. Bassett also gave superstars such as Wayne Gretzky and Steve Spurrier their first big breaks in sports.

"He was a pioneer, but he was a nice pioneer," said hockey great Wayne Gretzky. "There are many pioneers in sports who may not be good people. But Mr. Bassett was good people, very similar to Ralph Wilson of the Buffalo Bills. He paved the way for Wayne Gretzky to have a better life. It's just as simple as that."[19]

"Johnny was a builder of professional sports whether it was tennis, football or hockey," said business partner John Eaton. "I think he should be in the Hockey Hall of Fame and the Pro Football Hall of Fame. He may have been a pain in the ass, but he helped make those sports what they are today. And undeniably, he helped the athletes and for that he deserves recognition. He never begrudged the athlete his fair share and a good wage. He always thought of the players."[20]

In an age in which success is too often measured by the size of a person's wallet, balance sheet, or trophy case, Johnny F. Bassett's life of endeavor could be easily dismissed as the actions of an eccentric dilettante. After all:

- He never won a major tournament in tennis.
- None of his football teams ever won a playoff game and both folded.
- His hockey team won one playoff series and folded.

Yet despite these apparent shortcomings, Johnny F. Bassett is remembered by those closest to him with wonder and pleasure. Fans of a certain age also recall his teams with real fondness. Some of those believe his legacy should be his imagination, integrity, and zest for life.

"I think he was a man ahead of his time," said Paul Godfrey, Toronto politician. "I've always been a fan of Johnny Bassett. He loved the city of Toronto and was such an enthusiast."[21]

"I think he was an innovator," said lifelong friend Peter Eby. "He tried to appeal to the interests of the average guy, he wasn't an elitist. Johnny tried to the best of his ability to provide a product that was of value to his customers."[22]

"Too often we learn of people who were successful in business but are not nice," Wayne Gretzky said. "But he was the opposite. His word was his signature. He changed a lot of people's lives. He never flaunted his money. He opened doors for people who were less fortunate, and I was one of them. I can't say enough nice things about him."[23]

"There was so much more to his legacy than just giving us an opportunity," said Rick Vaive, whose one year with the Birmingham Bulls catapulted him to a successful hockey career. "I remember looking forward to him coming to the locker room because he was bigger than life. He was a big, good-looking guy who was always tanned. There was just something about him that I can't even come up with a word for. To us, when we were 18 and 19-years old, he was just a charismatic, bigger than life individual. We loved being around him because it was always exciting and fun."[24]

Others believe Bassett's legacy should be the lessons he imparted on how to run a professional team. "He had such an influence on my life," said Steve Ehrhart, now executive director of the Liberty Bowl. "I tried to follow his creativity. Don't always do things the way they used to be done. Be creative. I've always been ready to go the creative route and that's because of the influence Johnny Bassett had on my life."[25]

What all these paeans to Johnny F. Bassett have in common is the binding theme that he was a decent, honest, and straightforward innovator who never forgot that sports are supposed to entertain. He was a complex man who did not always have the best idea but was capable of learning from mistakes and putting those lessons to work on his next project. Bassett's time in sports is probably best summed up by Carole Goss-Taylor, his co-host on *After Four*, an *American Bandstand*–style show Bassett created for CFTO in the 1960s, and an admirer of his career.

"There were business and public accomplishments and failures," said Goss-Taylor. "But you should make sure people are aware of what a fun person he was. Johnny always had a twinkle in his eye."[26]

For all the reasons Johnny F. Bassett is remembered perhaps no other is more important than the simple fact that he dared to live his life to the fullest while doing so in a very open manner. Johnny F. Bassett dreamt big and he invited people to come along with him, changing the trajectory of sports in the United States and Canada. Those that did were never the same and never forgot. To have that kind of influence is the hallmark of a life well-lived.

And that is a life worth writing about.

Chapter Notes

Preface

1. Michael O'Brien, *Vince: A Personal Biography of Vince Lombardi* (New York: William Morrow & Co., 1987), 379.

Introduction

1. Dave Reeves, "Don't Look Now, But Football's Starting," *Lakeland Ledger* (Lakeland, FL), January 9, 1984.
2. Mike Flanagan, "Even Critics Can't Ignore USFL Now," *The Evening Independent* (St. Petersburg, FL), March 7, 1984.
3. Silvio Brondoni, "Innovation and Imitation: Corporate Strategies for Global Competition," *Emerging Issues in Management* no. 1 (2012): 10–11.
4. Ramon Casadesus-Masanell and Feng Zhu, "Business Model Innovation and Competitive Imitation: The Case of Sponsor-Based Business Models," *Strategic Management Journal* 34, no. 4 (2013): 465.
5. Terry Pluto, *Our Tribe: A Baseball Memoir* (Cleveland, OH: Gray & Co., 1999), 132–136.
6. Paul Dickson, *Bill Veeck: Baseball's Greatest Maverick* (New York: Walker & Co., 2012), 48, 111, 240–241.
7. Fifth Organizational Meeting of the American Football League Minutes, November 23, 1959, AFL Meeting Minutes, Professional Football Hall of Fame, Canton, OH.
8. Michael MacCambridge, *Lamar Hunt*, 161.
9. U.S. Congress, House of Representatives, Sports Broadcasting Act of 1961, 87th Congress, 1st Session, 1961, Public Law 87–331. http://uscode.house.gov/statviewer.htm?volume=75&page=732.

Chapter One

1. A.H. Saxon, *P.T. Barnum: The Legend and the Man* (New York: Columbia University Press, 1989), 335–336.
2. Jack Dulmage, "Sickness and Fines," *Windsor Star*, December 3, 1975.
3. Ken McKee, "No Need for a Desk in Johnny F's Office," *Toronto Star*, February 9, 1974.
4. Ken McKee, *ibid.*
5. *The Producers*, directed by Susan Stroman (2005; Universal City, CA: Universal, 2006), DVD.
6. Peter Eby, interview, October 8, 2013.
7. John C. Bassett, interview, July 24, 2013.
8. Neil Harris, *The Art of P.T. Barnum* (University of Chicago Press, 1973), 3–4.
9. Michael Kimmel, *Manhood in America: A Cultural History* (New York: Oxford University Press, 2018), 22.
10. Phineas Taylor Barnum, *Struggles and Triumphs: Sixty Years' Recollections of P.T. Barnum* (Buffalo, NY: The Courier Company, 1889; Seattle, WA: CreateSpace Independent Publishing Platform, 2012), 37. Citations refer to the CreateSpace edition.
11. P.T. Barnum, 17.
12. P.T. Barnum, 27.
13. Dale A. Somers, *The Rise of Sports in New Orleans, 1850–1900* (Baton

Rouge: Louisiana State University Press, 1972), vi.

14. P.T. Barnum, 37–38.

15. P.T. Barnum, 39.

16. P.T. Barnum, 131.

17. Barry McDermott, "Here Comes Carling, Her Daddy's Darling," *Sports Illustrated*, June 27, 1983, 86.

18. Maggie Siggins, *Bassett: John Bassett's 40 Years in Politics, Publishing, Business and Sports* (Toronto: James Lorimer & Co.,1979), 14.

19. Siggins, 50.

20. Siggins, 229.

21. George Gross, "Goodbye to a Friend" *Toronto Sun*, May 15, 1986.

22. Gross, "Goodbye to a Friend."

23. Paul Rimstead, "Johnny F., Man of Legendary Mettle," *Toronto Sun*, March 23, 1986.

24. *Ibid.*

25. Rimstead, "Johnny F., Man of Legendary Mettle."

26. Rimstead, "Johnny F., Man of Legendary Mettle."

27. John MacDonald, "Family Affair in Junior Tennis," *Toronto Star*, July 11, 1955.

28. Gross, "Goodbye to a Friend."

29. Rimstead, Johnny F., "Man of Legendary Mettle."

30. Bassett-Klauber, telephone interview.

31. *Ibid.*

32. John C. Bassett, personal interview, 24 July 2013.

33. Richard O. Davies, *Sports in American Life: A History* (West Sussex, UK: Blackwell Publishing, 2017), 1.

34. Davies, *Sports in American Life*, 1.

35. Allen Guttman, *From Ritual to Record: The Nature of Modern Sports* (New York: Columbia University Press, 1978), 59.

36. Charles Samuels, *The Magnificent Rube: The Life and Gaudy Times of Tex Rickard* (New York: McGraw-Hill, 1957), 251.

37. Davies, *Sports in American* Life, 150.

38. Samuels, 185.

Chapter Two

1. Maggie Siggins, *Bassett: John Bassett's 40 Years in Politics, Publishing, Business and Sports* (Toronto: James Lorimer & Co., 1979), 173.

2. Siggins, 173.

3. Gross, "Farewell to a Friend."

4. Carole Goss Taylor, interview, February 24, 2014.

5. Siggins, 230.

6. Fran Zimniuch, *Baseball's New Frontier: A History of Expansion, 1961–1998* (Lincoln, NE: University of Nebraska Press, 2013), 115.

7. Allan Levine, *Toronto: Biography of a City* (Madeira Park, BC: Douglas & McIntyre, 2014), 7, 146.

8. Levine, 147.

9. Levine, 189.

10. "First Beer Sold at Blue Jays Game," UPI, July 30, 1982, https://www.upi.com/Archives/1982/07/30/First-beer-sold-at-Blue-Jays-game/6892396849600/.

11. David A. Charters, *The Chequered Past: Sports Car Racing and Rallying in Canada, 1951–1991* (Toronto: University of Toronto Press, 2007), 125.

12. Charters, 235.

13. Charters, 216.

14. Frank Orr, "Auto Racing Plans Announced for CNE," *Toronto Star*, September 16, 1968.

15. Frank Orr, "Lamport Provides Opposition to Proposed CNE Track," *Toronto Star*, September 17, 1968.

16. "Controllers Okay CNE Raceway," *Toronto Star*, October 17, 1968.

17. Frank Orr, "Auto Racing Plans Announced for CNE."

18. "Parkdale Residents Plan to Boycott Promoters of CNE Auto Raceway," *Toronto Star*, November 11, 1968.

19. "Residents Will Ask Court to Stop Raceway Scheme," *Toronto Star*, January 14, 1969.

20. Frank Orr, "Lamport Provides Opposition to Proposed CNE Track."

21. "Promoters Abandon Plans for CNE Raceway," *Toronto Star*, February 7, 1969.

22. *Ibid.*

23. John C. Bassett, interview, February 10, 2014.

24. *Ibid.*

25. Siggins, 229.

26. Siggins, 228.

27. Siggins, 228.

28. Scott Surgent, *The World Hockey*

Association Fact Book (Tempe, AZ: Xaler Press, 2010), 5.

29. Mark Speck, *... and a Dollar Short: The Empty Promises, Broken Dreams and Somewhat-Less than Comical Misadventures of the 1974 Florida Blazers* (Haworth, NJ: St. Johann Press, 2014), 4.

30. Siggins, 229.

31. Al Nickelson, "Bassett Group Buys WHA Nats," *Toronto Star*, May 3, 1973.

32. *Ibid.*

33. Peter Eby, interview, October 8, 2013.

34. *Ibid.*

35. Todd Maher and Mark Speck, *The World Football League Encyclopedia* (Haworth, NJ: St. Johann Press, 2006), 16–17.

36. John C. Bassett, interview, July 20, 2013.

37. George Gross, "Goodbye to a Friend"; Al Sokol, "Sportsman Johnny F. Bassett Dead at 47"; Paul Rimstead, "At Tely, He Foresaw the Rise of the Sun."

38. Douglas Bassett, interview, October 11, 2013.

39. Gross, "Goodbye to a Friend."

40. *Ibid.*

41. Jim Kernaghan, "Newly Named Toros Bullish on Leafs Center," *Toronto Star*, June 12, 1973.

42. Ken Rappoport, *The Little League that Could: A History of the American Football League* (New York: Taylor Trade Publishing, 2010), 10.

Chapter Three

1. Michael McKinley, *Hockey Night in Canada: 60 Seasons* (Toronto: Viking Press, 2012), 33.

2. Bob Pennington, "Ballard's World is Tough—And That's How He Likes It," *Toronto Star* February 2, 1974.

3. Peter Eby, interview, October 8, 2013.

4. Jesse Lawrence, "Maple Leafs Have Most Expensive Tickets for 2014–2015 Season," *Forbes* September 19, 2014, https://www.forbes.com/sites/jesselawrence/2014/09/19/leafs-top-canadian-team-blackhawks-top-american-team-in-2014-15-nhl-tickets-on-secondary-market/#5871619b5668.

5. Milt Dunnell, "Bassett Believes His Rookies Best," *Toronto Star*, January 1, 1974.

6. John C. Bassett, interview, July 24. 2013.

7. Elaine Kenney, "Toros Night in Toronto: 'Terrific, Super-Duper,'" *Toronto Star*, October 8, 1973.

8. *Ibid.*

9. Jim Kernaghan, "Toros Tie in WHA Debut," *Toronto Star*, October 8, 1973.

10. *Ibid.*

11. Jim Proudfoot, "Toros Catching on This Survey Says," *Toronto Star*, February 26, 1974.

12. *Ibid.*

13. Al Nickelson, "Bassett Group Buys WHA Nats," *Toronto Star*, May 3, 1973.

14. Allan Levine, *Toronto: Biography of a City* (Madeira Park, BC: Douglas and McIntyre), 251.

15. Jim Kernaghan, "Toros Know Gardens Well," *Toronto Star*, April 2, 1974.

16. *Ibid.*

17. Jim Kernaghan, "Late-Season Drive a Harris Trademark," *Toronto Star*, April 9, 1974.

18. Jim Kernaghan, "Oshawa Slams Arena Doors on Toros," *Toronto Star*, March 6, 1974.

19. *Ibid.*

20. Jim Kernaghan, "Toros to Play Home Games Next Year at the Gardens," *Toronto Star*, April 3, 1974.

21. Bob Pennington, "Ballard's World is Tough—And That's How He Likes It."

22. *Ibid.*

23. John C. Bassett, interview, July 24, 2013.

24. Ed Willes, *Rebel League: The Short and Unruly Life of the World Hockey Association* (Toronto: McClelland & Stewart, 2004), 148.

25. Peter Eby, interview, October 8, 2013.

26. John C. Bassett, interview, July 24, 2013.

27. Peter Eby, interview, October 8, 2013.

28. *Ibid.*

29. John Eaton, interview, September 1, 2014.

30. Jim Proudfoot, "Toronto's Best? Could be Toros if They Keep On," *Toronto Star*, July 25, 1974.

Chapter Four

1. Jim Proudfoot, "Toronto's Best? Could be Toros if They Keep On," *Toronto Star*, July 25, 1974.
2. Scott Surgent, *The World Hockey Association Fact Book* (Tempe, AZ: Xaler Press, 2010), 111.
3. Peter McAskile, interview, May 1, 2014.
4. *Ibid.*
5. Jim Kernaghan, "Toros Whacked by Fans and Mariners," *Toronto Star*, April 10, 1975.
6. Jim Kernaghan, "Lack of Support May Chase Toros Out of Toronto," *Toronto Star*, February 3, 1976.
7. *Ibid.*
8. Jim Proudfoot, "Here is Why Toros are Going Off to Sweden," *Toronto Star*, August 20, 1975.
9. Gilles Leger, interview, February 24, 2015.
10. Surgent, 138.
11. Peter Eby, interview, October 8, 2013.
12. Bob Baun, interview, August 29, 2015.
13. Jim Kernaghan, "Toros Fined $500 Each After Blowing 6-Goal Lead," *Toronto Star*, December 1, 1975.
14. *Ibid.*
15. Jim Kernaghan, "Is Baun Being Ousted by Toros?" *Toronto Star*, December 23, 1975.
16. Jim Kernaghan, "Toros Fire Man They Didn't Help," *Toronto Star*, February 17, 1976.
17. *Ibid.*
18. Jim Kernaghan, "Lack of Support May Chase Toros Out of Toronto."
19. Ed Willies, *Rebel League: The Short and Unruly Life of the World Hockey Association* (Toronto: McClelland & Stewart, 2004), 148, 151.
20. Gilles Leger, interview, August 29, 2015.
21. John C. Bassett, interview, July 24, 2013.
22. Sue Bassett-Klauber, interview, October 3, 2013.
23. Carling Bassett-Seguso, interview, June 10, 2014.
24. Victoria Bassett, interview, February 13, 2014.

Chapter Five

1. Paul Warfield, interview, June 19, 2013; John C. Bassett, interview, July 24, 2013.
2. Marc Gunther and Bill Carter, *Monday Night Mayhem: The Inside Story of ABCs Monday Night Football* (New York: William Morrow, 1988), 129–130.
3. Mark Kriegel, *Namath: A Biography* (New York: Viking, 2004), 357–358.
4. David Harris, *The League: The Rise and Decline of the NFL* (New York: Bantam Books, 1986), 177.
5. Mark Speck, *...And a Dollar Short: The Empty Promises, Broken Dreams and Somewhat-Less Than Comical Misadventures of the 1974 Florida Blazers* (Haworth, NJ: St. Johann Press, 2011), 4.
6. Speck, 5.
7. Michael MacCambridge, *America's Game: The Epic Story of How Pro Football Captured a Nation* (New York: Anchor Books, 2004), 326.
8. Speck, 5.
9. Speck, 4.
10. Speck, 4–5.
11. Speck, 5.
12. Maggie Siggins, *Bassett: John Bassett's Forty Years in Politics, Publishing, Business, and Sports* (Toronto: James Lorimer & Co., 1979), 120–121.
13. John Eaton, interview, September 1, 2014.
14. Steve O'Brien, *The Canadian Football League: The Phoenix of Professional Sports Leagues* (Morrisville, NC: Lulu Enterprises, 2005), 1.
15. *Ibid.*
16. O'Brien, 9.
17. O'Brien, 5.
18. O'Brien, 212.
19. O'Brien, 6–7.
20. *Ibid.*
21. O'Brien, 11.
22. Erik Barnouw, *Tube of Plenty: The Evolution of American Television* (New York: Oxford University Press, 1990), 235.
23. *Ibid.*
24. Siggins, 206.
25. O'Brien, 214.
26. Colin Woodard, *American Nations: The History of the Eleven Rival Regional Cultures of North America* (New York: Penguin Books, 2011), 4, 154.

27. Woodard, 155.

28. Steven J. Jackson, "Gretzky, Crisis, and Canadian Identity in 1988: Rearticulating the Americanization of Culture Debate," *Sociology of Sport Journal* 11, no. 4 (1994): 434–435.

29. Jack L. Granastein, *Yankee Go Home? Canadians and Anti-Americanism* (Toronto: Harper Collins, 1996), 4.

30. Bob Hughes, "Government May Move Against WFL," *The Leader Post* (Regina, Saskatchewan), February 22, 1974.

31. Milt Dunnell, "Johnny F. Out, Joe's Deal Off," *Toronto Star*, January 22. 1974.

32. Paul Godfrey, interview, January 30, 2014.

33. *Ibid.*

34. Katharyne Mitchell, "In Whose Image? Transnational Capital and the Production of Multiculturalism in Canada," in *Global/Local: Cultural Production and the Transnational Imaginary*, eds. Rob Wilson and Wimal Dissanayake (Durham, NC: Duke University Press, 1996), 237–239.

35. Al Sokol, "Argo Position Worries CFL," *Toronto Star*, January 23, 1974.

36. O'Brien, 8–9.

37. Siggins, 115–116.

38. *Ibid.*

39. Bob Hughes, "Government May Move Against WFL."

40. Siggins, 231.

41. *Ibid.*

42. Siggins, 232.

43. Ken McKee, "Toronto's New Football Club Can Veto Canadian Entries," *Toronto Star*, January 16, 1974.

44. Milt Dunnell, "Johnny F. Out, Joe's Deal Off."

45. Ken McKee, "Toronto's New Football Club Can Veto Canadian Entries."

46. *Ibid.*

47. Siggins, 232.

48. Al Sokol, "Leo Cahill is Back in Action," *Toronto Star*, February 2, 1974.

Chapter Six

1. Jack L. Granatstein, *Yankee Go Home? Canadians and Anti-Americanism* (Toronto: Harper Collins, 1996), 135, 164–166.

2. Marc Lalonde, interview, September 26, 2014.

3. *Ibid.*

4. Bob Hughes, "Government May Move Against WFL," *The Leader Post* (Regina, Saskatchewan), February 22, 1974.

5. Paul Godfrey, interview, January 30, 2014, JFB Audio Collection.

6. John Robertson, "No Hearing for Bassett," *Montreal Star*, February 28, 1974.

7. Bob Hughes, "Government May Move Against WFL."

8. John Robertson, "No Hearing for Bassett," *Montreal Star*, February 28, 1974.

9. *Ibid.*

10. Larry Csonka, interview, March 11, 2014.

11. David Harris, *The League: The Rise and Decline of the NFL* (New York: Bantam Books, 1986), 168.

12. Larry Csonka, Jim Kiick and Dave Anderson, *Always on the Run* (New York, Bantam Books, 1974), 175, 186–187.

13. Larry Csonka, interview, March 11, 2014.

14. Paul Warfield, interview, June 19, 2013.

15. *Ibid.*

16. Harris, 168.

17. Larry Csonka, interview, March 11, 2014.

18. Paul Warfield, interview, June 19, 2013.

19. *Ibid.*

20. Harris, 170.

21. Brad Schultz, *Year One: The 1970 Season and the Dawn of Modern Football* (Washington D.C.: Potomac Books, 2013), 144.

22. Herb Solway, interview, April 22, 2014.

23. Harris, 170.

24. Mark Speck, *...And a Dollar Short: The Empty Promises, Broken Dreams and Somewhat-Less Than Comical Misadventures of the 1974 Florida Blazers* (Haworth, NJ: St. Johann Press, 2011), 65.

25. Herb Solway, interview, April 22, 2014.

26. Paul Warfield, interview, June 19, 2013.

27. Larry Csonka, interview, March 11, 2014.

28. *Ibid.*

29. Paul Warfield, interview, June 19, 2013.

30. Larry Csonka, interview, March 11, 2014.

31. Judi Timson, "Bassett's Big Coup No Hustle, He Says 'They Dig Canada,'" *Toronto Star*, April 1, 1974.

32. Jim Proudfoot, "WFL Ready to Share Cost of Miami Stars," *Toronto Star*, March 30, 1974.

33. Larry Csonka, Jim Kiick, and Dave Anderson, 233.

34. Paul Warfield, interview, June 19, 2013.

35. Harris, 170.

36. Judi Timson, "Bassett's Big Coup No Hustle, He Says 'They Dig Canada.'"

37. Harris, 170.

38. Herb Solway, interview, April 22, 2014.

39. "Lalonde Insists Those Miami Stars Won't Play Here," *Toronto Star*, April 1, 1974.

40. Larry Csonka, interview, March 11, 2014.

41. Paul Warfield, interview, June 19, 2013.

42. Judi Timson, "Bassett's Big Coup No Hustle, He Says 'They Dig Canada.'"

43. Peter Eby, interview, October 8, 2013.

44. "Lalonde Insists Those Miami Stars Won't Play Here."

45. Steve O'Brien, *The Canadian Football League: The Phoenix of Professional Sports Leagues* (Morrisville, NC: Lulu Enterprises, 2005), 14.

46. O'Brien, 15.

47. *Ibid.*

48. Marc Lalonde, interview, September 26, 2014.

49. Rick Matsumoto, "Northmen Still Hope to Stay," *Toronto Star*, April 11, 1974.

50. *Ibid.*

51. Mary Forbes, *Gentle Giants: The Selmon Brothers* (Tampa, FL: Mariner Publishing, 1981), 88.

52. Jim Proudfoot, "Northmen Pledge to Stop WFL Raids—If They Stay," *Toronto Star*, April 5, 1974.

53. *Ibid.*

54. Doug Gilbert, "No Football Change—But Does it Matter?" *Montreal Gazette* May 9, 1974.

55. *Ibid.*

56. Harris, 174–175.

57. "Memphis Will Vote on Northmen Bid," (UPI) *Toronto Star*, May 3, 1974.

58. Milt Dunnell, "The Beer Money is Big in Memphis," *Toronto Star*, May 15, 1974.

59. "Memphis Will Vote on Northmen Bid."

60. Doug Gilbert, "No Football Change—But Does it Matter?"

61. "Northmen Off to U.S., They'll be Southmen," *Toronto Star*, May 7, 1974.

62. O'Brien, 16.

63. Marc Lalonde, interview, September 26, 2014.

64. "WFL—Pig in Poke is Selling," (UPI) *The Evening Independent* (St. Petersburg, FL), June 27, 1974.

65. "Northmen to Become Southmen," *Milwaukee Journal* May 8, 1974.

66. Sue Bassett-Klauber, interview, October 3, 2013.

67. Peter Eby, interview, October 8, 2013.

68. John Gault, "'I'm Going to Fight,' Says Bassett," *Toronto Star*, March 16, 1974.

69. Marc Lalonde, interview, September 26, 2014.

70. *B'nai B'rith Sportsmen Lodge #1977 John F. Bassett Celebrity Dinner* (program), Royal York Hotel, Canadian Room, November 5, 1974.

Chapter Seven

1. Tod Maher and Mark Speck, *World Football League Encyclopedia* (Haworth, NJ: St. Johann Press, 2006), 33.

2. *Ibid.*

3. William Oscar Johnson, "The Day the Money Ran Out," *Sports Illustrated*, December 1, 1975, 88.

4. *Lost Treasures of NFL Films: The World Football League*, directed by Dave Petrellius (2001; Mt. Laurel, NJ: NFL Films, 2001), DVD.

5. Scott Surgent, *The World Hockey Association Fact Book* (Tempe, AZ: Xaler Press, 2010), 4.

6. David George Surdam, *Run to Glory and Profits: The Economic Rise of*

the NFL During the 1950s (Lincoln, NE: University of Nebraska Press, 2013), 126–130.

7. Stephen R. Lowe, *The Kid on the Sandlot: Congress and Professional Sports, 1910–1992* (Bowling Green, OH: Bowling Green State University Popular Press, 1995), 36.

8. David Harris, *The League: The Rise and Decline of the NFL* (New York: Bantam Books, 1986), 121–124.

9. Surdam, 18–20; Jeff Miller, *Going Long: The Wild 10-Year Saga of the Renegade American Football League in the Words of Those Who Lived it* (New York: McGraw-Hill, 2003), 163–175

10. William N. Wallace, "Stabler of Raiders Joins WFL for '76," *New York Times*, April 3, 1974.

11. *Ibid.*

12. "Toronto of WFL Gets Memphis Home," (AP) *New York Times*, May 7, 1974.

13. Victor Zarnowitz and Geoffrey H. Moore, "The Recession and Recovery of 1973–1976," *Explorations in Economic Research* 4, no. 4 (1977): 471–472.

14. Hubert Mizell, "Jacksonville Attorney Tampa NFL Owner," *St. Petersburg Times*, December 6, 1974.

15. Harris, 129–130.

16. Mark Speck, *...And a Dollar Short: The Empty Promises, Broken Dreams and Somewhat-Less Than Comical Misadventures of the 1974 Florida Blazers* (Haworth, NJ: St. Johann Press, 2011), 72–73.

17. Speck, 73.

18. John McVay, interview, October 14, 2013.

19. *Ibid.*

20. *Lost Treasures of NFL Films: The World Football League.*

21. Bill Livingston, "Bell Crowd Control Plan: More Cops, Less Freebies," *Philadelphia Inquirer*, July 27, 1974.

22. "High-Flying WFL: Full of Hot Air," (AP) *St. Petersburg Times*, August 7, 1974.

23. Buddy Martin, "Inferior Surroundings Hamper WFL at the Gate," *St. Petersburg Times*, July 19, 1974.

24. Hubert Mizell, "Defense Hands Sharks a Win," *St. Petersburg Times*, July 12, 1974.

25. Buddy Martin, "Gary Davidson a Proud Papa," *St. Petersburg Times*, July 12, 1974.

26. "Rookies, Free Agents May Be Keys to NFL Strike," (AP) *Philadelphia Inquirer*, July 2, 1974.

27. Beano Cook, "WFL: Maybe on Sundays," *St. Petersburg Times*, July 12, 1974.

28. Buddy Martin, "Gary Davidson a Proud Papa."

29. Arnold Moss, "Jewels from a Box Office: The Language of Show Business," *American Speech* 11, no. 3 (1936): 221–22.

30. "Bell Tolls a Lie," (AP) *St. Petersburg Times*, August 6, 1974.

31. Buddy Martin, "Padding One Thing, But Wall-to-Wall?" *St. Petersburg Times*, August 7, 1974.

32. William Oscar Johnson, 88.

33. "Bell Tolls a Lie."

34. *Ibid.*

35. Jim Kernaghan, "Bassett Defends Free Tickets," *Toronto Star*, January 3, 1976.

36. "High Flying WFL Full of Hot Air."

37. Rob Manker, "After 40 Years, Can We Slam the Door on '-Gate' Already?" May 29, 2012, http://articles.chicagotribune.com/2012-05-29/news/ct-talk-gate-words-manker-0529-20120529_1_scandal-nixon-speechwriter-william-safire.

38. Frank Dolson, "Bell's Attendance Isn't What It's Cracked Up to Be," *Philadelphia Inquirer*, August 4, 1974; Frank Dolson, "Will Paper-Gate Topple President," *Philadelphia Inquirer*, August 6, 1974.

39. "High-Flying WFL: Full of Hot Air."

40. *Ibid.*

41. Frank Dolson, *The Philadelphia Story: A City of Winners* (South Bend, IN: Icarus Press, 1981), 151–152.

42. "High Flying WFL Full of Hot Air."

43. William Oscar Johnson, 88.

44. Maher and Speck, 24–29.

45. Ed Willes, *Rebel League: The Short and Unruly Life of the World Hockey Association* (Toronto: McClelland & Stewart, 2004), 147.

46. Sue Bassett-Klauber, interview, April 1, 2014.

47. Gordon Lightfoot, interview, February 24, 2014.

48. *Ibid.*

49. Sue Bassett-Klauber, interview, April 1, 2014.

50. Paul Warfield, interview, June 19, 2013.

51. William Oscar Johnson, 92.

52. John McVay, interview, October 14, 2013.

Chapter Eight

1. Mark Speck, ...And a Dollar Short: The Empty Promises, Broken Dreams and Somewhat-Less Than Comical Misadventures of the 1974 Florida Blazers (Haworth, NJ: St. Johann Press, 2011), 72.

2. Speck, 166–167.

3. Speck, 167.

4. Tod Maher and Mark Speck, World Football League Encyclopedia (Haworth, NJ: St. Johann Press, 2006), 49.

5. Maher and Speck, 82.

6. Speck, 173.

7. Speck, 180.

8. Speck, 185.

9. Speck, 188.

10. Maher and Speck, 40.

11. Speck, 198.

12. Speck, 198.

13. Ibid.

14. John McVay, interview, October 14, 2013.

15. Speck, 184.

16. Speck, 206.

17. William Oscar Johnson, "The Day the Money Ran Out," Sports Illustrated, December 1, 1975, 88.

18. Larry Csonka, interview, March 11, 2014.

19. Ibid.

20. Maher and Speck, 142.

21. William Oscar Johnson, 88.

22. Robert F. Jones, "They're Grinning and Bearing It," Sports Illustrated, July 28, 1975, 17.

23. Paul Warfield, interview, June 19, 2013.

24. Larry Csonka, interview, March 11, 2014.

25. John McVay, interview, October 14, 2013.

26. Larry Csonka, interview, March 11, 2014.

27. Maher and Speck, 146.

28. William Oscar Johnson, 91.

29. Larry Csonka, interview, March 11, 2014.

30. William Oscar Johnson, 86.

31. Gene Klein and David Fisher, First Down and a Billion: The Funny Business of Pro Football (New York: William Morrow & Co., 1987), 82.

32. David Harris, The League: The Rise and Decline of the NFL (New York: Bantam Books, 1986), 206.

33. Harris, 215.

34. Larry Csonka, interview, March 11, 2014.

35. Ibid.

36. Paul Warfield, interview, June 19, 2013.

37. John McVay, interview, October 14, 2013.

38. Larry Csonka, interview, March 11, 2014.

39. Paul Warfield, interview, June 19, 2013.

40. Larry Csonka, interview, March 11, 2013.

41. "Memphis in Two," (UPI) The Evening Independent (St. Petersburg, FL), June 3, 1974.

42. Ibid.

43. Milt Dunnell, "Stadium Sold Out if There's a Game," Toronto Star, February 3, 1976.

44. Harris, 229.

45. "NFL Freezes Out John Bassett," (AP) Toronto Star, March 17, 1976.

46. Ibid.

47. Ibid.

48. Klein and Fisher, 282.

49. Harris, 243.

50. Klein and Fisher, 284.

51. Steve Ehrhart, interview, September 4, 2013.

Chapter Nine

1. Harold Baldwin, Slim and None: My Wild Ride from the WHA to the NHL and all the Way to Hollywood (Toronto: Anansi Press, 2014), 120.

2. Barry McDermott, "Here's Carling, Her Daddy's Darling," Sports Illustrated, June 27, 1983, 94.

3. Ibid.

4. Frank Falkenberg, interview, May 1, 2014.

5. Sue Bassett-Klauber, interview, April 16, 2014.

6. Paul Rimstead, "Johnny F., Man of

Legendary Mettle," *Toronto Sun*, March 23, 1986.

7. Sue Bassett-Klauber, interview, April 16, 2014.

8. Peter McAskile, interview, May 1, 2014.

9. Andrew Doyle "An Atheist in Alabama is Someone Who Doesn't Believe in Bear Bryant: A Symbol for an Embattled South," in *The Sporting World of the Modern South*, ed. Patrick B. Miller (Urbana: University of Illinois Press, 2002), 260.

10. Frank Falkenburg, interview, May 1, 2014.

11. John C. Bassett, interview, July 24, 2013.

12. Scott Surgent, *The World Hockey Association Fact Book* (Tempe, AZ: Xaler Press, 2010), 163.

13. Peter McAskile, interview, May 1, 2014.

14. Ed Willes, *Rebel League: The Short and Unruly Life of the World Hockey Association* (Toronto: McClelland and Stewart, 2004), 152.

15. Peter Eby, interview, October 8, 2013.

16. Peter McAskile, interview, May 1, 2014.

17. Peter Eby, interview, October 8, 2013.

18. *Ibid.*

19. Surgent, 12.

20. Surgent, 15.

21. John C. Bassett, interview, July 24, 2013.

22. Todd Maher and Mark Speck, *World Football League Encyclopedia* (Haworth, NJ: St. Johann Press, 2006), 34–35.

23. Wes Borucki, "You're Dixie's Football Pride: American College Football and the Resurgence of Southern Identity," *Identities: Global Studies on Culture and Power* 10, no. 4 (2003): 477.

24. Peter McAskile, interview, October 7, 2014.

25. Paul Henderson, interview, August 29, 2015.

26. Peter McAskile, interview, October 7, 2014.

27. Dave Hanson and Ross Bernstein, *Slap Shot Original: The Man, the Foil, the Legend* (Chicago: Triumph Books, 2008), 132.

28. Stephen Cole, *Hockey Night Fever: Mullets, Mayhem, and the Game's Coming*

of Age in the 1970s (Toronto: Doubleday Canada, 2015), 200–201.

29. Ed Willes, *Rebel League: The Short and Unruly Life of the World Hockey Association* (Toronto: McClelland and Stewart, 2004), 154.

30. Jim Kernaghan, "WHA Players Hit Goons," *Toronto Star*, June 11, 1976.

31. Hanson and Bernstein, 134.

32. Hanson and Bernstein, 133.

33. Peter McAskile, interview, May 1, 2014.

34. Willes, 153.

35. Hanson and Bernstein, 133.

36. Frank Falkenburg, interview, May 1, 2014.

37. Hanson and Bernstein, 140–141.

38. Hanson and Bernstein, 139.

39. Hanson and Bernstein, 134.

40. John C. Bassett, interview, July 24, 2013.

41. Willes, 151.

42. Doyle, 248.

43. Willes, 151.

44. "McKegney Released," (AP) *Montgomery Advertiser*, June 19, 1978.

45. Victoria E. Johnson, *Heartland TV: Primetime Television and the Struggle for U.S. Identity* (New York: New York University Press, 2008), 143.

46. Peter McAskile, interview, May 1, 2014.

47. *Ibid.*

48. Scott Surgent, 163.

49. Peter McAskile, interview, 1 May 2014.

Chapter Ten

1. Scott Surgent, *The World Hockey Association Fact Book* (Tempe, AZ: Xaler Press, 2010), 17.

2. Howard Baldwin, interview, May 26, 2015.

3. Howard Baldwin, *Slim and None: My Wild Ride from the WHA to the NHL and all the Way to Hollywood* (Toronto: Anansi Press, 2014), 81.

4. Ed Willes, *Rebel League: The Short and Unruly Life of the World Hockey Association* (Toronto: McClelland and Stewart, 2004), 73.

5. John C. Bassett, interview, July 24, 2013.

6. Surgent, 11.

7. Gus Badali, interview, February 19, 2014,

8. Willes, 150.

9. Harold Baldwin, interview, May 26, 2015.

10. Willes, 150.

11. "WHA Suspends Bassett," (AP) *Montgomery Advertiser*, November 18, 1977.

12. Willes, 153.

13. John C. Bassett, interview, April 25, 2014.

14. *Ibid.*

15. Harold Baldwin, interview, May 26, 2015.

16. *Ibid.*

17. Baldwin, 120.

18. John C. Bassett, interview, July 24, 2013.

19. Wayne Gretzky, interview, October 23, 2014.

20. *Ibid.*

21. Gus Badali, interview, February 19, 2014.

22. *Ibid.*

23. John C. Bassett, interview, July 24, 2013.

24. Wayne Gretzky, interview, October 23, 2014.

25. Gus Badali, interview, February 19, 2014.

26. Alan Thicke, interview, March 6, 2014.

27. Wayne Gretzky, interview, October 23, 2014.

28. Peter Eby, interview, October 8, 2013.

29. John Eaton, interview, September 1, 2014.

30. John Brophy, interview, September 4, 2013.

31. John Brophy, interview, September 4, 2013.

32. John Brophy, interview, September 4, 2013.

33. Peter Eby, interview, October 8, 2013.

34. Barry McDermott, "Here Comes Carling, Her Daddy's Darling," *Sports Illustrated*, June 27, 1983, 88.

35. John Brophy, interview, September 4, 2013.

36. John Brophy, interview, September 4, 2013.

37. Gilles Leger, interview, August 29, 2015.

38. Steve Ehrhart, interview, September 4, 2013.

39. Wayne Gretzky, interview, October 23, 2014.

40. Surgent, 203.

Chapter Eleven

1. Gary R. Mormino, *Land of Sunshine, State of Dreams: A Social History of Florida* (Gainesville, FL: University Press of Florida, 2005), 20.

2. Heidi Bassett-Blair, interview, June 29, 2014.

3. Bassett, Victoria, interview, February 13, 2014.

4. Carling Bassett-Seguso, interview, June 10, 2014.

5. Heidi Bassett-Blair, interview, June 29, 2014.

6. Victoria Bassett, interview, February 13, 2014.

7. Carling Bassett-Seguso, interview, June 10, 2014.

8. John C. Bassett, interview, June 24, 2013.

9. Mormino, 131.

10. Susan Burns, "The Collapse of the Colony," *Sarasota Magazine*, October 31, 2010, https://www.sarasotamagazine.com/news-and-profiles/2010/10/the-collapse-of-the-colony.

11. Barry McDermott, "Here's Carling, Her Daddy's Darling," *Sports Illustrated*, June 27, 1983, 90.

12. Donald Dell, interview, April 22, 2014.

13. Sue Bassett-Klauber, interview, April 16, 2014.

14. Nick Bollettieri, interview, April 22, 2014.

15. Peter Eby, interview, October 8, 2013.

16. John C. Bassett, interview, July 24, 2013.

17. Jim Byrne, *The $1 League: The Rise and Fall of the USFL* (New York: Prentice Hall Press, 1986), 8.

18. William Oscar Johnson, "Whole New League, Whole New Season," *Sports Illustrated*, May 23, 1982, 84.

19. George Becnel, *When the Saints Came Marching In: What the New Orleans NFL Franchise Did Wrong (and Sometimes Right) in its Expansion Years*

(Bloomington, IN: Author's House, 2009), 2.

20. Jeff Miller, *Going Long: The Wild 10-Year Saga of the Renegade American Football League in the Words of Those Who Lived it* (New York: McGraw Hill, 2003), 155–160.

21. Byrne, 8.

22. William Oscar Johnson, 84.

23. Byrne, 9–10.

24. Stuart Mieher, "Sports Teams Hardly Ever Score Big Bucks, but Who Cares?" *Florida Trend,* February 1985, 77.

25. John C. Bassett, interview, July 24, 2013.

26. "Bassett, Tampa Team Ready," *Sarasota Journal,* May 12, 1982.

27. Mike Flanagan, "Taking Stock in USFL," *Evening Independent* (St. Petersburg, FL), June 25, 1982.

28. *Ibid.*

29. Chris Harry and Joey Johnston, *Tales from the Bucs Sideline* (Chicago: Sports Publishing LLC, 2004), 89.

30. John C. Bassett, interview, July 24, 2013.

31. Mormin, 125.

32. Mormino, 125; John Rothchild, "The Distinguished States of Florida," *Forum: The Magazine of the Florida Humanities Council* 17, no. 2 (1993): 8.

33. Tracy J. Revels, *Sunshine Paradise: A History of Florida Tourism* (Gainesville, FL: University of Florida Press, 2011), 4.

34. Revels, 133, 137.

35. Revels, 113.

36. Gregory Jason Bell, "Ye Mystic Krewe of Historical Revisionists: The Origins of Tampa's Gasparilla Parade," in *Zlín Proceedings in Humanities, Volume 5,* eds. Roman Trušník, Gregory Jason Bell, and Katarína Nemčoková (Zlín, Czech Republic: Thomas Bata University, 2015), 191.

37. Revels, 117.

38. Jim McVay, interview, November 19, 2013.

39. *Ibid.*

40. Mike Tierney, "Bucs Tabbed as a Rich, Low-Paying Club," *St. Petersburg Times,* February 27, 1982.

41. Mic Huber, "Bandits Sign Sarasota Policeman," *Sarasota Herald-Tribune,* October 26, 1982.

42. Mike Flanagan, "Dreams Put to Test," *Evening Independent* (St. Petersburg, FL), October 25, 1982.

43. Jimmy Jordan, interview, October 17, 2013.

44. Mike Flanagan, "Reaves Tries to Recapture Potential He Wasted," *Evening Independent* (St. Petersburg, FL), March 4, 1983.

45. *Ibid.*

46. Mark Johnson, "Bandit-Ball: The Thing in Spring," *St. Petersburg Times,* September 14, 1982.

47. Flanagan, "Taking Stock of the USFL."

48. Steve Spurrier, interview, August 20, 2013.

49. *Ibid.*

50. Patrick Zier, "It's Official, Spurrier Bandits' Man," *Lakeland Ledger,* November 23, 1982.

51. Denis M. Crawford, *Hugh Culverhouse and the Tampa Bay Buccaneers: How a Skinflint Genius with a Losing Team Made the Modern NFL* (Jefferson, NC: McFarland, 2011), 103.

52. Zier, "It's Official, Spurrier Bandits' Man."

53. Patrick Zier, "Bandits on the Run as Bucs go into Stall," *Lakeland Ledger,* October 31, 1982.

54. Jim McVay, interview, November 19, 2013.

55. Ron Martz, "The Community Owns Nothing," *St. Petersburg Times,* August 15, 1979.

56. "Robbie Calls Truce in Battle of Florida," *Ocala Star-Banner,* August 11, 1979.

57. Patrick Zier, "Bucs Don't Care for the New Kid in Town," *Lakeland Ledger,* March 28, 1983.

58. Jim McVay, interview, November 19, 2013.

59. Leo Suarez, "USFL Bandits Making a Big Hit with Tampa's Sports Fans," *The Miami News,* February 12, 1983.

60. Mike Flanagan, "So Much for Quarterback Equality in Bandits' Camp," *Evening Independent* (St. Petersburg, FL), February 16, 1983.

61. Suarez, "USFL Bandits Making a Big Hit with Tampa's Sports Fans."

62. Steve Ehrhart, interview, September 4, 2013.

63. Mike Flanagan, "It Was a Different Kind of Football," *Evening Independent* (St. Petersburg, FL), February 14, 1983.

64. *Ibid.*

65. Steve Ehrhart, interview, September 4, 2013.

66. Jim McVay, interview, November 19, 2013.

67. John C. Bassett, interview, July 24, 2013.

68. Mike Flanagan, "Bandits' Non-Game Makes League and Television History," *Evening Independent* (St. Petersburg, FL), February 14, 1983.

69. Flanagan, "It Was a Different Kind of Football."

70. *Ibid.*

Chapter Twelve

1. Tracy J. Revels, *Sunshine Paradise: A History of Florida Tourism* (Gainesville, FL: University of Florida Press, 2011), 66.

2. Revels, 70.

3. Gary R. Mormino, *Land of Sunshine, State of Dreams: A Social History of Florida* (Gainesville, FL: University Press of Florida, 2005), 132.

4. Buddy Martin, "Tampa Gets NFL Franchise for '76," *St. Petersburg Times,* April 25, 1974.

5. Jim Byrne, *The $1 League: The Rise and Fall of the USFL* (New York: Prentice Hall Press, 1986), 25.

6. Byrne, 47.

7. Huber, "Bandits Sign Sarasota Policeman."

8. Steve Ehrhart, interview, September 4, 2013.

9. Mike Flanagan, "Beach Boys Teach Arizona a Lesson," *Evening Independent* (St. Petersburg, FL), March 3, 1984.

10. *Ibid.*

11. Paul Reeths, *The United States Football League, 1982–1986* (Jefferson, NC: McFarland, 2017), 107.

12. Jeff Pearlman, *Football for a Buck: The Crazy Rise and Crazier Demise of the USFL* (Boston: Mariner Books, 2018), 104–105.

13. Bob Gilmore, "Despite Losses the USFL Just Keeps on Truckin,'" *The Altus Times* (Altus, OK), April 26, 1984.

14. Doug Lasswell, "Bandits' Bassett Wears Many Hats," *Sarasota Herald-Tribune,* June 17, 1984.

15. Mike Flanagan, "State of the USFL is Healthy: Bassett," *Evening Independent* (St. Petersburg, FL), June 30, 1984.

16. Byrne, 35.

17. Byrne, 37–38.

18. Mic Huber, "Bandits in Final Preseason Tune-up," *Sarasota Herald-Tribune*, February 26, 1983.

19. Steve Ehrhart, interview, September 4, 2013.

20. *Ibid.*

21. Flanagan, "Taking Stock in USFL."

22. John C. Bassett, interview, July 24, 2013.

23. Mark Johnson, "Doggone, Burt. They're the Tampa Bay Bandits," *St. Petersburg Times,* August 5, 1982.

24. *Ibid.*

25. *Ibid.*

26. *Ibid.*

27. Bruce J. Schulman, *The Seventies: The Great Shift in American Culture, Society, and Politics* (Boston: De Capo Press, 2002), xiv.

28. Schulman, 105–106.

29. Peter Applebome, *Dixie Rising: How the South Is Shaping American Values, Politics, and Culture* (San Diego: Harcourt Brace & Co., 1997), 244.

30. Schulman, 115.

31. Greg Fielden, *NASCAR: The Complete History* (Lincolnwood, IL: Publications International, 2015), 212.

32. Stuart Mieher, "Sports Teams Hardly Ever Score Big Bucks, but Who Cares? *Florida Trend*, February 1985, 78.

33. Steve Spurrier, interview, August 20, 2013.

34. Jimmy Jordan, interview, October 17, 2013.

35. *Small Potatoes: Who Killed the USFL?* directed by Mike Tollin (2009; Bristol, CT: ESPN, 2009), DVD.

36. "Bandit-Ball Pays Off for Tampa Bay, 27–22," *Ocala Star-Banner*, March 28, 1983.

37. Tim McDonald and Mike Flanagan, "Bits and Pieces," *Evening Independent* (St. Petersburg, FL), March 7, 1983.

38. Byrne, 57.

39. Bob Chick, "Bandits Debut Like a Grown-up," *Evening Independent* (St. Petersburg, FL), March 7, 1983.

40. Dave Reeves, "Spurrier Considered a Comeback," *Lakeland Ledger*, May 10, 1983.

41. Jim McVay, interview, November 19, 2013.

42. Jimmy Jordan, interview, October 17, 2013.

Chapter Thirteen

1. Jim Byrne, *The $1 League: The Rise and Fall of the USFL* (New York: Prentice Hall, 1986), 78.
2. Jeff Pearlman, *Football for a Buck: The Crazy Rise and Crazier Demise of the USFL* (Boston: Mariner Books, 2018), 78–79.
3. Paul Reeths, *The United States Football League, 1982–1986* (Jefferson, NC: McFarland, 2017), 100.
4. Bob Chick, "How Hot Was it? Just Ask any Sunburned Fan," *Evening Independent* (St. Petersburg, FL), June 6, 1983.
5. Paul Warfield, interview, June 19, 2013.
6. Stuart Mieher, "Sports Teams Hardly Ever Score Big Bucks, But Who Cares?" *Florida Trend*, February 1985, 77.
7. Dave Reeves, "Bandits Want to be Attractive," *Lakeland Ledger*, January 14, 1983.
8. Mike Flanagan, "So Much for Quarterback Equality in Bandits' Camp," *Evening Independent* (St. Petersburg Times), February 16, 1983.
9. Leo Suarez, "USFL Bandits Making a Big Hit with Tampa's Sports Fans," *Miami News*, February 12, 1983.
10. Reeves, "Bandits Want to be Attractive."
11. *Ibid.*
12. Pearlman, 76–77.
13. Pam Yonge, interview, April 23, 2013.
14. "Bandit Burnout Winner Picked in Draw," *Lakeland Ledger*, May 19, 1983.
15. Mike Flanagan, "It Doesn't Matter Who Takes the Snap for the Bandits," *Evening Independent* (St. Petersburg, FL), May 23, 1983.
16. Mike Flanagan, "Burned Out? Bandits Have a Remedy—A Good Dose of Bandit-Ball," *Evening Independent* (St. Petersburg, FL), January 27, 1984.
17. Dave Reeves, "Don't Look Now, But Football's Starting," *Lakeland Ledger*, January 9, 1984.
18. Steve Ehrhart, interview, September 4, 2013.

19. "Miami-Florida Game Is a Sell-Out," *Palm Beach Post* (AP), May 9, 1984.
20. *Ibid.*
21. Mike Flanagan, "State of the USFL is Healthy: Bassett," *Evening Independent* (St. Petersburg, FL), June 30, 1984.
22. Doug Lasswell, "Bandits' Bassett Wears Many Hats," *Sarasota Herald-Tribune*, June 17, 1984.
23. Jim McVay, interview, November 19, 2013.
24. Doug Lasswell, "Simmons Predicts Tampa Sell-Out," *Sarasota Herald-Tribune*, April 11, 1984.
25. Michael Tollin, interview, August 14, 2013.
26. Patrick Zier, "Bandits Are Best of a Very Bad Group," *Lakeland Ledger*, May 31, 1984.
27. Mike Flanagan, "Bandits' New Idea: Win a Million Bucks," *Evening Independent* (St. Petersburg, FL), April 2, 1985.
28. Mike Flanagan, "Bandits Owner John Bassett Ends Mystery, Admits He's Ill," *Evening Independent* (St. Petersburg, FL), April 8, 1985.
29. Jim McVay, interview, November 19, 2013.
30. Fred Nordgren, interview, October 10, 2013.
31. Steve Ehrhart, interview, September 4, 2013.
32. Reeths, 220.
33. Fred Nordgren, interview, October 10, 2013.
34. *Ibid.*
35. Reeths, 220.
36. Reeths, 289.
37. Jane Feuer, *Seeing Through the Eighties: Television and Reaganism* (Durham, NC: Duke University Press, 1995), 131.
38. Doug Rossinow, *The Reagan Era: A History of the 1980s* (New York: Columbia University Press, 2015), 6.
39. Michael Kimmel, *Manhood in America: A Cultural History* (New York: Oxford University Press, 2018), 246.
40. Diana Kendall, *Framing Class: Media Representations of Wealth and Poverty in America* (Plymouth, UK: Rowman & Littlefield, 2011), 39.
41. Rossinow, 125.
42. *Wall Street*, directed by Oliver

Stone (1987; Los Angeles: Twentieth Century Fox, 2000), DVD.

43. Richard O. Davies, *America's Obsession: Sports and Society Since 1945* (Fort Worth, TX: Harcourt Brace & Co., 1994), 146–147.

44. David George Surdam, *The Age of Landis and Ruth: The Economics of Baseball During the Roaring Twenties* (Lincoln: University of Nebraska Press, 2018), 87.

45. Davies, 146.

46. Rossinow, 126.

47. Byrne, 101–102.

48. Dave Reeves, "Don't Look Now, But Football's Starting."

49. Steve Ehrhart, interview, September 4, 2013.

Chapter Fourteen

1. Donald J. Trump and Tony Schwartz, *Trump: The Art of the Deal* (New York: Ballantine Books, 1987), 274.

2. Trump and Schwartz, 53.

3. Jim Byrne, *The $1 League: The Rise and Fall of the USFL* (New York: Prentice Hall, 1986), 109.

4. Jeff Pearlman, *Football for a Buck: The Crazy Rise and Crazier Demise of the USFL* (Boston: Mariner Books, 2018), 118.

5. Byrne, 98.

6. Pearlman, 124.

7. Bruce Lowitt, "Tampa Bay USFL Owner Wants Erasing of Contracts as League Reacts to New Deal," (AP) *Kentucky New Era* (Hopkinsville, KY), March 7. 1984.

8. Reeves, "Don't Look Now, But Football's Starting."

9. Fred Nordgren, interview, October 10, 2013.

10. Jimmy Jordan, interview, October 17, 2013.

11. John C. Bassett, interview, July 24, 2013.

12. "Bassett Denies USFL Will Switch to Fall Play," (AP) *Lakeland Ledger*, April 16, 1984.

13. Byrne, 97.

14. Byrne, 119–120.

15. Pearlman, 181.

16. "Bassett Denies USFL Will Switch to Fall Play."

17. Trump and Schwartz, 59.

18. Byrne, 143.

19. Trump and Schwartz, 277.

20. Trump and Schwartz, 288–289.

21. Pearlman, 209–210.

22. Flanagan, "State of the USFL is Healthy: Bassett."

23. "Bassett Denies USFL Will Switch to Fall Play."

24. Pearlman, 182.

25. Byrne 203–204.

26. Steve Ehrhart, interview, September 4, 2013.

27. Larry Guest, "Orlando's USFL Hopes Have Died," *Lakeland Ledger* (*Orlando Sentinel* re-print), September 11, 1984.

28. "Bassett Denies USFL Will Switch to Fall Play."

29. Fred Goodall, "Flutie on Sidelines for Exhibition," *Schenectady Gazette*, February 11, 1985.

30. Mike Flanagan, "For Bassett, the USFL Just Isn't Fun Anymore," *Evening Independent* (St. Petersburg, FL), April 5, 1985.

31. "If No Spring, Then No Bandits," (AP) *Eugene Register-Guard* (Oregon), March 27, 1985.

32. John Luttermoser, "Bandits Spring from USFL After League Insists on Fall," *St. Petersburg Times*, April 30, 1985.

33. John C. Bassett, interview, July 24, 2013.

34. John C. Bassett, interview, August 14, 2015.

35. "If No Spring, Then No Bandits."

36. John Luttermoser, "Bassett Says He Never Indicated USFL Would Abandon Autumn Plans," *St. Petersburg Times*, April 16, 1985.

37. John C. Bassett, interview, June 24, 2013.

38. Flanagan, "For Bassett, the USFL Just Isn't Fun Anymore."

39. Steve Ehrhart, interview, September 4, 2013.

40. Jim Armstrong, "Bassett Threatens Breakoff if USFL Goes to Fall Schedule," *The Sun* (Vancouver, BC), April 23, 1985.

41. Luttermoser, "Bandits Spring from USFL After League Insists on Fall."

42. Luttermoser, "Bandits Spring from USFL After League Insists on Fall.

43. *Ibid.*

44. *Ibid.*
45. John C. Bassett, interview, July 24, 2013.
46. Steve Ehrhart, interview, September 4, 2013.
47. Trump and Schwartz, 297.
48. Pearlman, 308.
49. *Small Potatoes: Who Killed the USFL?* directed by Mike Tollin (2009; Bristol, CT: ESPN 30 for 30, 2009), DVD.
50. Jim McVay, interview, November 19, 2013.
51. Sue Bassett-Klauber, interview, April 16, 2014.
52. Douglas Bassett, interview, October 11, 2014.
53. Sue Bassett-Klauber, interview, April 16, 2014.
54. Sue Bassett-Klauber, interview, October 3, 2013.
55. "Bandits' John Bassett Said Recovering from Brain Tumors," (AP) *Gainesville Sun* (Florida), April 8, 1985.
56. Peter Eby, interview, October 8, 2013.
57. *The Final Season*, directed by Mike Tollin (1988; Los Angeles, CA: Halcyon Days Productions, 2014), DVD.
58. John C. Bassett, interview, July 24, 2013.
59. Mike Flanagan, "Bandits Owner John Bassett Ends Mystery, Admits He's Ill," *Evening Independent* (St. Petersburg, FL), April 8, 1985.
60. *The Final Season.*
61. Fred Nordgren, interview, October 10, 2013.
62. Jimmy Jordan, interview, October 17, 2013.
63. Flanagan, "Bandits Owner John Bassett Ends Mystery, Admits he's Ill."
64. "Bandits' John Bassett Said Recovering from Brain Tumors."
65. *The Final Season.*
66. Sue Bassett-Klauber, interview, October 3, 2013.
67. Steve Ehrhart, interview, September 4, 2013.
68. Mark Todd, "Bassett in Intensive Care as Condition Worsens," *Sarasota Herald Tribune*, May 13, 1986.
69. Sue Bassett Klauber, interview, August 7, 2014.
70. John C. Bassett, interview, August 6, 2014.
71. Sue Bassett Klauber, interview, October 3, 2014.

Chapter Fifteen

1. Sigmund Levy, interview, August 7, 2014.
2. Bill Lankhof, "John F. Bassett: A Triumphant End," *Toronto Sun*, May 18, 1986.
3. "In Praise of Johnny F.," *Toronto Sun*, May 15, 1986.
4. Donald J. Trump and Tony Schwartz, *Trump: The Art of the Deal* (New York: Ballantine Books, 1987), 288.
5. Douglas Bassett, interview, October 11, 2013.
6. Steve Spurrier, interview, August 20, 2013.
7. "In Praise of Johnny F."
8. Richard Ian Kimball, *Legends Never Die: Athletes and Their Afterlives in Modern America* (Syracuse, NY: Syracuse University Press, 2017), 2.
9. Michael Tollin, interview, August 14, 2013.
10. *Small Potatoes: Who Killed the USFL?* directed by Mike Tollin (2009; Bristol, CT: ESPN 30 for 30, 2009), DVD.
11. Michael Tollin, interview, August 14, 2013.
12. Paul Warfield, interview, June 19, 2013.
13. Larry Csonka, interview, March 11, 2014.
14. Carl Peterson, interview, October 9, 2013.
15. Jim McVay, interview, November 19, 2013.
16. John C. Bassett, interview, July 24, 2013.
17. J.C.H Jones and William D. Walsh, "Salary Determination in the National Hockey League: The Effects of Skill, Franchise Characteristics, and Discrimination," *Industrial and Labor Relations Review*, 41, no. 4 (1988): 601.
18. "Average NFL Salary is $90,102, Survey Says," *New York Times*, January 29, 1982, https://www.nytimes.com/1982/01/29/sports/average-nfl-salary-is-90102-survey-says.html.
19. Wayne Gretzky, interview, October 23, 2014.

20. John Eaton, interview, September 1, 2014.

21. Paul Godfrey, interview, January 30, 2014.

22. Peter Eby, interview, October 8, 2013.

23. Wayne Gretzky, interview, October 23, 2014.

24. Rick Vaive, interview, February 24, 2015.

25. Steve Ehrhart, interview, September 4, 2013.

26. Carole Goss-Taylor, interview, February 24, 2014.

Bibliography

Archival Resources

American Football League Fifth Organizational Meeting Minutes, November 23, 1959. Professional Football Hall of Fame, Canton, OH.

John F. Bassett Celebrity Dinner Program, B'nai B'rith Sportsmen Lodge #1977, November 5, 1974. Royal York Hotel. Bassett Family Archives.

U.S. Congress, House of Representatives, Sports Broadcasting Act of 1961, 87th Congress, 1st Session, 1961, Public Law 87–331. http://uscode.house.gov/statviewer.htm?volume=75&page=732.

Interviews

Badali, Gus. February 19, 2014.

Baldwin, Howard. May 26, 2015.

Bassett, Douglas. October 11, 2013.

Bassett, John C. July 24, 2013, and February 10, 2014.

Bassett-Blair, Heidi. June 29, 2014.

Bassett-Klauber, Sue. October 3, 2013, April 1, 2014, and April 16, 2014.

Bassett-Seguso, Carling. June 10, 2014.

Baun, Bob. August 29, 2015.

Bollettieri, Nick. April 22, 2014.

Brophy, John. September 4, 2013.

Consoli, Sylvia. April 27, 2013.

Csonka, Larry. March 11, 2014.

Dell, Donald. April 22, 2014.

Eaton, John. September 1, 2014.

Eby, Peter. October 8, 2013.

Ehrhart, Steve. September 4, 2013.

Falkenberg, Frank. May 1, 2014.

Godfrey, Paul. January 30, 2014.

Goss-Taylor, Carole. February 24, 2014.

Gretzky, Wayne. October 23, 2014.

Henderson, Paul. August 29, 2015.

Jordan, Jimmy. October 17, 2013.

Lalonde, Marc. September 26, 2014.

Leger, Gilles. February 24, 2015, and August 29, 2015.

Levy, Sigmund. August 7, 2014.

Lightfoot, Gordon. February 24, 2014.

McAskile, Peter. May 1, 2014.

McVay, Jim. October 14, 2013, and November 19, 2013.

McVay, John. October 14, 2013.

Nordgren, Fred. October 10, 2013.

Peterson, Carl. October 9, 2013.

Solway, Herb. April 22, 2014.

Spurrier, Steve. August 20, 2013.

Thicke, Alan. March 6, 2014.

Tollin, Michael. August 16, 2013.

Vaive, Rick. February 24, 2015.

Warfield, Paul. June 19, 2013.

Yonge, Pam. April 23, 2013.

Films

The Final Season. Directed by Mike Tollin. Los Angeles: Halcyon Days Productions, 1988.

Lost Treasures of NFL Films: The World Football League. Directed by Dave Petrellius. Mt. Laurel, NJ: NFL Films, 2001.

The Producers. Directed by Susan Stroman. Universal City, CA: Universal, 2005.
Small Potatoes: Who Killed the USFL? Directed by Mike Tollin. Bristol, CT: ESPN, 2009.
Wall Street. Directed by Oliver Stone. Los Angeles: Twentieth Century Fox, 1987.

Newspapers

Armstrong, Jim. "Bassett Threatens Breakoff If USFL Goes to Fall Schedule." *The Sun* (Vancouver, BC), April 23, 1985.
"Bandit Burnout Winner Picked in Draw." *Lakeland Ledger* (Lakeland, FL), May 19, 1983.
"Bandit-Ball Pays Off for Tampa Bay, 27–22." *Ocala Star-Banner* (Ocala, FL), March 28, 1983.
"Bandits' John Bassett Said Recovering from Brain Tumors." (AP) *Gainesville Sun* (Gainesville, FL), April 8, 1985.
"Bassett Denies USFL Will Switch to Fall Play." (AP) *Lakeland Ledger* (Lakeland, FL), April 16, 1984.
"Bassett, Tampa Team Ready." *Sarasota Journal*, May 12, 1982.
"Bell Tolls a Lie." (AP) *St. Petersburg Times*, August 6, 1974.
Chick, Bob. "Bandits Debut Like a Grown-up." *The Evening Independent* (St. Petersburg, FL), March 7, 1983.
_____. "How Hot Was It? Just Ask Any Sunburned Fan." *The Evening Independent* (St. Petersburg, FL), June 6, 1983.
"Controllers Okay CNE Raceway." *Toronto Star*, October 17, 1968.
Cook, Beano. "WFL: Maybe on Sundays." *St. Petersburg Times*, July 12, 1974.
Dolson, Frank. "Bell's Attendance Isn't What It's Cracked Up to Be." *Philadelphia Inquirer*, August 4, 1974.
_____. "Will Paper-Gate Topple President?" *Philadelphia Inquirer*, August 6, 1974.
Dulmage, Jack. "Sickness and Fines." *Windsor Star*, December 3, 1975.
Dunnell, Milt. "Bassett Believes His Rookies Best." *Toronto Star*, January 1, 1974.
_____. "The Beer Money Is Big in Memphis." *Toronto Star*, May 15, 1974.
_____. "Johnny F. Out, Joe's Deal Off." *Toronto Star*, January 22, 1974.
_____. "Stadium Sold Out If There's a Game." *Toronto Star*, February 3, 1976.
Flanagan, Mike. "Bandits' New Idea: Win a Million Bucks." *The Evening Independent* (St. Petersburg, FL), April 2, 1985.
_____. "Bandits' Non-Game Makes League and Television History." *The Evening Independent* (St. Petersburg, FL), February 14, 1983.
_____. "Bandits Owner John Bassett Ends Mystery, Admits He's Ill." *The Evening Independent* (St. Petersburg, FL), April 8, 1985.
_____. "Beach Boys Teach Arizona a Lesson." *The Evening Independent* (St. Petersburg, FL), March 3, 1984.
_____. "Burned Out? Bandits Have a Remedy—A Good Dose of Bandit-Ball." *The Evening Independent* (St. Petersburg, FL), January 27, 1984.
_____. "Dreams Put to Test." *The Evening Independent* (St. Petersburg, FL), October 25, 1982.
_____. "Even Critics Can't Ignore USFL Now." *The Evening Independent* (St. Petersburg, FL), March 7, 1984.
_____. "For Bassett, the USFL Just Isn't Fun Anymore." *The Evening Independent* (St. Petersburg, FL), April 5, 1985.
_____. "It Doesn't Matter Who Takes the Snaps for the Bandits." *The Evening Independent* (St. Petersburg, FL), May 23, 1983.
_____. "It Was a Different Kind of Football." *The Evening Independent* (St. Petersburg, FL), February 14, 1983.
_____. "Reaves Tries to Recapture Potential He Wasted." *The Evening Independent* (St. Petersburg, FL), March 4, 1983.
_____. "So Much for Quarterback Equality in Bandits' Camp." *The Evening Independent* (St. Petersburg, FL), February 16, 1983.

_____. "State of the USFL Is Healthy: Bassett." *The Evening Independent* (St. Petersburg, FL), June 30, 1984.

_____. "Taking Stock in USFL." *The Evening Independent* (St. Petersburg, FL), June 25, 1982.

Gault, John. "'I'm Going to Fight,' Says Bassett." *Toronto Star*, March 16, 1974.

Gilbert, Doug. "No Football Change—But Does It Matter?" *Montreal Gazette*, May 9, 1974.

Gilmore, Bob. "Despite Losses the USFL Just Keeps on Truckin.'" *The Altus Times* (Altus, OK), April 26, 1984.

Goodall, Fred. "Flutie on Sidelines for Exhibition." *Schenectady Gazette*, February 11, 1985.

Gross, George. "Goodbye to a Friend." *Toronto Sun*, May 15, 1986.

Guest, Larry. "Orlando's USFL Hopes Have Died." *Orlando Sentinel* reprint in *Lakeland Ledger* (Lakeland, FL), September 11, 1984.

"High-Flying WFL: Full of Hot Air." (AP) *St. Petersburg Times*, August 7, 1974.

Huber, Mic. "Bandits in Final Preseason Tune-up." *Sarasota Herald-Tribune*, February 26, 1983.

_____. "Bandits Sign Sarasota Policeman." *Sarasota Herald-Tribune*, October 26, 1982.

Hughes, Bob. "Government May Move Against WFL." *The Leader Post* (Regina, Saskatchewan), February 22, 1974.

"If No Spring, Then No Bandits." (AP) *Eugene Register-Guard* (Eugene, OR), March 27, 1985.

"In Praise of Johnny F." *Toronto Sun*, May 15, 1986.

Johnson, Mark. "Bandit-Ball: The Thing in Spring." *St. Petersburg Times*, September 14, 1982.

_____. "Doggone Burt. They're the Tampa Bay Bandits." *St. Petersburg Times*, August 5, 1982.

Kenney, Elaine. "Toros Night in Toronto: 'Terrific, Super-Duper.'" *Toronto Star*, October 8, 1973.

Kernaghan, Jim. "Bassett Defends Free Tickets." *Toronto Star*, January 3, 1976.

_____. "Is Baun Being Ousted by Toros?" *Toronto Star*, December 23, 1975.

_____. "Lack of Support May Chase Toros Out of Toronto." *Toronto Star*, February 3, 1976.

_____. "Late-Season Drive a Harris Trademark." *Toronto Star*, April 9, 1974.

_____. "Newly Named Toros Bullish on Leafs Center." *Toronto Star*, June 12, 1973.

_____. "Oshawa Slams Arena Doors on Toros." *Toronto Star*, March 6, 1974.

_____. "Toros Fined $500 Each After Blowing 6-Goal Lead." *Toronto Star*, December 1, 1975.

_____. "Toros Fire Man They Didn't Help." *Toronto Star*, February 17, 1976.

_____. "Toros Know Gardens Well." *Toronto Star*, April 2, 1974.

_____. "Toros Tie in WHA Debut." *Toronto Star*, October 8, 1974.

_____. "Toros to Play Home Games Next Year at the Gardens," *Toronto Star*, April 3, 1974.

_____. "Toros Whacked by Fans and Mariners." *Toronto Star*, April 10, 1975.

_____. "WHA Players Hit Goons." *Toronto Star*, June 11, 1976.

"Lalonde Insists Those Miami Stars Won't Play Here." *Toronto Star*, April 1, 1974.

Lankhof, Bill. "Johnny F. Bassett: A Triumphant End." *Toronto Sun*, May 18, 1986.

Lasswell, Doug. "Bandits' Bassett Wears Many Hats." *Sarasota Herald-Tribune*, June 17, 1984.

_____. "Simmons Predicts Tampa Sell-Out." *Sarasota Herald-Tribune*, April 11, 1984.

Livingston, Bill. "Bell Crowd Control Plan: More Cops, Less Freebies." *Philadelphia Inquirer*, July 27, 1974.

Lowitt, Bruce. "Tampa Bay USFL Owner Wants Erasing of Contracts as League Reacts to New Deal." (AP) *Kentucky New Era* (Hopkinsville, KY), March 7, 1984.

Luttermoser, John. "Bandits Spring from USFL After League Insists on Fall." *St. Petersburg Times*, April 30, 1985.

_____. "Bassett Says He Never Indicated USFL Would Abandon Autumn Plans." *St. Petersburg Times*, April 16, 1985.

MacDonald, John. "Family Affair in Junior Tennis." *Toronto Star*, July 11, 1955.

_____. "Gary Davidson a Proud Papa." *St. Petersburg Times*, July 12, 1974.

_____. "Inferior Surroundings Hamper WFL at the Gate." *St. Petersburg Times*, July 19, 1974.

_____. "Padding One Thing, but Wall-to-Wall?" *St. Petersburg Times*, August 7, 1974.

_____. "Tampa Gets NFL Franchise for '76." *St. Petersburg Times*, April 25, 1974.

Martz, Ron. "The Community Owns Nothing." *St. Petersburg Times*, August 15, 1979.

Matsumoto, Rick. "Northmen Still Hope to Stay." *Toronto Star*, April 11, 1974.

McDonald, Tim and Mike Flanagan. "Bits and Pieces." *The Evening Independent* (St. Petersburg, FL), March 7, 1983.

McKee, Ken. "No Need for a Desk in Johnny F's Office." *Toronto Star*, February 9, 1974.

_____. "Toronto's New Football Club Can Veto Canadian Entries." *Toronto Star*, January 16, 1974.

"McKegney Released." (AP) *Montgomery Advertiser*, June 19, 1978.

"Memphis in Two." (UPI) *The Evening Independent* (St. Petersburg, FL), June 3, 1974.

"Memphis Will Vote on Northmen Bid." (UPI) *Toronto Star*, May 3, 1974.

"Miami-Florida Game Is a Sell-Out." (AP) *Palm Beach Post*, May 9, 1984.

Mizell, Hubert. "Defense Hands Sharks a Win." *St. Petersburg Times*, July 12, 1974.

_____. "Jacksonville Attorney Tampa NFL Owner." *St. Petersburg Times*, December 6, 1974.

"NFL Freezes Out John Bassett." (AP) *Toronto Star*, March 17, 1976.

Nickelson, Al. "Bassett Group Buys WHA Nats." *Toronto Star*, May 3, 1973.

"Northmen Off to U.S., They'll Be Southmen." *Toronto Star*, May 7, 1974.

"Northmen to Become Southmen." *Milwaukee Journal*, May 8, 1974.

Orr, Frank. "Auto Racing Plans Announced for CNE." *Toronto Star*, September 16, 1968.

_____. "Lamport Provides Opposition to Proposed CNE Track." *Toronto Star*, September 17, 1968.

"Parkdale Residents Plan to Boycott Promoters of CNE Auto Raceway." *Toronto Star*, November 11, 1968.

Pennington, Bob. "Ballard's World Is Tough—And That's How He Likes It." *Toronto Star*, February 2, 1974.

"Promoters Abandon Plans for CNE Raceway." *Toronto Star*, February 7, 1969.

Proudfoot, Jim. "Here Is Why Toros Are Going Off to Sweden." *Toronto Star*, August 20, 1975.

_____. "Northmen Pledge to Stop WFL Raids—If They Stay." *Toronto Star*, April 5, 1974.

_____. "Toronto's Best? Could Be Toros If They Keep On." *Toronto Star*, July 25, 1974.

_____. "Toros Catching on This Survey Says." *Toronto Star*, February 26, 1974.

_____. "WFL Ready to Share Cost of Miami Stars." *Toronto Star*, March 30, 1974.

Reeves, Dave. "Bandits Want to Be Attractive." *Lakeland Ledger* (Lakeland, FL), January 14, 1983.

_____. "Don't Look Now, but Football's Starting." *Lakeland Ledger* (Lakeland, FL), January 9, 1984.

_____. "Spurrier Considered a Comeback." *Lakeland Ledger* (Lakeland, FL), May 10, 1983.

"Residents Will Ask Court to Stop Raceway Scheme." *Toronto Star*, January 14, 1969.

Rimstead, Paul. "At Tely, He Foresaw Rise of the Sun." *Toronto Sun*, March 25, 1986.

_____. "Johnny F., Man of Legendary Mettle." *Toronto Sun*, March 23, 1986.

"Robbie Calls Truce in Battle of Florida." *Ocala Star-Banner* (Ocala, FL), August 11, 1979.

Robertson, John. "No Hearing for Bassett." *Montreal Star*, February 28, 1974.

"Rookies, Free Agents May Be Keys to NFL Strike." (AP) *Philadelphia Inquirer*, July 2, 1974.

Sokol, Al. "Argos Position Worries CFL." *Toronto Star*, January 23, 1974.

_____. "Leo Cahill Is Back in Action." *Toronto Star*, February 2, 1974.

_____. "Sportsman Johnny F. Bassett Dead at 47." *Toronto Star*, May 15, 1986.

Suarez, Leo. "USFL Bandits Making a Big Hit with Tampa's Sports Fans." *The Miami News*, February 12, 1983.

Tierney, Mike. "Bucs Tabbed as Rich, Low-Paying Club." *St. Petersburg Times*, February 27, 1982.

Timson, Judi. "Bassett's Big Coup No Hustle, He Says 'They Dig Canada.'" *Toronto Star*, April 1, 1974.

Todd, Mark. "Bassett in Intensive Care as Condition Worsens." *Sarasota Herald-Tribune*, May 13, 1986.

"Toronto of WFL Gets Memphis Home." (AP) *New York Times*, May 7, 1974.

Wallace, William N. "Stabler of Raiders Joins WFL for '76." *New York Times*, April 3, 1974.

"WFL—Pig in Poke Is Selling." UPI *The Evening Independent* (St. Petersburg, FL), June 27, 1974.

"WHA Suspends Bassett." AP *Montgomery Advertiser*, November 18, 1977.

Zier, Patrick. "Bandits Are Best of a Very Bad Group." *Lakeland Ledger* (Lakeland, FL), May 31, 1984.

_____. "Bandits on the Run as Bucs Go Into Stall." *Lakeland Ledger* (Lakeland, FL), October 31, 1982.

_____. "Bucs Don't Care for the New Kid in Town." *Lakeland Ledger* (Lakeland, FL), March 28, 1983.

_____. "It's Official, Spurrier Bandits' Man." *Lakeland Ledger* (Lakeland, FL), November 23, 1982.

Periodicals

Borucki, Wes. "You're Dixie's Football Pride: American College Football and the Resurgence of Southern Identity." *Identities: Global Studies on Culture and Power* 10, no. 4 (2003): 477–494.

Brondoni, Silvio. "Innovation and Imitation: Corporate Strategies for Global Competition." *Emerging Issues in Management* no. 1 (2012): 10–24.

Casadesus-Masanell, Ramon, and Feng Zhu. "Business Model Innovation and Competitive Imitation: The Case of Sponsor-Based Business Models." *Strategic Management Journal* 34, no. 4 (2013): 464–482.

Doyle, Andrew. "Causes Won, Not Lost: College Football and the Modernization of the American South." *International Journal of the History of Sport* 11, no. 2 (1994): 231–251.

Jackson, Steven J. "Gretzky, Crisis, and Canadian Identity in 1988: Rearticulating the Americanization of Culture Debate. *Sociology of Sport Journal* 11, No. 4 (1994): 428–446.

Johnson, William Oscar. "The Day the Money Ran Out." *Sports Illustrated*, December 1, 1975: 84–94.

_____. "Whole New League, Whole New Season." *Sports Illustrated*, May 23, 1982: 82–87.

Jones, J.C.H., and William D. Walsh. "Salary Determination in the National Hockey League: The Effects of Skills, Franchise Characteristics, and Discrimination." *Industry and Labor Relations Review* 41, no. 4 (1988): 592–604.

Jones, Robert F. "They're Grinning and Bearing." *Sports Illustrated*, July 28, 1975: 16–18.

McDermott, Barry. "Here Comes Carling, Her Daddy's Darling." *Sports Illustrated*, June 27, 1983: 84–98.

Mieher, Stuart. "Sports Teams Hardly Ever Score Big Bucks, but Who Cares?" *Florida Trend*, February 1985: 75–78.

Moss, Arnold. "Jewels from a Box Office: The Language of Show Business." *American Speech* 11, no. 3 (1936): 219–222.

Newman, Joshua I. "Old Times There Are Not Forgotten: Sport, Identity, and the Confederate Flag in the Dixie South." *Sociology of Sport Journal* 24, no. 3 (2007): 261–282.

Rothchild, John. "The Distinguished States of Florida." *Forum: The Magazine of the Florida Humanities Council* 17, no. 2 (1993): 4–9.

Zarnowitz, Victor and Geoffrey H. Moore. "The Recession and Recovery of 1973–1976." *Explorations in Economic Research* 4, no. 4 (1977): 471–557.

Secondary Sources

Applebome, Peter. *Dixie Rising: How the South Is Shaping American Values, Politics, and Culture*. San Diego: Harcourt Brace, 1997.

Baldwin, Harold. *Slim and None: My Wild Ride from the WHA to the NHL and All the Way to Hollywood*. Toronto: Anansi, 2014.

Barnouw, Erik. *Tube of Plenty: The Evolution of American Television*. New York: Oxford University Press, 1990.

Barnum, Phineas Taylor. *Struggles and Triumphs: Sixty Years' Recollections of P.T. Barnum*. Buffalo, NY: Courier, 1889; Seattle: CreateSpace Independent Publishing Platform, 2012.

Becnel, George. *When the Saints Came Marching In: What the New Orleans Saints Did Wrong (and Sometimes Right) in Its Expansion Years*. Bloomington, IN: Authors House, 2009.

Bell, Gregory Jason. "Ye Mystic Krewe of Historical Revisionists: The Origins of Tampa's Gasparilla Parade." In *Zlin Proceedings in Humanities, Volume 5*, edited by Roman Trušník, Gregory Jason Bell, and Katarína Nemčoková, 191–199. Zlín, Czech Republic: Thomas Bata University, 2015.

Byrne, Jim. *The $1 League: The Rise and Fall of the USFL*. New York: Prentice Hall, 1986.

Cash, W.J. *The Mind of the South*. New York: Vintage, 1941 [1991].

Charters, David A. *The Chequered Past: Sports Car Racing and Rallying in Canada, 1951–1991*. Toronto: University of Toronto Press, 2007.

Cole, Stephen. *Hockey Night Fever: Mullets, Mayhem, and the Game's Coming of Age in the 1970s*. Toronto: Doubleday Canada, 2015.

Cowie, Jefferson. *Stayin' Alive: The 1970s and the Last Days of the Working Class*. New York: New Press, 2010.

Csonka, Larry, Jim Kiick, and Dave Anderson. *Always on the Run*. New York: Bantam, 1974.

Davies, Richard O. *America's Obsession: Sports and Society Since 1945*. Fort Worth: Harcourt Brace, 1994.

———. *Sports in American Life: A History*. West Sussex, UK: Wiley Blackwell, 2017.

Dickson, Paul. *Bill Veeck: Baseball's Greatest Maverick*. New York: Walker, 2012.

Dixon, Phil S. *Andrew "Rube" Foster: A Harvest on Freedom's Fields*. Bloomington, IN: Xlibris Corporation, 2010.

Dolson, Frank. *The Philadelphia Story: A City of Winners*. South Bend, IN: Icarus, 1981.

Doyle, Andrew. "An Atheist in Alabama Is Someone Who Doesn't Believe in Bear Bryant: A Symbol for an Embattled South." In *The Sporting World of the Modern South*, edited by Patrick B. Miller, 247–275. Urbana: University of Illinois Press, 2002.

Feuer, Jane. *Seeing Through the Eighties: Television and Reaganism*. Durham, NC: Duke University Press, 1995.

Fielden, Greg. *NASCAR: The Complete History*. Lincolnwood, IL: Publications International, 2015.

Forbes, Mary. *Gentle Giants: The Selmon Brothers*. Tampa, FL: Mariner, 1981.

Granastein, Jack L. *Yankee Go Home? Canadians and Anti-Americanism*. Toronto: HarperCollins, 1996.

Gunther, Marc, and Bill Carter. *Monday Night Mayhem: The Inside Story of ABCs Monday Night Football*. New York: William Morrow, 1988.

Guttman, Allen. *From Ritual to Record: The Nature of Modern Sports*. New York: Columbia University Press, 1978.

Hanson, Dave, and Ross Bernstein. *Slap Shot Original: The Man, the Foil, the Legend*. Chicago: Triumph, 2008.

Harris, David. *The League: The Rise and Decline of the NFL*. New York: Bantam, 1986.

Harris, Neil. *The Art of P.T. Barnum*. Chicago: University of Chicago Press, 1973.

Harry, Chris, and Joey Johnston. *Tales from the Bucs Sideline*. Chicago: Sports Publishing LLC, 2004.

Johnson, Victoria. *Heartland TV: Primetime Television and the Struggle for U.S. Identity*. New York: New York University Press, 2008.

Kemper, Kurt Edward. *College Football and American Culture in the Cold War Era*. Urbana: University of Illinois Press, 2009.

Kendall, Diana. *Framing Class: Media Representation of Wealth and Poverty in America*. Plymouth, UK: Rowman and Littlefield, 2011.

Kimball, Richard Ian. *Legends Never Die: Athletes and Their Afterlives in Modern America*. Syracuse, NY: Syracuse University Press, 2017.

Kimmel, Michael. *Manhood in America: A Cultural History*. New York: Oxford University Press, 2018.

Klein, Gene, and David Fisher. *First Down and a Billion: The Funny Business of Pro Football*. New York: William Morrow, 1987.

Kriegel, Mark. *Namath: A Biography*. New York: Viking, 2004.

Kyriakoudes, Louis M., and Peter A. Coclanis. "The Tennessee Test of Manhood: Professional Wrestling and Southern Cultural Stereotypes." In *The Sporting World of the Modern South*, edited by Patrick B. Miller, 276–293. Urbana: University of Illinois Press, 2002.

Lester, Larry. *Rube Foster in His Time: On the Field and in the Papers with Black Baseball's Greatest Visionary*. Jefferson, NC: McFarland, 2012.

Levine, Allan. *Toronto: Biography of a City*. Madeira Park, BC: Douglas & McIntyre, 2014.

Lowe, Stephen R. *The Kid on the Sandlot: Congress and Professional Sports, 1910–1992*. Bowling Green, OH: Bowling Green State University Popular Press, 1995.

MacCambridge, Michael. *America's Game: The Epic Story of How Pro Football Captured a Nation*. New York: Anchor, 2004.

_____. *Lamar Hunt: A Life in Sports*. Kansas City, MO: Andrews McMeel, 2012.

Maher, Todd, and Mark Speck. *The World Football League Encyclopedia*. Haworth, NJ: St. Johann, 2006.

McKinley, Michael. *Hockey Night in Canada: Seasons*. Toronto: Viking, 2012.

Miller, Jeff. *Going Long: The Wild 10-Year Saga of the Renegade American Football League in the Words of Those Who Lived It*. New York: McGraw-Hill, 2003.

Mitchell, Katharyne. "In Whose Image? Transnational Capital and the Production of Multiculturalism in Canada." In *Global/Local: Cultural Production and the Transnational Imaginary*, edited by Rob Wilson and Wimal Dissanayake, 219–251. Durham, NC: Duke University Press, 1996.

Moffett, Samuel. *The Americanization of Canada*. New York: Columbia University Press, 1907.

Mormino, Gary R. *Land of Sunshine, State of Dreams: A Social History of Florida*. Gainesville: University Press of Florida, 2005.

Nash, Roderick Frazier. *Wilderness and the American Mind*. New Haven, CT: Yale University Press, 1967.

Nielsen, Kim E. *A Disability History of the United States*. Boston: Beacon, 2012.

O'Brien, Michael. *Vince: A Personal Biography of Vince Lombardi*. New York: William Morrow, 1987.

O'Brien, Steve. *The Canadian Football League: The Phoenix of Professional Sports Leagues*. Morrisville, NC: Lulu Enterprises, 2005.

Pearlman, Jeff. *Football for a Buck: The Crazy Rise and Crazier Demise of the USFL*. Boston: Mariner, 2018.

Pluto, Terry. *Our Tribe: A Baseball Memoir*. Cleveland: Gray, 1999.

Pollard, Edward A. *The Lost Cause: A New Southern History of the World of the Confederacy*. New York, 1866.

Rappoport, Ken. *The Little League That Could: A History of the American Football League*. New York: Taylor Trade, 2010.

Reeths, Paul. *The United States Football League, 1982–1986.* Jefferson, NC: McFarland, 2017.

Revels, Tracy J. *Sunshine Paradise: A History of Florida Tourism.* Gainesville: University Press of Florida, 2011.

Rossinow, Doug. *The Reagan Era: A History of the 1980s.* New York: Columbia University Press, 2015.

Rydell, Robert W. and Rob Kroes. *Buffalo Bill in Bologna: The Americanization of the World, 1869–1922.* Chicago: University of Chicago Press, 2005.

Samuels, Charles. *The Magnificent Rube: The Life and Gaudy Times of Tex Rickard.* New York: McGraw-Hill, 1957.

Saxon, A.H. *P.T. Barnum: The Legend and the Man.* New York: Columbia University Press, 1989.

Schulman, Bruce J. *The Seventies: The Great Shift in American Culture, Society, and Politics.* Boston: De Capo, 2002.

Schultz, Brad. *Year One: The 1970 Season and the Dawn of Modern Football.* Washington, D.C.: Potomac, 2013.

Siggins, Maggie. *Bassett: John Bassett's 40 Years in Politics, Publishing, Business, and Sports.* Toronto: James Lorimer, 1979.

Somers, Dale A. *The Rise of Sports in New Orleans, 1850–1900.* Baton Rouge: Louisiana State University Press, 1972.

Speck, Mark. *...and a Dollar Short: The Empty Promises, Broken Dreams, and Somewhat-Less Than Comical Misadventures of the 1974 Florida Blazers.* Haworth, NJ: St. Johann, 2014.

Surdam, David George. *Run to Glory and Profits: The Economic Rise of the NFL During the 1950s.* Lincoln: University of Nebraska Press, 2013.

Surgent, Scott. *The World Hockey Association Fact Book.* Tempe, AZ: Xaler, 2010.

Trump, Donald J. and Tony Schwartz. *Trump: The Art of the Deal.* New York: Ballantine, 1987.

Willes, Ed. *Rebel League: The Short and Unruly Life of the World Hockey Association.* Toronto: McClelland & Stewart, 2004.

Woodard, Colin. *American Nations: The History of the Eleven Rival Regional Cultures of North America.* New York: Penguin, 2011.

Zimniuch, Fran. *Baseball's New Frontier: A History of Expansion, 1961–1998.* Lincoln: University of Nebraska Press, 2013.

Web Articles

"Average NFL Salary Is $90,102, Survey Says," *New York Times*, January 29, 1982. https://www.nytimes.com/1982/01/29/sports/average-nfl-salary-is-90102-survey-says.html.

Burns, Susan. "The Collapse of the Colony," *Sarasota Magazine*, October 31, 2010. https://www.sarasotamagazine.com/news-and-profiles/2010/10/the-collapse-of-the-colony.

"First Beer Sold at Blue Jays Game." UPI. July 30, 1982. https://www.upi.com/Archives/1982/07/30/First-beer-sold-at-Blue-Jays-game/6892396849600/.

Lawrence, Jesse. "Maple Leafs Have Most Expensive Tickets for 2014–2015 Season." *Forbes*, September 19, 2014. https://www.forbes.com/sites/jesselawrence/2014/09/19/leafs-top-canadian-team-blackhawks-top-american-team-in-2014-15-nhl-tickets-on-secondary-market/#5871619b5668.

Manker, Rob. "After 40 Years, Can We Slam the Door on '-Gate' Already?" *Chicago Tribune*, May 29, 2012. http://articles.chicagotribune.com/2012-05-29/news/ct-talk-gate-words-manker-0529-20120529_1_scandal-nixon-speechwriter-william-safire.

Taylor, Vincent. "Bandits, They're Back." WFTS-TV, originally aired February 25, 2014.

Index